WHEN LOVE COMES TO LIGHT

Also by Richard Freeman and Mary Taylor

The Art of Vinyasa: Awakening Body and Mind through the Practice of Ashtanga Yoga

Also by Richard Freeman

The Mirror of Yoga: Awakening the Intelligence of Body and Mind

Also by Mary Taylor

WITH LYNN GINSBURG:
What Are You Hungry For? Women, Food, and Spirituality

New Vegetarian Classics: Soups

New Vegetarian Classics: Entrees

WHEN LOVE COMES TO LIGHT

Bringing Wisdom from the Bhagavad Gītā to Modern Life

RICHARD FREEMAN
AND MARY TAYLOR

SHAMBHALA

Shambhala Publications, Inc.
4720 Walnut Street
Boulder, Colorado 80301
www.shambhala.com

Cover art: Robert Beer
Interior design: Steve Dyer

9 8 7 6 5 4 3 2

Printed in the United States of America

♾ This edition is printed on acid-free paper that meets the American National Standards Institute Z39.48 Standard.
♻ This book is printed on 30% postconsumer recycled paper.
For more information please visit www.shambhala.com.
Shambhala Publications is distributed worldwide by
Penguin Random House, Inc., and its subsidiaries.

LIBRARY OF CONGRESS CATALOGING-IN-PUBLICATION DATA

Names: Freeman, Richard, 1950– author. | Taylor, Mary (Yoga teacher), author.
Title: When love comes to light: bringing wisdom from the Bhagavad Gītā to modern life / Richard Freeman and Mary Taylor.
Description: First. | Boulder: Shambhala, 2020.
Identifiers: LCCN 2019056555 | ISBN 9781611808179 (trade paperback)
Subjects: LCSH: Bhagavadgītā—Commentaries. | Yoga. | Religious life—Hinduism. | Lifestyles.
Classification: LCC BL1138.67 .F74 2020 | DDC 294.5/44—dc23
LC record available at https://lccn.loc.gov/2019056555

Dedicated to dialogue and
endless inquiry in service to others.

CONTENTS

INTRODUCTION

WHAT *DOES* IT MEAN to be human in the twenty-first century? Extremes are surfacing throughout the world, and there are schisms between the rich and poor, the educated and uneducated, and the healthy and those unable to access medical care. There are deep divides and internal conflicts within and between nations, religions, genders, and even closely knit families. Due to improved technology we are more able to communicate and physically connect than ever before, yet paradoxically, many of us feel an overwhelming sense of isolation that is combated only by perpetuating, through social media, a sort of personal propaganda as to how clever, how special, and how above average we are. Mountains of information are readily available; however, knowing whose word to trust is becoming more and more difficult with the ever-increasing presence of those possessing a shameless desire and willingness to stretch the truth or deceive others for personal gain. Perhaps one day we will look back and see this as the age of extremes that catapulted us into a new age of insight because beneath this chaos and separatism, woven into the strands of divisiveness that seem to be tearing us apart, there is also a palpable craving for connectedness, truth, and sustainability.

The funny thing is that, even though we may fear that the world has plummeted into the darkest time in history—as some days it does indeed feel that way—in many ways, our modern time isn't that different from life at any other point in history. There have always been tricksters and thieves, saints and sinners, and those gliding through life on waves of complacency and ignorance alongside others fervently searching for meaning and truth. Human suffering, and equally, hope and kindness, are nothing new. Granted, the particulars have changed, but the underlying difficulties—and joys—of being on this remarkable planet, in this extraordinary human form, are pretty much the same today as they've always been.

We're born. We think we're the center of the universe—and in some ways we are. We find our "selves" and begin to feel whole. But then one day most of us have the rude awakening that there are countless others out there who also think *they* are the center of creation. A seed of doubt about our own omnipotence and importance is planted: "How can this be?" But we shrug it off when our own habitual thought patterns and storyline—the insufferably boring-to-everyone-else "Story of Me"—come solidly back into focus. We struggle, we question, we suffer, we laugh, and we love. We have great insight and good fortune, feeling terrific as our ego swoops in to claim credit for successes and to rationalize oversights and failures. When things don't go according to plan, perhaps we do get angry, closed-minded, or stubborn. We may dip our toe into the streams of avoidance, denial, or experimentation, testing waters from one end of the spectrum of life to the other until we become nauseous from the aftereffect of swinging in our isolated biosphere on the pendulum of impulse and ill-planned dreams. When things get particularly severe, we may even abandon it all, turning the whole operation over to a parental figurehead, drugs, a confidence trickster, a system, or a formula that we find in a disparate moment of disconnect.

But if we're lucky, at some point in there we begin to wake up. We experience the paradox of living alone encased in the sack of skin we call "me" while simultaneously recognizing the immeasurable beauty of being an integral part of a limitless, interconnected, finely tuned web of existence. Quite by accident we taste the nectar of trusting the process of life with an open heart and open mind, realizing that we *are* the center, yet part of a unified whole. Separate, but not separate at all. The prospect of waking up and moving through and beyond our own self-absorption and suffering is alluring. It is confusing, inspiring, and challenging all at once. If we don't take the dare, we are likely to suffer even more and in not waking up are prone to doing harm to ourselves and to others. In either case, awake or sleepwalking through life, we are part of the kaleidoscoping pattern of birth, life, and death and the inherent internal chaos that *is* the human condition. The same today as it was in the time of Homer and as it will be into the foreseeable future.

As unsettling as the inner turmoil may be, it is quite possible to find a path to follow that will quell our seeds of discontent. The passageway toward freedom from suffering turns out to be a process of learning to trust and let go of habitual patternings of mind, perception, and emotion that keep us trapped in loops of self-absorbed separation. Our burning desire to be happy is the key and can be the impetus we need to get us rolling. Deciding it's time we find our way out of suffering is the very first step we must take and when we do, we discover in an instant that the path is right at our fingertips. It all begins with the sincere intention to relentlessly cultivate compassion, to sharpen our capacity for discriminating awareness, and to honestly desire to free all others from suffering as well.

It is nothing new for humankind to crave this kind of freedom. Religions and great thinkers have contemplated happiness since the beginning of time. Wars, monarchies, cultural norms, dogmas, and traditions have arisen from generations of pursuing this very question of what it is to be in this embodied human condition. So, too, mythological imagery and intricate stories, poignant poetry and brilliant hymns have flowed forth because always there have been the dreamers and the mystical thinkers of the time; those who dare question and risk waking up.

The hymn of the Bhagavad Gītā (often called simply the Gītā) is one such piece of writing. It is a section of the great Indian epic known as the Mahābhārata, which has its early roots in stories dating back as far as the eighth or ninth century B.C.E. The full teaching was later told as a compelling narrative—stories within stories—filled with deceit and bravery, love and betrayal, and puzzles and paradoxes that turned it into a classic text for Hindus and others in search of freedom from suffering. The myth, which in many ways was a critique of religious extremism, the caste system, and social injustice, was told by the sage Vyāsa to his early disciples and was recorded by his scribe, the elephant-headed god, Gaṇeśa. It is the story of the interlinked Kaurava and Pāṇḍava families and their struggles within the complexity of jousting for power over the land and victory in the ensuing war.

The Gītā, which appears in the middle of this epic, teaches that all possible disparate approaches to enlightenment culminate in *bhakti*, or love. It is the story of Arjuna, a Pāṇḍava brother, who is faced with the dilemma of what to do when he finds himself—a warrior—in the center of an unfolding battle with people he loves and admires on both sides. The powerful tale—both compelling and touching—describes how Arjuna faces his doubts and fears while questioning tradition, duty, cultural values, and even his own perceptions and the teachings themselves at every step of the way. His dear friend and teacher, Kṛṣṇa (who happens to be the Hindu deity of delight and compassion), carefully guides Arjuna toward insight, transformation, love, and compassion.

But the Gītā also serves as a guide for any of us when we find ourselves perilously dangling between the horns of dilemma within a crisis or difficult situation. Should we act or not? And if so, how do we know the correct course of action to take? This ancient text has served for generations as a foundational guidebook within the yoga traditions, helping eager students address the complexity not only of what Arjuna himself faces, but perhaps even more so, the complexity of what each of us confronts in the human condition as we struggle to awaken.

Translating the wisdom of the Gītā for the modern age is a longstanding dream of ours. In part one of this book we follow and explore the traditional sequence of teachings from the original text, while interweaving insight into how the teachings are relevant in and serve as a practical guide for today's complex world. Part two is a brand new verse-by-verse translation of the full text. And since one of the primary teachings of the Gītā is the importance of tangible contemplative practices that enable one to embody and thereby fully assimilate the teachings, we also include an appendix of embodiment exercises that reflect essential themes from the Gītā, such as impermanence and the nature of change, as well as simple practices to foster stillness and the stability of mind and body. We hope these exercises will not only shed light on the teachings but also be helpful when facing challenges that arise in everyday life, offering practical ways to stay focused, grounded, and in the present moment.

PART ONE

When Love Comes to Light

[1]

Caught between Conscience and Crisis

IMAGINE YOU AWAKEN one morning from a long, luxuriously comfortable sleep. Taking in a deep breath, you stretch your arms and yawn, beginning to transition slowly into the day. But then you notice the distant noise of voices raised in anger. As your focus sharpens you recognize the nature of the insults being tossed out and familiar voices amid a cacophony of sound—feet shuffling on a graveled surface, coughs, and some laughter and small talk off in the distance. The light is far brighter than it should be at this time of day, and you slowly realize that you're not in your bed at all but instead are standing in a field with dirt roads around the perimeter and a crowd of people watching you wake up. You're with your closest friend in the very center of a chaotic standoff that is obviously about to augment into blows. Your friend seems calm and clear, strong. But you are swept by waves of doubt and fear. You feel clammy and nauseous and find it difficult to breathe. You pinch yourself to see if you can escape the situation, which must be part of a horrible dream, yet there you are! No dream, no misperception, no way out, and if you don't act soon, you know you'll be crushed in the ensuing battle.

On one side you see your beloved family, close friends, and respected members of your community. On the other are the faces of distant relatives along with many you've considered teachers and mentors over the years. You recall that a conflict had bubbled up because of political differences, but you had thought it would be sorted out by negotiations instead of what now seems to be an impending battle. Overcome by confusion, sadness, and dread you know full well this isn't a dream, that indeed you *are* awake like never before, and you are at the epicenter of a crisis, precariously perched on the precipice of action or nonaction.

This ominous situation, along with the knowledge that regardless of what action is taken people we respect and love will be killed, is more extreme than most of us face in our everyday lives. Yet we can experience the same sense of insurmountable dilemma when we find ourselves in the midst of *any* crisis—a family feud, an emergency, a brutal work environment, or being attacked, abused, or unjustly accused by another. Feelings of confusion, sadness, and despair are likely to surface when we are faced by the push and pull of any dilemma, but particularly when we get a taste of the impermanent, interconnected nature of life. There is seldom a simple, formulaic answer as to how we should act. Instead, as we pay close attention to any struggle we encounter, it becomes clear that there are always multiple actions—some of which invariably seem conflicting—that we might take, yet we must choose a single direction if we are to step forth.

When we are called to take decisive action while being pulled in contradictory directions, we have reached a crossroads where we have the opportunity to "wake up" and fully engage in the experience of life as relationship dependent. If we tune in to circumstances as they arise and manage to loosen our preconceptions and predispositions (even for just a moment), then insight is possible and perhaps we can act in relation to the whole rather than from habitual patterns and self-oriented, ego-driven motivations.

However, at these important junctures, doubts, fears, and confusions often take over, and we often have the impulse to avoid the difficulty and fall back asleep into the comfortable illusion of ourselves as somehow separate or above it all—an absolutely independent phenomenon and the center of our own very small story and even more minuscule privately imagined universe. And this is exactly where Arjuna, the protagonist of the Bhagavad Gītā, finds himself as the story and teachings of the epic hymn start. He begins a journey of awakening wondering, "What did my people (army) and the Sons of Pāṇḍu do, gathered together eager to fight on the field of dharma, on the field of action" (1.1)?

In many Indian texts or teachings, the very beginning—sometimes even the first words—give you a clue as to the underlying message of the entire scripture, and so it is with this first verse of the Gītā. As Arjuna enters the field of *dharmakṣetre kurukṣetre*, the field of dharma and action, he is stunned to see two opposing legions, fully armed and ready to fight over rights to the kingdom. Arriving in his chariot with his close friend, Kṛṣṇa, as the charioteer, Arjuna is flooded by excitement, imagining the thrill of battle with a sense that he will be fulfilling his duty; as a Kṣatriya (a member of the warrior or ruling caste), he has been primed for this moment his whole life. We can imagine him pulling out his trusty bow and plucking the bowstring, making sure the tenor of the twang indicates it is well tuned. In the distance he hears the sound of thousands of conch shells being blown by the opposition, so he and Kṛṣṇa blow their conchs as well, indicating their readiness for battle.

But just then the scene comes more clearly into focus for Arjuna and he hesitates, asking Kṛṣṇa to draw the chariot into the middle of the field between the two sides, so he can assess the situation more closely. He sees friends, family, teachers, and trusted advisers lined up and forming the side he will be fighting on. They are pitted against an opposing army, which he soon realizes is also composed of relatives from his very own family, as well as many others he admires and loves. Envisioning the horror that lies ahead if they all proceed into battle, Arjuna's palms become clammy, and his hands begin to tremble. He feels his legs quivering, his skin intensely burning as his mouth goes dry, and his hair standing on end.

From the outset of the story, Arjuna realizes, on a deep visceral level, that something is very wrong. He does not want "victory in battle," in spite of the fact that if his side wins, his elder brother will become king, meaning Arjuna himself will be second in line for full power of the land. Instead, he understands that there is no point in killing and that it does not make sense to harm friends and family with whom he would want to share the delights of the kingdom. He sees through the lure of power and wealth, which—especially when tempted by the potential of personal benefit—would be difficult for any of us to resist under similar circumstances.

Suppose, for instance, that you were about to get a better job. The occupation requires that you travel a lot and work a great deal of overtime, but you think, "Well, at least I'll make lots of money and be able to buy a bigger house." But then you realize that if you take this new job, you'll ruin your relationship with your family because you'll never be home. You'll be working twenty hours a day, seven days a week, flying all over the world, and possibly feeling quite special and pleased with yourself and your position, wealth, and power, but all of the people you would want to share the bigger house and better social standing with are going to suffer.

The initial teaching of the Gītā, therefore, is one showing us that, like this new job, all of these types of plans for sovereignty—which is what the ego wants, some sort of kingdom—destroy our relationships with the people that we would then enjoy the fruits of our actions with. This is actually the situation that the modern materialist is often in. All over the world, *so* many people in so many different cultures are succeeding economically—particularly in capitalist countries—but they've destroyed their relationships with other people. So what sort of fun can they have? "Oh! I've got my modern mansion with my own swimming pool. Too bad I've abandoned all of my friendships, and nobody will come over to visit. I'm all alone."

Likewise, with the global push for infinite economic expansion, we are actually destroying the environment that allows us to enjoy it. If we decide to grow more food through modern industrialized agriculture and in doing so destroy the environment and prevent all of our children for countless generations from enjoying a high quality of food or life, then we are being quite shortsighted and ultimately rather stupid. Any organism that destroys its own relationships with others along with its habitat in order to get *more* of what it thinks it wants is poisoning itself. So, in one sense, Arjuna is actually seeing the toxic nature and stupidity of this ego-based approach to self-fulfillment. He arrives on the battlefield and immediately understands this primary importance of relationship. Arjuna doesn't want anything for himself. He is realizing love. Yet because of his culture, his upbringing, and his doubts he doesn't trust his gut feeling, his instinctual understanding that something is terribly wrong with the situation. Arjuna tells Kṛṣṇa that he sees only bad omens and unjust outcomes if they move into battle. In this state of distress and overwhelming conflict, knowing in his heart that the situation is immoral yet holding tightly on to his identity as a warrior, Arjuna is impaled by the horns of a dilemma. Should he engage in killing or not? He asks himself, "Alas! We are determined to commit a great sin in resolving to kill our own people through greed for the pleasures of a royal kingdom. If the fully armed Sons of Dhṛtarāṣṭra should kill me, unarmed and unresisting in battle, it would be a greater happiness for me" (1.45–46). Seeing the futility of the situation, Arjuna, thinking out loud to Kṛṣṇa, declares he would rather die a pacifist than kill. And here the first chapter draws to a close, and the once vibrant young warrior collapses into the seat of his chariot, dropping his bow from his hand, frozen by uncertainty and unable to act.

Remember that in Indian mythology the bow represents the tuned body and mind. Like a bow the mind is the tool used to launch the arrows of the mind—your thoughts. When the *prāṇas* (in this context, perceptions) of the body are tuned through *āsana* (yoga posture), meditation, and *prāṇāyāma* (breathing practices), then the mind gradually clears with an increased capacity to move quickly between thought and counterthought, distress and calm, action and nonaction. With this focus and resiliency of mind we can also become more one pointed and precise in thought, sharpening the arrows of intelligence and concentration so as to know how to take more skillful action. The story of the Gītā, therefore, opens with Arjuna in utter confusion, as he is beginning to wake up spiritually, intellectually, and personally.

This is precisely why the myth is set on a battlefield of both dharma and action. The word *dharma* can mean many things, but initially in this context it means the field of duty or law, what Arjuna *should* be doing. It also means the field of idealism, or ideas, and the field of structure, of cognitive knowledge, and of technique. Dharma can refer to foundational teachings or the cosmic order of things. It defines one's individual purpose in the world and implies a capacity for discernment that informs ethical action. When we become intimately familiar with our own purpose or dharma—which is necessarily defined by our circumstances—we then begin to see that the ultimate structure of existence is ever changing and always rooted in relationship. When we cultivate the intelligence to contextualize, we establish the ground from which acting with kindness and connectedness—with compassion—naturally arises. In this sense dharma is then the glue that holds everything together.

The other characteristic of the field is that of action: What should Arjuna *do*, and what should any of us actually do once we discern a course of action for any given situation? No matter how much we agonize over the specifics of a conflict or situation, no matter how carefully we weigh our options as to what the best course of action might be, it is when we actually take that first step that our actions truly count. The first step, where the rubber meets the road, is where the rewards, and failures, of our efforts are revealed. At that point, of course, as much as when we are gearing up for action, staying attentive and awake, listening to feedback, and discerning the next appropriate step (which is sometimes in the exact opposite direction from what we originally thought was best) are equally important. For instance, if you are a designer of cars, or wheels, or tires, it is all meaningless until you test-drive the vehicle. If the tire flies apart or the car crashes into a flaming fireball, you realize you must begin again because it wasn't correctly designed. So *kurukṣetra* (or the field of action) is not only action, but more specifically, the capacity to discern while stepping into action. It means taking action in the context of the moment; being steadied by an awareness of your moral ground—your intentions in life—so that your motivations and actions reflect and align with your intentions. This provides a clear sense of what specific actions will serve in any given moment, and when it is most appropriate to act.

The Gītā unfolds in the middle of this extraordinary field—the very field upon which such an important confrontation *must* take place. The teachings do not occur in an idyllic setting, such as a rose garden, but instead are deliberately set on a battlefield. This extreme situation represents the crisis that every one of us is in if we really start to wake up, facing with an open mind and clear heart the difficulties we encounter in a world that is utterly intertwined within the chaos of relationship to others. Looking closely we see that truth, knowledge, patience, action, trust, and kindness—love itself—are all present as guidelines for action.

At that point, as we begin to awaken, if we are lucky, we take refuge initially in what could be referred to as a field of dharma *and* action, or a structure for harmony between dharma and action that informs us of what to do. Of course it turns out that within the dilemmas we all face, just as is taught in the Gītā, whatever the situation, our action cannot be reduced to one single dharma or a single formula, technique, or style. But one must start somewhere, so the first step must be taken.

Though in the story of the Gītā Kṛṣṇa is the teacher, it is Arjuna who, by refusing to fight, provides this preliminary profound teaching, one that is supposed to hit you right in the heart. Kṛṣṇa immediately overrides the hesitation by telling Arjuna that he is totally ignorant, which sets up the teachings in an even more interesting way. As readers, from the onset most of us feel aligned with Arjuna and his reluctance to rush into battle, senselessly killing others. This is particularly true for those of us who've been practicing yoga for a while and have decided we agree with the first *yama*, or ethical principle, put forth in the Yoga Sūtras of Patañjali—that of nonviolence. We've started mellowing out, becoming more tolerant of others, and may even have become vegetarian in a gesture toward nonharming other sentient beings. In response to Arjuna falling apart—dropping his beloved bow and exposing his vulnerability by proclaiming his unwillingness to kill—instead of congratulating him on being such a good *yogī*, Kṛṣṇa just smiles his beautiful smile and says, "You grieve for those for whom you should not grieve. And yet you speak about wisdom. The paṇḍits do not mourn for those who have gone or for those who have not yet gone" (2.11). So at the very start of the Gītā Kṛṣṇa becomes incredibly irritating, which is interesting too. Why would the story be constructed to portray Kṛṣṇa as such? Many scholars—Hindu and Buddhist alike—reject the Gītā for this very reason, considering Kṛṣṇa and the Gītā to be promoting senseless killing. At first glance, it seems to be true that Kṛṣṇa is advising Arjuna to ignore his conscience—his moral compass—by strong-arming him into standing up to fight and to kill. Indeed, he does tell Arjuna that it doesn't really matter if he kills others on the battlefield because everything is impermanent; they're as good as dead anyway: "One who thinks that they kill and one who thinks that this is killed; they both do not understand. This neither kills nor is killed. . . . One who knows this as indestructible and eternal, unborn and undecaying; how could such a person kill, causing whom to kill and killing whom" (2.19; 2.21)? Yet if you contemplate the message given as the full text unfolds, it is quite clear that Kṛṣṇa is teaching something far more complex, not simply encouraging Arjuna to blindly uphold his duty as a warrior and to therefore kill.

If we become too absorbed by the particulars of the account, the mythology of the Gītā, it is easy to forget that the teaching is intended to be instructive to *all* of us within our own unique circumstances. In a sense it is the story of one's inner conflict when faced with any crisis, and in times of crisis we must all stand up and fight. Considering the Gītā metaphorically we can imagine our own body as our chariot carrying us through life. Kṛṣṇa represents our intelligence; the *buddhi* and our capacity to understand the context of complicated situations. As such he is ultimately the *paramātman*, or pure consciousness, which within Hindu mythology is thought of as the "supreme or primordial self." In this sense, the Kṛṣṇa within us is the witness, the friend, the beloved—the other. In the telling of the myth he is the charioteer and the chariot and therefore represents Arjuna's body. The horses pulling the chariot symbolize the senses, and the reins, held in Kṛṣṇa's competent hands, represent the mind with an ever-present need to guide the senses so as not to be pulled hither and thither. As the paramātman, Kṛṣṇa represents intelligence, and he chooses to work with Arjuna as he is—sincere, eager, and beginning to awaken to a deeper level of understanding of the world but also still captive to his thoughts and senses. Rather than assuming the powerful role of God, or that of a teacher who could try to shove tradition and dogma—or even truth—down Arjuna's throat, Kṛṣṇa instead takes on the role of a servant and guide. This in and of itself is a teaching; in particular, a teaching for those of us interested in being teachers.

The particular self, or self-awareness, what would be called the *jivātman*, is represented by Arjuna. We, like Arjuna, are all intimately familiar with our individual jivātman because it is our unique capacity for thought construction; subtle and gross thoughts, desires, and aversions and the experiential interplay between the body, mind, and senses. The jivātman is what we imagine our True Selves to be, transmigrating body to body, life to life, situation to situation. It is a constant reminder of the tangible reality of our unique experiences that necessarily exists in conversation with the less palpable, intuitive, mystical, deeply selfless sense of impermanence and interconnectedness. When we find a balance between these two aspects of experience—our existence as both an individual (the jivātman) and as part of something far bigger than our own corporeal and imaginary self (the paramātman)—then struggles of identity and discernment begin to subside, and this is what gradually happens for Arjuna as the Gītā unfolds.

Kṛṣṇa arrives with Arjuna on the battlefield, ready to steer his dear friend toward remembering, reacquainting himself with what he already knows—his innate humanness and the natural capacity for compassion. In this way, from the start Kṛṣṇa is also teaching all of us the need to find our underlying sense of truth, meaning, and openhearted compassion (our true dharma) by means of directly experiencing all aspects of interconnectedness rather than through theoretical, detached dogma.

In terms of applying the teachings of the Gītā to our own experience, from the very onset of the story we find two very important buried teachings. The first is the value of becoming clear, embodied, and grounded in the face of crisis. As Arjuna and Kṛṣṇa pull up onto the battlefield they experience a huge sense of excitement, what these days we might consider to be an adrenaline rush. They've been groomed for battle and here they are! The electrifying sound of conch shells being blown by members of the two sides signifies the beginning of battle, so Kṛṣṇa and Arjuna get out their own conchs and blow them as well. Blowing the conch shell is used to indicate the beginnings or endings of many things in traditional Indian rituals and is customarily used while making offerings in temples. The sound is a way of communicating to a great many others, and it demands that others listen. It also has the practical and immediate effect of waking up the senses of the one who is blowing the shell, requiring focus and a long, smooth exhalation of breath. It is, therefore, virtually impossible to blow a conch without becoming absorbed in the physical sensations that spontaneously occur throughout your body due to the vibration of sound and the grounding effect of the exhalation of breath itself. Whether blowing or listening, the sound of a conch has the effect of waking us up into the present moment, focusing the runaway mind—our *citta vṛttis*—and quelling distracted states that so often sabotage our capacity to stay present.

Within the story of the Gītā it is just after Arjuna blows his conch that the teachings begin. He hesitates, asking Kṛṣṇa to draw the chariot up in the middle, between the two opposing armies, so that he may see those "who have come together here ready to fight and hoping to achieve in battle that which is wanted by the evil-minded Son of Dhṛtarāṣṭra" (1.23).

And it is at this point that Arjuna begins to question the situation. Perhaps his hesitation is initiated because he has become embodied due to the vibration of sound; momentarily his mind becomes still as the long exhale brings him down to earth and into the present. This is the moment that he starts to wake up and where his story—our story—of awakening begins to unfold. So from the outset of the text we are taught the importance of pausing, being attentive to the visceral experience of our senses, and finding a way to become grounded. Blowing the conch represents the importance of trusting our full, embodied experience and our intuitive sense (our conscience, as it were) in the face of crisis and dilemma.

As the first chapter of the Gītā draws to a close we find Arjuna frozen by the reeling of his untrained mind and wild senses and by his inability to see beyond his ego—his perceived identity as a warrior. Though he experiences a gut sense that something is wrong, his mind will not loosen its grip long enough for him to fully explore his misgivings. He swoons, revealing to Kṛṣṇa that he must be walked through, step-by-step, an understanding of how to make sense of the conflicting sides of his story.

Kṛṣṇa witnesses that Arjuna, like so many of us when we're in the throes of a dilemma, cannot commit to one course of action or another. So he begins to teach a manifold understanding of insight and the path toward liberation by pointing out to Arjuna, and any of us following the text, that neither his beliefs nor his ethical underpinnings—*our* beliefs and moral ground—should be prescribed, formulaic, or dictatorial. Instead, they should be deeply rooted in a clear understanding of who we are, our dharma, as part of the context of each moment and situation within the ever-changing landscape of relationship. As such, Kṛṣṇa starts the careful process of ushering his beloved student, Arjuna, through a firsthand experience of understanding the complexity and interrelatedness of dharma and action.

But because Arjuna is just *beginning* to awaken (and Kṛṣṇa, by the way, is actually secretly happy that he's resisting battle because that is a sign of Arjuna's insight into interconnectedness), Kṛṣṇa cannot go straight to the punch line of the entire text, revealing that compassion and love are the answer when Arjuna collapses into the chariot. If he were to say, "Fine! You're right. Killing is atrocious and we should just go out for coffee!" then Arjuna wouldn't really get the direct experience of the complexity of his situation, and he might not learn how to apply the teachings to future crises and dilemmas. To make matters worse, his psychopathic cousin, who is the leader of the opposing army, would likely cause deep suffering to countless beings. So as we move into chapter 2 of the Gītā, Kṛṣṇa meets Arjuna where he is and proceeds to give the simplistic answer within which Arjuna's well-trained, conventional mind is likely to find footing. He reminds Arjuna that he is a warrior, so it is his duty to fight. When this doesn't work, he turns to tenets of Sāṁkhya (the first Indian philosophical tradition) and the idea of impermanence within an ever-changing, interpenetrating system, in order to try to convince Arjuna he must act with clarity. In an almost offhanded way in verses 2.11–13, Kṛṣṇa tells Arjuna it is hypocritical of him to speak of wisdom and yet still grieve for those who will die on the battlefield. He says that those who are truly wise understand that though the body gives out at some point, because of reincarnation we are reborn with a new life and a new body to once again work toward insight and enlightenment. Essentially he tells Arjuna to wise up, to use his intelligence!

The underlying simplified theory of Sāṁkhya is that there are two aspects of reality: *puruṣa*, which is divine or pure consciousness, and *prakṛti*, which is creative energy or all that manifests. From this perspective, within the *jivā* (a living entity) puruṣa and prakṛti are related in a way that facilitates individual experience. One's experience is often incorrectly interpreted as the whole of reality when, in fact, Sāṁkhya shows us that it is an impermanent composition of mind. In Sāṁkhya theory pure consciousness, or puruṣa, exists outside of time and space, infinitely present and unending. Anything that manifests and/or is perceived, including each of us as individuals, our thoughts, forces of nature, and everything else we think, feel, perceive, or imagine, is just a form of creative energy, or prakṛti. All prakṛti is impermanent and therefore not real in an absolute sense of the word.

Kṛṣṇa continues by pointing out that life (puruṣa) has no beginning and no end, so it does not really matter if we kill one particular being or not. Seeing that Arjuna is confused and his eyes are glazing over as he tries to understand (which, by the way, is the typical response for any of us when we first begin trying to understand the truth of impermanence and Sāṁkhya theory), Kṛṣṇa then tries to explain further. He says that, yes, we take on the form of a body when we are born and from that limited point of view we live, and we die. But really, he clarifies, those who are wise see that the puruṣa takes on different bodies that eventually are cast aside like the garments one casts off day to day. It is this, the puruṣa, the divine consciousness or what from a Western perspective might be thought of as the soul, that is lasting. Sāṁkhya proposes that it is the subtle body, composed of prakṛti, that transmigrates body to body and the death or killing of a particular body is like discarding an article of clothing. Sāṁkhya would say that prakṛti, manifesting in the form of a particular gross body, ceases to be in death, but the underlying subtle body transmigrates, and the pure consciousness, puruṣa, is completely unharmed. So logically "killing" a body does no harm to pure consciousness. Of course, from a personal perspective there are severe problems with this view, and later in the text Kṛṣṇa addresses what it means to be born into this world in the embodied human form.

Having laid this part of the groundwork of understanding his dilemma by introducing to Arjuna this underlying tenet of Sāṁkhya, Kṛṣṇa next reveals the necessity of considering context when deciding how to act skillfully and with integrity. The best action is seldom if ever taken based on one perspective or one dharma alone but from a multiplicity of viewpoints and from the embodiment of love. For many studying the Gītā it is a relief to hear that the text's foundational teaching is one of love, rather than a call to senseless killing. Yet driven by habitual patterns of thought, our ego is likely at that point to slip in, and suddenly we find ourselves wanting to understand love in order to master it so that the next time a crisis arrives we will be able to avoid the situation altogether by knowing exactly what to do. It is *so* difficult to resist the temptation to know rather than trust not knowing. Yet in this case, we want to know the unknowable.

If we stick with the text, we, like Arjuna, will learn through the teachings that in order to be adept at operating from a foundation of love, one must be seasoned enough in life to see the broader context of what love actually means. Beyond the ecstatic experience of finding another we feel so powerfully connected to that we fall "in love," true love is tenderness, mercy, forgiveness, and the capacity to see others for who they really are rather than from our narrative of who we think they are. Love is an open acceptance and connection to everyone and everything else from a place so deep within ourselves that we lose track of our illusion of self along with our definition of love. Like a Möbius strip, true love has no beginning and no end and is completely free from identity. With this, at the beginning of chapter 2, Kṛṣṇa takes the first step in a process of ushering his beloved student, Arjuna, through his own doubts, fears, understandings, and misunderstandings until finally he can fully comprehend the complexity of taking action in the midst of life's inevitable crises.

[2]

The Nature of Harmony: Not Two, Not One

As CHAPTER 2 of the Gītā opens, Arjuna is in the midst of a crisis of conscience. Immobilized by conflicting ideals and collapsed in a state of utter despair at the prospect of the impending deaths that doubtlessly lie ahead, he finds himself impaled by the horns of dilemma—to act or not to act. As a warrior, yet equally a man of strength and integrity who is filled with compassion, no clear course of action, no suitable path that combines his defining traits so that he might act in integrity with his sense of meaning and truth, seems possible. Feeling anguish and empathy for those on the battlefield, yet gripped by the responsibility he feels as a warrior, Arjuna asks Kṛṣṇa how he can justify killing his opponent, Droṇa, the great teacher of virtually every warrior on either side of the battle. Worse yet, he cannot fathom what good it would do for anyone to kill his great uncle, Bhīṣma, one of the greatest warriors of all time, who happens also to be a rival in this battle. Arjuna is faced with the impossible, and his predicament sets the stage for the interwoven layering of teachings that are presented throughout the text. He is overcome by despair laced with compassion and says, "My limbs sink down, my mouth dries up, my body trembles, and my hair stands up on end. Gāṇḍīva (the bow) drops from my hand

and my skin is burning all over. I am not able to stand steady, and my mind is flying about" (1.29–30).

This vivid account by Arjuna of what it feels like to be ripped apart mentally, emotionally, and physically is familiar territory to any of us who've been tossed into the center of a complex crisis of conscience. When our sense of cognitive and/or moral dissonance becomes undeniably pervasive it can be overwhelming. The Gītā addresses the all-too-human feelings of helplessness and confusion that can become embedded in every aspect of how we relate to the world if, when faced with a crisis, we separate ourselves from the full context of the situation due to fear, anger, or any other perceived imbalance. The text carefully presents a multidimensional approach to seeing through this reflexive behavior, piercing our own layered storyline within the context of an interwoven pattern of life. We are reminded to always pause and step back, to take a broadened view and recall that our perceptions and preconceptions shape our experience into one that is uniquely ours, yet remains embedded within the background of others and the whole. Separate yet intimately connected. If we allow ourselves to become comfortable with this type of paradoxical perspective we can foster more clarity and an ability to act more intelligently in difficult situations. Throughout the Gītā, therefore, we are encouraged to look closely, again and again, at intricate layerings of perception, history, theory, emotion, relationship, dogma, wisdom, and illusion as a means of gaining insight into what actions might be the most beneficial and least harmful.

Awareness of the layering usually begins superficially as we become absorbed by a storyline. In the Gītā Arjuna's immediate story is that he's on the battlefield seeking guidance from his dear friend, Kṛṣṇa. Arjuna identifies strongly with his position in life as a prince and a warrior, a member of the ruling class, yet his emotional attachment to those whom he loves and respects in combination with his naturally ethical and compassionate disposition make it virtually impossible for him to act. As the story progresses, time and again, Arjuna begins to theoretically grasp the breadth and complexity of the situation, but then he repeatedly loses the thread of understanding—seeing through his theories and emotions into the present moment—and is swept away by waves of doubt and fear that quell his ability to act.

Arjuna's story of crisis is our own story too. It represents the many crises all of us encounter while living in the complex modern world. Perhaps we are confronting a political, personal, or global conflict. Maybe our work requires us to make what seem to be impossible decisions that challenge our underlying beliefs and ethics. It could also be that we are facing the loss of someone we love dearly—or our own impending death. Whatever it is, when a crisis arises it leaps to the foreground of our own story, demanding attention. It can become painfully clear that even if we are confused by the circumstances we must act anyway and that our actions have far-reaching impact. Like Arjuna we may become immobilized by overwhelming uncertainty or by the thought of having to act in ways that go against what we feel is our true nature. The situation may seem to be out of our hands, and we may even be put in a position where our actions might cause harm. Perhaps we are driven by concepts of identity, duty, and status, theorizing to the point that we lose touch with the full context of our story—how we impact others, what is at stake and, equally, what is actually informing our perceptions and actions. We may be ruled by desires, ambitions, emotions, or fears that prevent us from seeing clearly and from maintaining any semblance of connection and responsibility to others. It is common to feel isolated, unsupported, or lost when in the throes of a crisis. So this storyline layer of the Gītā is everyone's story, everyone's predicament as a human being: shackled by the "ignorance" of imagining ourselves to be separate, driven by ego, and ruled by habit and emotion.

A second layer of the teachings in the Gītā is an examination of traditional Indian philosophical perspectives, such as *jñāna*, karma, and bhakti, and how they inform Arjuna's situation. Looking closely at our own lives, we see too that we all have philosophical stances and that from these our unique perspectives grow, creating scaffolding for the flow and comprehension of our own storyline. Unless we are deeply tied to a religion or other group that is fashioned around specific ideals, our philosophy is likely to be informal, so the perspectives we use as navigating tools through life may not be as polished as those of more formal schools of philosophical thought; they may not even be considered decent philosophy. But when we think we philosophize; the mere process of considering life is in and of itself a philosophical endeavor. Though this layer of understanding is sometimes considered the primary teaching of the Gītā—an overview of various traditional schools and paths one may take in search of insight and liberation—it is very interesting to consider the philosophical stances presented as they relate to Arjuna's (our) personal storyline, as well as how they interface with underlying, more global themes, which make up the third layer of teachings.

This important third layer of global themes, such as the truth of impermanence, the power of embodiment, and the necessity of embracing deep meaning—things like trust, love, and compassion—is critical to consider when studying the Gītā or our own lives. We can define "global themes" as deep-seated ethical, moral, aesthetic, and intellectual rubrics that serve as polestars; a guidance system through the seemingly unfathomable waters of crises and conflict that invariably arise. They help us to stay rooted within the present moment, and they provide ground for discernment by offering a nonpersonal perspective. Supported by our deep beliefs and a sense of meaning, we can begin to see through our ideas and constructed identities, so that clear and principled action becomes quite natural.

Within the story of the Gītā we follow Arjuna's fascinating process of evolving through the visceral experience of understanding impermanence, interconnection, and the need for compassion. These insights are made possible for him by Kṛṣṇa who gingerly guides him through, between, and within the layering of his own personal story and experience, in light of philosophical theories cradled within underlying truths or global themes. It is only possible for Arjuna to assimilate a full understanding in a step-by-step manner; through the slow process of repeatedly building temporary footholds of comprehension, a corner here, a corner there, from one layer to the next, then doubling back to his immediate experience, confusion, and eagerness to question. For example, Arjuna is vividly aware of his own story—what is expected of a royal warrior. Kṛṣṇa then emphasizes a philosophical context—the notion that life has no beginning and no end. However, Arjuna only begins to discern what action he must take by interfacing his understanding of the global theme of love with his personal storyline of feeling compelled to show compassion for his enemies within the context of his own dharma, duty, or philosophical stance as a princely warrior. We find time and again within the Gītā that the teachings unfold in this way: global themes pointing through and back around to specific details of Arjuna's story, then circling deeper and deeper within the story and classical schools of thought to touch on fallacies and insights as they relate to the nature of life and of being, before once again shedding light on the immediate experience and the story itself. We find layers being interwoven, twisting and turning back and around time and again in order to reveal paths we may take to dive in more deeply to a more subtle level where new insight appears. This story is, in a sense, our own predicament, and so it is revealed that there is a step-by-step process each of us must take if we are to fully absorb the content, tenor, and embodied feel of the teachings as they relate to our own personal life. How do we engage fully, ethically, and with great joy and compassion in life during both good times and bad? We are shown that this process of seeing clearly and taking action often requires patience, the determination to comprehend, and the capacity to let go of preconceptions in order to taste new perspectives.

Exploring the interconnected nature inherent in the layering of personal storyline, philosophy, and global themes reveals that this sort of patterning is what all life is actually about. As we mature, our foundational beliefs and ethical values—our own global themes—become the rudders that help us traverse life's waters. If we polish and upgrade them while also keeping an open mind, we become increasingly clear, strong, and compassionate. However, if we ignore them, they become encrusted with suffocating barnacles of prejudgment and may even fall away. When this happens we lose our ethically informed sense of inner guidance and direction and begin to become stuck within our own ego and our limited personal story, increasingly separated from the world as a whole. As we wither within life in this way, the heart—our humanness that has as its roots in kindness and compassion—begins to close because we have lost our connection to others and to a deeper meaning in life.

When we consider this layering of the storyline of "me," our personal beliefs, and philosophical underpinnings in concert with truths like birth, death, old age, and disease, we automatically begin to wake up. Of course "waking up" isn't always easy and comfortable because, at least at certain phases, by definition it will not fit with our preconceptions and conditioned behaviors. However, if we hold steady at precarious points of unfolding, there is the potential for insight. This is, perhaps, one of the most important messages of the Gītā: by actively participating in the interwoven process of mind, body, and spirit within our own storyline, we find hope and a chance not only to create our own happiness but also to contribute to the happiness of others. Within this there is the opportunity to live a fulfilled, relationship-based and compassionate life.

By the end of chapter 2 of the Gītā we have not only been introduced to Arjuna's story—the dilemma and specifics of his crisis—we have also been subject to a lengthy discussion of the principles of the Sāṁkhya school and given insight into interconnectedness, infinity, and the beauty of paradox. Kṛṣṇa has also given a nod to other philosophical theories and global themes of the Gītā. As the text progresses these layers of the teaching—storyline, philosophical underpinnings, and global themes—are visited and revisited, offered separately, then woven and rewoven together as a demonstration of the natural learning process. When we are sincerely looking for a path toward awakening, we must slowly lay a multidimensional foundation of interwoven understanding. Then we must set it down to look at it again more deeply or from different angles. This setting down is imperative if we are to comprehend and evolve before finally letting all of it go with a sense of trust in what it means to be part of an interpenetrating process of existence. So right from the start of the Gītā we see this pattern being taught. Kṛṣṇa advises us to study the classical legs of philosophy, pointing out that they were part of the ancient texts of the Vedas, but he cautions us not to become shackled into closed-minded thinking through these teachings. He says, "The activities of the three guṇas [the three phases of change in creative energy] are the realm of the Vedas. Be free of the three guṇas, Arjuna. Always abiding in truth, free of the dualities, not concerned for acquisition and preservation, and holding the True Self" (2.45).

He encourages Arjuna to stand steadily in wisdom (insight and what we have referred to as global themes), without becoming dogmatic. Kṛṣṇa encourages Arjuna to question philosophical systems, perceptions, and conclusions to avoid becoming stuck in any particular viewpoint.

The method for realizing this freedom from dogma is to cultivate a grounded, embodied experience of love. This is true for us too, as we persevere in our search for meaning. It is important to let go again and again, noticing when we're distracted from the truth by personal needs and ego attachments. In this way perhaps we get a taste for freedom by fully embodying a sense of what could be called the "True Self," which is everything, everywhere. Once submerged in this truth, we may discover pure bliss and that there is no need for the distractions of ego and attachment. Kṛṣṇa then offers a beautiful metaphor of this teaching to bring the idea into the realm of imagination: "As is the use of a well in a place flooded with water on all sides, such is the value in all of the Vedas (rituals) for a Brāhman who truly understands" (2.46).

One of the most important underlying themes that we find early on in the Gītā is that nothing happens in our awakening (what later is called yoga) without grace and compassion or in this case, the *kṛpa* of Mādhava, the grace of Kṛṣṇa. It turns out to be the same thing as openheartedness, the presence of pure awareness, or what Buddhists might call *śūnyatā* or emptiness. Nothing can happen, nothing can move without surrendering to it. This is the attitude of bhakti, or devotion, that you might absorb and then manifest from reading the Gītā. Even if we want to understand the storyline and its intricate teachings, there is no hope for us as readers to fully understand the teachings unless we surrender. In other words, the global theme is that understanding and insight in life are not acts of will, although you must have the will to understand. Deeper understanding—insight—will not occur without reaching a point of surrendering to the paradoxical truth that you *cannot* understand; life is delightfully incomprehensible. When finally you give in you realize that instead of striving to understand, you must trust, and that in trusting you allow concepts and theories of mind to dissolve into pure awareness and the direct experience of the present moment. It is only then that, suddenly, you will truly understand and be able to rest happily in the paradox of knowledge nested in the radiant background of not knowing. Learning to flourish while not knowing, no matter how uncomfortable it may be, is essential to truly knowing and ultimately to freedom.

In the story, as Arjuna begins to question and wake up to the reality of the situation before him, he sees the great generic tragedy that is war.

He also grasps the humanness of all of the participants, just as if you, if you're a parent, stop to think about war and actually begin to understand that all of the soldiers are children with parents—they could be *your* child. You might have insight into the depth of the situation; each one of these soldiers probably has a mother or father just like you. They may have a family and kids at home, and everyone impacted is worried to death! Soldiers on both sides are all praying, just like the warriors in the Gītā are praying to the same god that is metaphorically the father of all of the characters in the book. In Mahāyāna Buddhism it is said that sometime in the past you have been the mother of each being you now meet, and at another time they have been *your* mother. But it doesn't stop there. Within the Mahāyāna—which is the same view of impermanence and interconnectedness that Kṛṣṇa is using with Arjuna at the beginning of the Gītā to say he should fight—there is no beginning and no end to life. Consequently, you have been in every conceivable combination of relationships—daughter, friend, enemy, lover, and so on—with every other sentient being you meet. We are, after all, "made of stardust," particles that have been around since the formation of our planet and will long outlive us. Without question, from this theoretical or mystical perspective, the perceivable world is interconnected, interpenetrating, and unending. Looking deeply into the eyes of another—anyone—you can see infinity. You can sense the endless, interweaving pattern of connection that is life, not by way of your theories but through your heart.

That is the position Arjuna finds himself in when the Gītā begins. Fortunately for him, he's with his trusted friend, Kṛṣṇa, who happens to be one of the best yogīs of all time. Kṛṣṇa, like any sincere yoga practitioner, has taken the Mahāvrata, or the great ethical vow of the yamas that Patañjali describes in the Yoga Sūtras. First and foundational to all other yamas is *ahiṁsā*, which is a vow to not harm. Then there is *satya* (to be honest), *asteya* (to not steal from others), *brahmacarya* (to not exploit others as objects), and finally *aparigrahā* (to not grasp at things all around in all dimensions). This last yama is often overlooked, but one we all easily fall prey to: "I need this, I want that, I deserve the best, I, I, I, me, me, me." The Mahāvrata is the ethical vow that yogīs take to avoid the natural tendency to become slaves to our own small story of "me."

Each of the vows is built upon the idea of ahiṁsā, nonharming, and this is very important to look at deeply when trying to untangle ourselves from absorption in our own storyline. When our actions are motivated exclusively (or even primarily) from the perspective of "what is best for me," then it is inevitable we will act in harmful ways, not only to others, but also ultimately to ourselves—because if we perceive our self as separate and autonomous, by definition we have lost sight of the underlying truth of interconnectedness. Keeping the vow of ahiṁsā in the foreground of our thoughts is imperative, but it is ahiṁsā in the context of the whole. From the perspective of an individual, ahiṁsā and inherent interconnectedness can seem paradoxical because we think "I" am a person who does not harm others. Quickly this limited viewpoint can be ripped out of the contextual background and, if we become rigid in its definition and application, the idea of ahiṁsā can flip to manifest in harmful ways at the drop of a hat.

Arjuna's commitment to nonharming is buried deep in the situation before him and it plays a big part in his dilemma. He is a member of the ruling class—a noble—and a caring person, but his dharma is to be a warrior. Like Arjuna you too may run into situations where it is impossible to know what action is in accordance with dharma and the beliefs that steer you through life. Once you've taken the vow of ahiṁsā, you may feel some moral dissonance when faced with a situation that requires action that could harm others. Worse yet, what if your everyday job is one that places you in circumstances that might involve harming someone to help or protect others? Say, for example, you are a policeman. By definition at some point in your career you will likely be put in the position of restraining, if not hurting, someone for the safety of others. If you're a nonviolent or "softie" policeman, people will probably walk all over you. If you are to be effective and keep your job as a policeman, you'll have to be a little bit tough. "What to do? Oh dear! I wish I had a different job."

No matter what our dharma "dictates," what chosen profession or lot in life we have, these kinds of difficult situations will arise. To act skillfully we can and must identify and remain conscious of our moral ground—our ethics and values, our intentions and motivations. These are our guidance systems. They not only keep us navigating and on track in the world, but they are the fail-safe indicators that tell us on a visceral level when we have veered off track. Just as Arjuna hesitated on the battlefield because he had a gut sense that something was not right, whether you're a policeman, a politician, or a parent, learning to recognize, then pause and listen to feelings of internal discord and disharmony that arise, is imperative before taking action, especially in times of conflict or crisis. In a sense these indicators are what would be called our conscience—our moral, ethical, interpersonal, ecological markers that toss up red flags of caution when things just aren't right. If we repeatedly ignore our conscience due to carelessness, dogmatic beliefs, or circumstances beyond our control (such as a boss who asks us to do things we morally disagree with, like keeping a secret we feel is wrong to keep), signals from our intrinsic warning system, our moral compass, become more and more faint. Eventually we lose connection to and trust in ourselves until we (or concerned others) discover we have no conscience left at all. To complicate matters, when we are not focused and grounded we can become caught in a swirling quagmire of emotions, thoughts, and sense perceptions that can skew how we understand things as well, causing us to override our intuition. So simply saying "I'm going to uphold my ethical beliefs" needs to be counterbalanced by honesty, by looking as best we can at the big picture of the context of our situation and by calling ourselves on familiar patterns of self-deceit, denial, emotional upheaval, and mind games that skew our ability to perceive clearly. These types of self-deceit and internal mayhem cause feelings of isolation, separation, and even persecution, and they result in a great deal of confusion and miscommunication. If we are to trust our gut sense of things it must not only be rooted in a constructed understanding of our moral ground. We must also be willing, again and again, to take an honest appraisal of our personal quirks as they interface with basic characteristics of human nature—like attachment or the need to know and so forth—that might be clouding or shaping our perceptions. Once we have established a fertile ground of trusting the process of life and its interconnected nature, then insight and a natural feeling of harmony spontaneously arise and from there we can act more clearly—hopefully in service to others and in alignment with the truth of who we really are.

[3]

Karma: Intention, Attachment, and Letting Go

BACK IN 1975, Gary Dahl, an American advertising executive, gave birth to the idea of the perfect pet—the Pet Rock. Your new pet would arrive by mail within just a few days, snuggled in a nest of straw and kept safe in a well-ventilated box. No need to feed, bathe, or clean up after this one and, best of all, you'd know that this pet, this *friend*, would be one you'd never have to grieve for as it would long outlive you. Mind you, this was long before the invention of the Internet where fads come and go in seconds. Yet still, within a few months of conceiving the idea, Dahl became a millionaire, selling his "pets" for a meager four dollars each to those who "needed" one. It was a clever idea and perhaps more than a demonstration of the strange twist our capitalistic, pervasively bourgeois, world was taking. It was a testament to the fact that we are a species that, by the sheer power of mind, can become attached to just about anything.

The influence of mind is on vivid display when, after focusing on something like a Pet Rock with what invariably becomes a building intensity, we start to believe the story the mind has constructed around our need for or aversion to that object. With strong focus of mind on anything whatsoever, our whole being can become a closed system. Gradually our fabricated storyline transforms into "truth" and, like a freight train barreling down the tracks, our imagination determines our actions. If we are unable to release our attachment to ideas or outcomes, our ability to keep an open mind and to take in important and relevant information is derailed. First the mind and eventually the entire embodied experience and our actions (karma) become a field of responsiveness to and reinforcement of whatever our fabricated narrative may be.

Letting go of attachments to urges or preconceptions is like keeping the windows open in a house. When you're not attached (or rather not attached to attachments as they arise) there is a quality of spaciousness throughout your head, as if breezes of intelligence are circulating through the structures of your mind. Rather than feeling a claustrophobic sense of keeping windows tightly sealed around entrenched habitual patterns of thinking and doing, you feel free. Imagine visiting an elderly friend. Opening the front door you are met by a thick wall of stagnant air that is perfumed with rose or laden by the smell of last night's dinner atop a blanket of odors accumulated during years of isolation from the world. You gradually adjust to the smell, but later when you step outside into fresh air, you remember that you're part of something bigger. Understanding the nature of attachment is relevant to all of us because when we move out of our habituated patterns of seeing and interacting by keeping an open mind, we are required to interface with the world at large and our torpid, private view is tempered. When we're attached to ideas or "needs" triggered by sense perceptions, it's like we're closing ourselves in a house surrounded by remnants of a life gone by, unable to feel into the present moment and a sense of interconnectedness. This misperception of existence as one of separateness, from Indian and Buddhist perspectives, is called *avidyā*, or ignorance and the inability to see clearly, and it is seen as the taproot of suffering as we all search for happiness.

As a species we tend to equate happiness with the attachments we have to things—either objects or ideas. Yet paradoxically, it is letting go of attachments, especially attachments to the fruits of our actions, that facilitates the ability to find stability within chaos. This stability is what allows us the capacity to look deeply enough into our essence to find freedom and *therefore* happiness. By cultivating this sort of equanimity, we can fully experience our attachments, even enjoy and be motivated by them, and then we easily see through them and let them go.

The necessity of letting go of attachment to the fruits of our actions is another global theme that defines the teachings of the Gītā. Throughout the story we are shown that attachments are a primary catalyst for establishing and reinforcing the ego, which leads to the perception of separateness and ultimately to suffering.

Kṛṣṇa explains to Arjuna that the problem with attachments is that the mind is so easily carried away by them. When we are attached to things, the fabricated storylines we spin around them cause us to become stuck in imaginary realms of confusion, and this is the real cesspool of suffering—*saṃsāra*. For instance we want, or do not want, something and so we either grasp it or push it away. We suffer. Or things don't go according to our plan, and it makes us angry or confused and unable to see that the contexts of our desires are part of a bigger picture. When we lose sight of context—our interconnectedness—invariably we, and others, suffer. Kṛṣṇa underscores this by telling Arjuna, "For one contemplating the objects of the senses, attachment to them is born; from attachment desire arises, from desire anger is born. From anger delusion arises. From delusion memory and mindfulness wander away. From memory wandering there is destruction of the intelligence (buddhi). From destruction of the intelligence one is lost" (2.62–63).

However, as any of us who've ever been attached to anything—which is all of us—knows, it is not easy to truly let go of attachments, especially being attached to the fruits of our actions. This is true for Arjuna too and is a huge factor that keeps him confused and immobilized on the brink of battle. He is restrained by his own idea that he should fight not only because he's drawn to the excitement on the battlefield, but also because he defines himself as a warrior. He cannot see through these attachments. As the story progresses Kṛṣṇa carefully weaves a safety net of insight beneath Arjuna, who feels unsteady and unstable, impaled by the horns of dilemma and not knowing what action to take. It's as if Arjuna has climbed up the tree of his ideals—just like an enthusiastic kid might climb an apple tree—and suddenly he finds himself way up near the top where the sky's the limit and infinity is close at hand, yet the limbs are thinner and the breeze is a reminder of his immortality and impermanence. He freezes; he can't get down. If Arjuna just lets go abruptly and walks away from his responsibilities, family, and friends, it's a problem. But redefining his role and actions—in a sense backing down the tree of his imagined imperative—is a challenge too. Kṛṣṇa, like the supportive parent on the ground saying, "Climb down the way you got up," begins to gently guide Arjuna toward an understanding of how to let go of the limbs of his attachments to objects and ideas, so that he may carefully reassess the situation in full as he finds his way safely back down to earth and to happiness. Kṛṣṇa explains that it is through a disciplined practice that we find happiness: "However, by disengaging with desire and repulsion a person with self-awareness and control, even though the senses are engaged with sense objects, attains clarity and tranquility. In that tranquil clarity there is born for one a cessation of all suffering. For the clever mind the intelligence is quickly established. For one not linked in yoga, there is no singular intelligence and there is no deep meditation, and for one without meditation there is no peace. For one without peace, where is happiness" (2.64–66)?

As the story progresses—to the very end, in fact—we are reminded that letting go is a process of unraveling infinite layers of understanding, misperception, insight, preconception, dogma, and imagination. Letting go is ultimately the capacity to trust and to reconsider, to surrender and to embrace the unknown within a clear perception of whatever is arising. There is a lot of uncertainty associated with letting go of the fruits of our actions, and this can lead to fear until we recognize that the ability to hold steady during storms of mind and to let go at the right moment is the most skillful and safest action any of us can ever take toward not only healthy evolution but also liberation. We are reminded that often it is attachment to our sense perceptions that keeps us frozen or stuck. "When one's mind is continuously led around by the wandering senses, it carries away the discriminating wisdom like the wind carries away a ship on the water" (2.67).

Kṛṣṇa, seeing Arjuna's confusion, pulls back slightly from the abstract thought of simply letting go of the fruits of his actions and tries another tactic to help Arjuna grasp the idea of nonattachment. He explains that the wise ones (yogīs) train the mind to become comfortable in stillness and that this stillness supports them in becoming comfortable in not knowing. The teaching is that through yoga the mind becomes calm by focusing on one thing while not impulsively responding to the bidding of the senses and through this process it gradually becomes apparent that although we are constantly bombarded by input from the senses, most of what is presented through our senses is unexpected, unknown. When we observe this process of input from the sense fields arising, and we choose to remain focused on one thing—like the breath—then eventually we notice too that by not instantly responding to what arises, it then transforms into yet another unexpected, unknown manifestation. We begin to notice that not responding haphazardly lends clarity to our perception of what we observe arising so that we may more easily discern the best course of action when action is called for. One can focus on any object of attention—the breath, sounds, patterns of thought as they come and go—but the recommended focus is ultimately the *ātman*, or the True Self, which could initially be thought of as pure awareness into the interconnected nature of all things. Of course, interconnectedness is difficult to focus on because it, the ātman, is not a separate specific thing but is the true nature of any and all things. In the Yoga Sūtras and other classical texts that offer details on how to practice meditation, we are advised to choose one object or field upon which to settle the mind Fortunately, since everything is connected, by focusing on whatever is arising we are bringing the mind to rest on a representative portion of the entire interconnecting pattern. If we do so long enough, one day the pattern that, indeed, everything is interpenetrating is revealed, and that reality is who and what you and all others really are: joy, satisfaction, pure awareness. *This* is the ātman. In Buddhist thought, this is referred to as the idea of emptiness, and in Sāṁkhya theory it is the open nature of all creative energy. So it turns out that training the mind by focusing it on a chosen field is the first step in letting go of the fruits of our actions.

As we work our way through the Gītā we're shown that, just like focusing the mind, virtually everything is a step-by-step process—one's storyline, philosophical theories, even the ability to let go of attachments. Observing any of these processes rather than becoming entrenched in them takes practice. For most it's easier to exercise a little restraint and delayed gratification when it comes to urges that arise from sense perceptions than it is to act with nonattachment to ideas (though not always so with addictions, which fall into a related, but separate, category).

Typically sense objects produce more blatant visceral responses than theoretical attachments, which tend to cause emotional or mental attachments as well. Of course, the process of *how* all attachments emerge is the same. The mind rides impulses and becomes increasingly stuck in and attached to the imagined end, while progressively less engaged in what is actually arising in the present moment. Eventually theory or habitual response becomes the deciding factor in directing one's actions. The *yogīc* practice recommended in the Gītā is to notice the arising of sensations that lead to attachment so that the choice to act—to respond or not respond—becomes a conscious choice based on as clear a vision as we are capable of within the context of everything else that is arising. This is what it means to see through our attachments and is an important step toward relieving not only our own suffering, but that of others as well.

Suffering arises when we pull our beliefs, perceptions, and actions out of their background, seeing them as separate and thereby perceiving ourselves as separate. Observing the insidious power that reflexive responses to our senses in concert with our imagined separateness can have in determining our actions is quite revealing, if not embarrassing. When we're attached to our ideas it is extraordinarily easy to be driven by our preconceptions and predispositions while we ignore red flags indicating something is not right, and we are also likely to miss feedback from others and our immediate circumstances. However, if we notice the urge to be attached and the impulse to believe our storylines around imagined ideas and attachments, then perhaps suffering can be alleviated. Remembering that all life is sacred and seeing everything—even our attachments themselves—as sacred manifestations within our particular life and circumstance can relieve suffering.

If we consider attachments as one of the root causes of suffering, we see that the attachments themselves, no matter what form they take, are not actually tangible. They arise within the process of interacting with the world; they are part of the mystery of life and in that sense they too are sacred. Probably most of us have experienced visceral responses triggered by attachments to a stimulus or thought. There is actually nothing harmful with that part of the process. Where it goes awry is when the mind becomes trapped within a single-focused urge or idea and cannot move past it. The mind is like a well-tooled, diamond needle, the kind used in old-fashioned record players. Sometimes the needle becomes stuck, repeating the same small loop of music until gentle downward pressure applied to the phonograph's arm reminds the needle to pass through and beyond the groove of the record. When we train the mind to return focus to whatever is arising in the present moment, then we do not become slaves to our senses. It is like putting just the right pressure on the phonograph's arm to keep the music flowing smoothly. Not only is there a palpable effort to steady the mind, but there is also the feeling of letting go so that habitual loops of response can fall into place with the rest of the context of our life.

Until we truly experience the process of how we become attached, and until we honestly experience the desire to put attachments aside, to move past the grooves that keep us stuck and looping within our thinking, then letting go of the fruits of our actions can only be obligatory and formulaic, carried out as a means to an end and tinged with a flavor of renunciation, resentment, or self-serving sacrifice. In contrast, embracing our circumstances fully in selfless sacrifice—while keeping a sense of humor—plays an essential role in letting go of attachments. As the Gītā progresses and as a next step of understanding, Kṛṣṇa offers Arjuna insight into comprehending the benefits and drawbacks to ritual and sacrifice, exploring the tendency to turn both into dogma or a sort of fundamentalist approach to getting what we want.

Healthy ritual and sacrifice are tricky to frame, especially in modern times. We hear of the extreme sacrifice a terrorist believes they are making, the sense of martyrdom they experience by ritualistically blowing themselves up in a crowded marketplace, killing dozens of others in the name of a cause. There are business deals or acts of war steered in inhumane directions—sacrificing the benefit of many for the perceived gain of a few. On a pedantic level, one might make everyday "sacrifices" to accomplish a dream or a goal such as beauty or fitness—"no pain, no gain." Selfless, uncalculated, healthy sacrifices, however, are made instinctively and unconditionally and are fueled by love, like those of a parent who would give their life to save their child. This is the type of sacrifice we aspire to when letting go of the fruits of our actions. But given that we're prone to becoming attached to our ideals, we can easily slip into ritualistic behaviors that on a surface level make it appear like we're not attached, while in fact, possibly unconsciously, we are motivated by the fruits of the action, which are squarely driving our behavior. Until we honestly feel fulfilled by the attachment *and* the letting go of the attachment, then at best we're stuck in our ego and at worst we're driven by ritual as a means to an imagined outcome. Ritual and sacrifice are steps toward liberation only within the context and deliberate cultivation of discriminating awareness; the capacity to withstand the seemingly magnetic force of mind that so easily creates a separate self in the face of interconnectedness.

Rituals and sacrifices are effective when they wake us up, not when they put us to sleep. They work by bringing consciousness into a particular action, while keeping us grounded in an intention held close in the heart. Through Kṛṣṇa's careful tutelage in demonstrating to Arjuna the nature of attachment, we begin to see that in the most basic sense ritual is what we do, and sacrifice is how we frame what we do. Both can be liberating, but, when performed with attachment to the outcome or in a way that perpetuates self-aggrandizement, when carried out with ignorance or in an uninspired manner, rituals and sacrifices become a meaningless means of bondage. They can serve the purpose of releasing the mind from habitual thinking, but in an instant can flip to become rigid, sewing seeds for even more habituated thoughts and behaviors than before. Like so many things in life and yoga, both ritual and sacrifice are slippery slopes.

Within the Indian tradition the important term *yajña* means "sacrificial worship," "devotion," or "the selfless offerings made through ritual." The most common Hindu sacrificial ritual is the fire sacrifice, or *homa*, during which objects with symbolic value, such as ghee, rice, and mantra are offered to the god of fire, Agni, who passes the offerings along to other gods and goddesses. In Vedic times, Agni was said to have the ultimate transformative power, existing on earth as fire, in the atmosphere as lightning, and in the sky as the sun associated with the mysterious, alchemical power to turn water into gas, solid into ash, and so on. Eventually Agni came to represent the ever-changing nature of being and of life itself, again metaphorically represented through the fire ceremony. The fire ceremony also plays a large part in Buddhist practices where Agni sometimes appears as Agni-kumara (the fire prince). It was the Buddhists who, thankfully, first rejected the ancient cross-cultural idea of sacrificing actual living creatures into a fire because killing was not in keeping with the systems underlying tenets of unity, kindness, and compassion.

A primary benefit of any ritual is that it organizes and orders complex situations, beliefs, or relationships. Rituals create a steady state, a stable ground from which to take action, and as such they still the mind. From a yogīc perspective, rituals may lead us to direct experience of what is arising and expose the mind's tendency to grasp, reject, create, and confuse. Whether it's a fire ceremony or a simple daily ritual of having coffee in the morning while reading the news, when carried out with conscious attention to the details of one's present circumstances during the "ritual" itself—the perception of the coffee's rich aroma as the cup is brought toward your lips, for example—everyday rituals of life are turned into moments of insight.

Consciously performing our rituals (tiny or complex) reminds us of the fact that everything in life is in a constant pattern of transformation and is profoundly sacred. An underlying benefit of performing rituals is that we bring focus to the experience of transformation, impermanence, and change. But if our rituals become routine rather than revered, they are useless—and that's the catch. We are ritualistic beings, and we're going to perform rituals—like having our morning coffee—whether we plan on it or not, so the trick is to dovetail on the natural tendency to ritualize by bringing new focus and curiosity to rituals and all actions over and over, again and again. Healthy sacrifices and rituals are those performed for the benefit of others rather than as a matter of habit, a means of self-righteous display, or a way to achieve a goal. They remind us to look beyond the bondage of our own ego structure and to intuit the importance of relationship to others. They help us see more clearly, feel connected, and instinctively express compassion. Rituals and sacrifices that are performed by rote, in a habitual, rigid, and nonvibrant manner, become the opposite; obstacles to seeing clearly and roadblocks on a path toward true joy and happiness.

The idea of ritual and sacrifice as a training ground for releasing attachments is deeply rooted in the teachings of the Gītā. At the very beginning of chapter 3, Kṛṣṇa begins to teach about karma as work, and he explores the importance of offering thoughts, beliefs, and aspirations—*everything*—into the fire of pure awareness with a sincere, open heart—the earnest gesture of consciously letting go in the context of something far bigger than oneself. He says to Arjuna, "This whole world is in bondage to action except for action done as and for sacrifice. O Son of Kuntī, perform action for the sake of sacrifice, free from attachments" (3.9).

From this perspective Kṛṣṇa is implying that in a very basic sense all actions, every aspect of life, is in fact a sacrifice, and we learn later in the teachings that true sacrifice is love. Even a tiger choosing to turn in one direction while following a scent in the jungle is sacrificing the option of taking another direction. In order to get something you have to create a path, and by definition, sacrifice other paths or other objects and actions you encounter, in order to get to the destination. As we are possibly more realized beings than tigers, driven not only by animal instinct but, theoretically, by some form of intellect and compassion for others, we too make sacrifices in the actions we take in the world. This is the nature of decision making.

The difference between sacrifices made in the jungle and those made on the "streets" of daily life is that in the jungle there is usually no complex, theoretical ego investment in sacrificing one path for another. Jungle decisions are often quick, biological, survival reflexes. In daily life, however, where at the very least we've been programmed to present a façade of success and at worst to believe we are separate, entitled, and superior, the setup is ripe for ego stories to dictate our choices, impelling us to take actions and make sacrifices not out of love for the whole but to gain something in return.

The blind spot in this form of isolated sacrifice is our inability to take responsibility for how everything is affected by everything else. Even the smallest action we might take impacts outcomes that in turn influence increasingly larger outcomes and countless other beings. Our sacrifice may start out with something simple like foregoing our indulgences in order to stay healthy, which isn't so bad. But once the wheels of sacrifice in the name of ego are greased by self-serving motivations or attachments to outcome, we are always at risk of losing sight of the bigger picture and of others. It is human nature to slide into self-absorption, and the ability to see others is what draws us back out of ourselves. If we lose sight of the fact that everything is cause and effect (dependent in its arising; the guṇas acting on the guṇas), if we neglect to observe what is being sacrificed and the full impact of the sacrifice, then one day we are presented with the temptation to sacrifice our values or ethics, and we may find ourselves sacrificing truth, relationships, or others for personal gain; returning again to a brutal form of human sacrifice, perhaps not as bloody, but potentially as harmful as those carried out in some ancient civilizations!

[4]

Knowing When to Know

THE EXCITEMENT of a young child who's just connected new dots of cause and effect is infectious. Even when they're tiny you can feel it. Their full-body expression of delight, wiggling arms, legs, and torso as they stick out their tongue to move it around, or their utter absorption as they silently study their fingers and move them at will. For infants, every day seems to bring new joys as they interact and wake up to life. Connecting and interconnecting they experience little difference between themselves and the rest of the world; it's only later they begin to separate themselves out as distinct. Gradually, the illusory bubble that they are the center of the universe pops in no uncertain terms—usually assisted by their older sibling.

Poets and psychologists have perpetuated the belief that the end of innocence dawns when we see through the illusion that we're the center of the universe. But is that really true? Could it be that indeed, each of us *is* at the center of the universe and that there is no one center? The whole of space-time creations have been called the Jeweled Net of Indra. At each juncture of mind and action in the net is a multifaceted jewel that reflects and contains all the other junctures. When we see this, we stop grasping at the hallucinations of separate sense objects and are free of the net. Could it be that our innocence erodes and ignorance arises when we *stop* seeing that each and every one of us is in the center—a sacred and embodied reflection of the rest of the universe? The illusion that hinders us is not that we are the center of the universe, it is the belief that we are the *only* center and that we can act independently from the universe.

Kṛṣṇa's teaching in the Gītā encourages us to explore deeply this idea of where we fit in an interconnected, interdependent world. It's easy to walk into a room and think, "I turned on the light" because you flipped the power switch. But if you look even a little more closely, you see that in fact, it wasn't you who manifested the light out of darkness, you just flipped the switch. Without the switch itself, the electrician who set up the wires connecting power from the switch to the light, and the people who run the power plant, not to mention those who designed, manufactured, and delivered the light fixture to your house and those who generations before you discovered how to corral the forces of electricity and motion, you'd be in the dark. The message in the Gītā is that by looking ever more closely, by letting go of our dharmas, preconceptions, and egotistical attachments, we can remember that joyful feeling we had as an infant when not knowing was a delight; when, totally absorbed in whatever was right in front of our eyes, we first discovered that things seem to work in harmony with other things and that this interplay presented us with limitless connections and insights into the world.

Again and again in the story of the Gītā we watch as Arjuna almost grasps the concept of stilling the mind in the field of open awareness and letting go of expectations and attachments, but then he's overcome by the "need to *know*" with certainty. Whether it is in the very beginning of the story when he is defeated by his own doubts, not knowing with clarity what to do on the battlefield, or in the middle of the story, when he is attempting to understand the complex teachings on karma and sacrifice, he persists in wanting to know with certainty: "You extol the renunciation of actions, O Kṛṣṇa, and again you extol yoga. Of these two, which is the better one? Explain this in a definitive way to me" (5.1).

Arjuna's need to know is likely a state familiar to most of us. It's a natural human tendency to crave definitive answers even though we may understand doing so can hinder pursuing a path toward liberation. Learning to be comfortable while not knowing for certain requires that we see through the ego and release any sense of separate identity that ego creates. It also means that we reevaluate the illusion that we can have absolute control in making things happen. No wonder we resist. The very thing we experience as navigating us through life—our ego—is diminished when we reframe our perception to see that our illusions of self and our actions do not arise independently but are deeply nested in Indra's interlinked net. Our thoughts, emotions, dharma—even our character—do not define us. Instead, though we do have a responsibility to direct our actions from conception to implementation, they are not "us" at all; they are forces of the universe acting on forces of the universe. The misperception that we are separate from everything else and that our actions (along with their results) are strictly dependent on our own force of will with neither context nor consequences considered is actually where innocence ends and prejudice, cynicism, and suffering originate.

Fully understanding this aspect of interconnectedness, where ego is valued, seen as sacred, yet carefully put aside, is described as the guṇas acting on the guṇas, which as mentioned earlier, is one of the foundational theses of Sāṁkhya philosophy. The guṇas—*rajas*, *tamas*, and *sattva*—are defined as the three qualities of nature that make up everything that manifests. Rajas is the quality that initiates and drives things like a powerful wind in nature, anger, or strength in a person, or a spicy pepper in cooking. Tamas is a sluggish, disorganized, and destructive quality and is the dominant trait in things like a stagnant pool of water, a mood of depression and indecisiveness, or dead, dull foods like meat, alcohol, or overly processed foods. Sattva is considered to be the quality of balance, sweetness, or goodness and is experienced in nature as things like sparkling mountain streams, in people as the feeling of love, or in a dish of food when all the flavors merge into heavenly gastronomic congruence.

Everything that manifests is said to be an ever-changing combination of these three phases of creative energy, which include and emanate from levels of mind so, in a sense, the guṇas can be described as the functioning of thought and a process of transformation through movements of creative energy. Tamas is the single view, rajas is the counterview, and sattva is the view that synthesizes all views with their counterviews into harmonious relationship (thesis, antithesis, synthesis). When functioning well, the finely tuned but imaginary ego makes creative choices by surrendering to the fluidity of the guṇas. This produces a holographic view that easily adjusts to circumstances, interfacing seamlessly on all levels of action and consciousness. In this process the stuckness of tamas is booted into action through rajasic energy, leading to a sattvic, balanced state that eventually settles so much that it stagnates into a tamasic state, starting the entire cycle again. At any point in this chain of interacting energies if we interrupt the flow and pull something out of its background—even theoretically—the process of transformation, in fact what life itself is, comes to a standstill.

When we trust the relationships unfolding before us, we become an organic part of whatever it is we are considering, and it naturally becomes easier to release attachments and the need to know or control. This is especially so when we bear in mind that this form of releasing is not dismissal, denial, or disengagement; it is the careful observation of whatever is arising as it unfolds and transforms before us. Then, as a scientist might, we can study the ever-changing manifestation of the world and notice the complementary characteristics of the guṇas as they present themselves. The process of guṇas acting on the guṇas happens with everything, from emotional upheaval to political attachments and philosophical doctrine. If we clearly see this, by observing the arising of phenomena in the present moment, then releasing ego attachments and the need to know is spontaneous. This is how the world opens into a multifaceted mystery, and no matter what direction we look in, we see an infinite regress (or progress) of the guṇas acting on the guṇas in whatever is being contemplated. Insight gained through trust in not knowing is what allows us to viscerally experience our own interconnectedness and the dependent origination of all things—without feeling minimized. Instead, we feel inspired.

Kṛṣṇa refers to the guṇas early in the Gītā, tossing the idea out to Arjuna almost offhandedly as if taking a chance that it might strike a chord of insight to help him solve his dilemma and see that a strict dualistic viewpoint usually causes confusion and suffering. He says that even though the action of the threefold mode is the subject matter of the Veda. In other words very well established through ancient texts, he encourages Arjuna to be free of the three guṇas and to always abide in truth. Meaning, in part, to stay present moment by moment to the unfolding of life without becoming trapped into believeing things to be unchanging due to dualistic thinking, attachments, and aversions.

In offering this wisdom in the form of what can be considered a global theme—interpenetration—as it interfaces with philosophical underpinnings of Sāṁkhya and the guṇas, Kṛṣṇa is laying the groundwork for his student to reach a point of insight. This is how learning takes place. Just like the small child who figures out that the shape at the end of his arm is his hand and realizes that he can manipulate his fingers at will, Arjuna, like all of us, must work up to truly embracing paradoxical presentations of mind and nature such as complex concepts like nondualism and the value of "knowing" how to not know. Becoming comfortable with paradox takes practice. First we hear and then get accustomed to an idea; it floats around in the back of the mind. Then we begin to develop a context for understanding the concept as it becomes assimilated. Kṛṣṇa is relying on this process of insight and learning, setting the seeds for Arjuna early in his teaching, so that later, when he goes deeply into the distinguishing characteristics of the guṇas in chapter 16, Arjuna will not take what is a process and turn it into a duality.

The idea of the guṇas acting on the guṇas is firmly rooted in many aspects of Indian thought. It is foundational to the Ayurvedic perspective and its deepest teaching—that everything, including our own actions and all of our thoughts, is a manifestation of the interacting nature of the guṇas. The same idea is dangled in front of avid students as fodder for thought in texts such as the Kena Upaniṣad where the subtle-most layers of investigation are encouraged (eye of the eye). All this is relevant to Arjuna's dilemma because in order to fully surrender, as eventually he must, Arjuna slowly discovers that if he is to solve his dilemma, he must learn how to trust the process of life manifesting around him to the point that he can also remain clear and confident when not knowing.

For each of us too, in our own ongoing sagas of life, these are profound teachings. When we experience that we cannot fully control an outcome and that no one thing—not our thoughts, feelings, sensations, bodily functioning, or deeds—will alone guide us through the difficulties in life, we reach a crossroads. Either we panic and recoil and things get worse, or we learn to find a way to release preconceptions and wake up to circumstances so that we can skillfully navigate through the challenges we encounter. Realizing that there is no infallible, isolated answer to anything offers the opportunity to experience life fully, as part of something that is vast and mysterious, much bigger than our own limited imagination. From this perspective we are not diminished but set free into an abundant, spacious field of not knowing where we can look to the subtle-most layers of our mind, dreams, and especially our actions to see that though we initiate aspects of our life and identity, even *they* are the forces of the guṇas acting on the guṇas. If we are lucky enough to get a glimpse of this, then we can finally fully surrender to love—a trust in interconnectedness—as the taproot of life. Still we embrace the mind's vital function of categorizing and conjecturing without becoming attached to the finiteness of our thoughts, but we do not stop there. The concepts of "my finger," or "the thing itself," are useful and perhaps excellent theories, but they are not literally separate forces of a causal relationship. They are not a result within the vacuum of separate things but arise from entwinement—the guṇas acting on the guṇas.

The notion speaks to the Buddhist concept of emptiness, or that the nature of everything is one of dependent arising. Dependent arising and separateness or "independent arising" are mutually exclusive concepts; however, the nature of the human mind is to persist in reframing things from the perspective of our immediate experience—directed through our own personal sensual fields. Consequently there is an underlying tendency to create a separateness, a "self" that arises independently to experience the world. This can happen even when we conceptually see the truth of emptiness. However, things do not manifest as separate things or compositions of separate things. Not one, but not exactly two either, which creates a nondual paradox. Though most of us spend our lives functioning around a story of separate self or ego, if we entertain the notion that everything that manifests is a function of the guṇas acting on the guṇas—everything is in a relationship of dependent arising—we discover that no matter how closely we look, we can never really perceive a separate "doer." Eventually we may see with a sense of awe (or possibly alarm) that not only are the wind and the rain functioning complements of the laws of nature, but that we ourselves—even what we consider to be our soul—are actually expressions of the interconnected nature of life.

No wonder Arjuna resists the teachings when he's trapped by dilemma, petrified by the thought of not knowing for certain exactly what action to take. Neither is it surprising that on a personal level we too may resist fully grasping the idea that we are a function of the guṇas. To assimilate and benefit from this insight we must truly let go of our attachment to our own storyline: our representations or theories about our personality, our actions, our relationships, and even our soul.

The mind perpetually creates stories about who we are, when in fact we are never only the story itself. In an advanced meditative state, if the mind is still and becomes crystal clear, we may get a peek at all of this because we have momentarily let go of attachment to outcome. Zoom in on any part of your story and perhaps you see in truth, *you* didn't "make it happen," but when the mind has no experience of the state of deep trust necessary to let go and see this (which is one thing we may spontaneously experience from the stillness meditation offers), then ego function cannot let go to admit that it was not fully in charge. Instead, it creates the theory of you, the "doer," and it shuts out subtle aspects of potential change that have nothing to do with you *doing* anything at all.

The classic metaphor explaining this is that of a farmer irrigating a field of crops. When the rains come *he* does not water the crops, he simply removes the clod of soil blocking the flow of water between ditches, and the water runs freely. Yes, his directed actions are critical to the process of irrigation, but *he* is not watering the crops. Taking action in concert with nature he is successful, but if he doesn't participate, if he becomes rigid in his thinking or ignores the ever-changing circumstances, he is destined to fail. If the farmer has no plan for how to irrigate the field and he digs random ditches, things don't work out. So too if he calculates the placement of the ditches, digs them, and notices during the first big rainfall that his design is not accommodating the rain, but he refuses to adjust it because he is certain that "his" design is perfect and that the flow of water will eventually shift course, he is also making a huge mistake. Likewise, if he sets everything up but refuses to move the clod of dirt blocking the flow, he fails.

This metaphor not only speaks to the principle of the guṇas acting on the guṇas but also deepens the understanding of an earlier verse in the Gītā when Kṛṣṇa encourages Arjuna to look closely at the nature of his actions as a demonstration that his initiative, his directed actions matter. They are vital to the outcome of the pattern of guṇas acting on the guṇas. No matter what action we take—even if we do nothing at all—there is impact. Kṛṣṇa points out that "one who sees inaction in action and who sees action in inaction is awakened among humans and does all actions linked in yoga" (4.18). In other words, if we use our intelligence and whatever sincere understanding we possess of any situation, we may begin to see that all of our actions directly impact the world; they are our work.

The tricky interplay between action and inaction is a unifying thread of the teachings that runs through the storyline of the Gītā. It appears first in the very beginning when Kṛṣṇa encourages Arjuna to stand up and fight, then is reflected later when Kṛṣṇa instructs Arjuna to act but to let go of the fruits of his actions. That same thread is also central to the teachings at the culmination of the text when Arjuna is instructed to choose his own actions. The relationship of action and inaction is likely to cause confusion for anyone new to the idea of releasing the ego to become a deeper part of an interconnected whole. If we see that life is a process, and we understand that we are not the deciding center of the action, how does our action really matter? It is puzzling how our small gesture of either taking action or choosing inaction could play a critical role. Hearing "inaction in action and action in inaction," the ego and a scattered mind are, at best, likely to skate over the surface of meaning, setting it aside as a clever statement—a koan to be considered later. Buried beneath the superficial message, however, is an implicit understanding of the philosophical and global themes that have been introduced into the text to this point: interconnectedness, the teachings of the guṇas acting on the guṇas, the benefits of a healthy relationship to our dharma, *and* the awareness that we must always be willing to let go of the fruits of our actions. Action in inaction and inaction in action means that, like the farmer, we must take action (remove the clod of dirt blocking the flow of water) because doing nothing has consequences—action in inaction. It also means we have a critical role (digging and adjusting the trenches as needed—our dharma) in the context of the circumstances. Our aspirations for a particular outcome (metaphorically for all of us, the field being irrigated) will never be successful and satisfying if we hold so tightly onto the abstract idea of our actions (our master plan on paper for how the trenches in the field should be laid) that we cannot adapt in relation to circumstances and let go of the fruits of our actions.

Connecting all of these dots and taking shelter in the process of life, perhaps we can experience inaction in the very actions we think we are "taking," recognizing that our actions are our own individual expressions of the guṇas acting on the guṇas exposed as an integral part of the world. Though our actions are unique to us, it is ultimately impossible to separate them out from the interconnected whole, which is life. Just like we see our thumb as separate from our hand—a digit unlike any other—it is obviously part of the hand. Every one, every thought, every *thing* that manifests is a unique part of this whole we call life; an irreplaceable, sacred expression of creative energy. Seen in this light, all of our actions can be considered sacred offerings into the fire—the process—of life. When we experience everything we do, think, say, feel, imagine, encounter, or dream about as sacred, then sacrifice becomes real yoga. Life itself (including how we perceive it—what we "know") transforms from a matter of discipline or denial into a trusting act of generosity, insight, and love.

It is said that greater than any material sacrifice is the sacrifice of knowledge, which, it turns out, produces *true knowledge*, or the release of attachment to knowing itself. Knowing with unwavering certainty may be comfortable, but it eliminates the incentive to question and can therefore hamper the ability to see clearly. Of course, knowledge and "knowing with certainty" are vital if we are to successfully operate in the world. We couldn't even brush our teeth without definitively distinguishing between caulk and toothpaste, so it's vital to *know* with certainty the difference. But what if some trickster had put caulk in the toothpaste tube? Half asleep and brushing your teeth, you sense something's wrong but refuse to consider that your notoriously cunning cousin from your father's side of the family is visiting, so you ignore the impulse to check the tube more closely and continue brushing.

You *know* it is toothpaste because it's in the toothpaste tube, so why check? Letting go of attachment and sacrifice of knowledge hinge on the ability to release and reframe definitions and preconceptions, to let go and wake up to circumstance and feedback from others and the environment. In a healthy situation we are able to make theories about the world, ourselves, and others and equally able to let the theories go—over and over and over. This turns out to be a cornerstone of discriminating awareness, the quality Kṛṣṇa refers to when describing to Arjuna one of the benefits of meditation.

Discriminating awareness, in a broad sense, is the ability to discern between two things, to not confuse name and form; for example, you wouldn't eat the menu at a restaurant. When discernment is well polished you even have discriminating awareness about your systems of knowledge. Seeing that your theories are systems, even if they are good systems, you know they are not solid or permanent, nor can they contain themselves, so you can let them go when appropriate. As you still the mind through meditation, at a certain point you see that all systems of knowledge have to be released and that this is done through discriminating awareness; not confusing the name (the scaffolding or the system) with the form (the substance or knowledge itself). You see through the storyline that served the function of allowing you to understand to a certain point, but because you know the story is just that—a story—you have the flexibility of mind to dissolve the story into not knowing. Letting go reveals two levels of knowledge: knowing stuff within a system along with knowledge that sets you free from the system and the knowledge itself. This second form could be considered Knowledge (with a capital *k*) because it is true knowledge and is, in fact, enlightenment.

Knowing with the freedom to not know is an art form that involves taking little steps of knowing with certainty (the story) before shifting awareness and trust back into the field of not knowing (closing that chapter or story) and stepping again into the stream of action dictated (the new story). Within this process the egotistical theories of who we are can remain secure in knowing what's going on step-by-step until eventually even the process of letting go between steps becomes another familiar step or story—the story of not knowing. Then there is a sense of ease with putting everything, even the ego itself, down while releasing the perpetual urge to separate things out from their background. Over time, the feeling of satisfaction associated with knowing for certain, which from a beginner's perspective can be equated with a sense of safety and happiness, turns out to be not so gratifying at all. Instead, it becomes evident that not needing to know is where real intelligence, satisfaction, and liberation reside.

[5]

Taming the Mind through Classical Yoga

THOUGH IT IS POSSIBLE to have a leap in understanding and direct insight into profound subjects, especially for the inner two-year-old that dwells within each of us and asks "Why?" for eternity, sudden insight can sometimes raise more questions, more doubt. So it is with Arjuna, who consistently within the story of the Gītā has a moment of brilliant insight and then slips back into the desperate need to know for certain. Being infinitely patient, Kṛṣṇa, therefore, takes the stable path with his friend and student, repeatedly layering together tiers of theoretical, ethereal, and practical understanding of wisdom, work, and devotion so that the nonexclusionary relationship of all of these approaches is revealed. He slowly builds a foundation for Arjuna to assimilate and eventually embody unshakable insight into interconnectedness, compassion, and life.

As the story progresses, chapters 5 and 6 of the Gītā present practical ways for applying to everyday life the theories presented up to this point in the text. We recall that Kṛṣṇa and Arjuna are still standing in the middle of the battlefield discussing whether or not Arjuna should stand up and fight. It's been a long conversation! And the fact that they're still standing in the middle of the field of dharma and action discussing philosophy, while opposing armies stand ready on both sides and horses chomp at their bits, is one of those "don't try this at home" teaching moments, i.e., once you've gotten a taste for how love interfaces with everything within the web of life, you should stand up quickly, consider what will serve the whole, and act in spite of not knowing definitively how things will turn out, otherwise you could be at risk of being caught in the crossfires of life.

Up to this point Arjuna has followed along relatively well with Kṛṣṇa's teachings of dharma, karma, the guṇas, nonattachment, and more. Yet still he is not satisfied. He's heard that through meditation the sage or yogī can quiet the mind and have remarkable insight and epiphanies, and he's coming to grips with the fact that his role as a Kṣatriya does not necessarily mean that he must kill. Nonetheless he's not sure exactly how his calling best interfaces with the importance of taking action and embracing the unknown. Arjuna now knows he must act—either enter the battle or make the conscious decision not to—and he understands that if he chooses not to, he is still acting by default. However, doubts remain within him; he is plagued by the need to know with certainty and the only thing he feels certain of is that there must be a particular, specific answer that will solve his dilemma.

Kṛṣṇa has spoken repeatedly about yogīs as the wise ones and of yoga as the path to awakening, but he has not given Arjuna details. Earlier in the story, in chapter 2, Arjuna asked for specifics, a description of how yogīs speak, sit, and walk. At that point Kṛṣṇa breezed over the inquiry without giving many tangible details, offering instead clues into the nature of the wise. He replied, "When one abandons all desires coming from the mind, O Pārtha, when the self is content in the self (itself), then one is called stable in intelligence" (2.55). He said this in an effort to teach Arjuna the necessity of letting go of formulas and preconceptions he might concoct about what it looks like to "be" a yogī or to "do" yoga. Kṛṣṇa alluded to yoga as the sacrifice of pouring prāṇa into *apāna* or offering the inhale and the exhale into one another sacrificially. He counseled Arjuna to consider his dharma not as set in stone but instead to see it in context. Kṛṣṇa also made it very clear that the human tendencies of needing to know, of turning sacrifice and ritual into formulas—rendering them meaningless—and of losing the capacity for compassion by becoming attached to the fruits of one's actions were not yoga.

So in many ways he had offered Arjuna great insight into what it means to practice yoga, and perhaps if he'd explained what a yogī looked like in greater detail too early in the teachings, Arjuna would have become content to behave in contrived and meaningless ways, identifying himself as a yogī without the incentive to give up the fruits of his yogic actions and to inquire ever deeper into the aim of attaining intelligence as a means of serving others. But now, with some capacity to understand the subtle process of yoga as a means of awakening, Arjuna is on the verge of insight. So Kṛṣṇa becomes more specific about what yoga looks like.

There is something to be said for imagining yourself as taking on particular attributes associated with something you aspire toward, such as "being" a yogī, a good athlete, or a strong leader. Doing whatever you are intending to do by observing and modeling yourself after others who are more skilled in a particular path can be part of the learning process. It is like you are playacting the part, becoming the understudy of your dreams until you transform on deeper levels to express a full embodiment of the role you are studying. In fact, Kṛṣṇa gives reference to the power of this method for learning earlier in the text when he says, "Whatsoever the great person does, the rest of humanity does. Whatever standards that one sets the world follows" (3.21).

This verse came when Kṛṣṇa was speaking about those who perform actions without attachment, instead acting for the benefit of others and motivated by something beyond their own gain and satisfaction. It is not intended as a superficial teaching, but rather it suggests that one doorway into understanding might be through mimicking (which is essentially visualizing and embodying) the actions of another who is wise or enlightened. Actually, this is one important way we all begin to learn, usually from copying the behavior of our parents and siblings who appear to know everything. So in this verse there is a hint that if you don't understand how to deal with a particular difficulty, one method of finding your way is to observe an intelligent role model and go through the motions of acting intelligently until you figure things out. "Fake it till you make it."

Needless to say, there are inherent pitfalls in this approach to learning, especially if it is taken out of context or used exclusively. First, what if your "model" isn't actually as good at whatever it is you are aspiring to as you originally thought? If you look at the surface actions of another without noticing and learning from the mistakes even the best are bound to make, then you risk clinging steadfastly to formulaic actions or thoughts at the expense of yourself and others. Also, it is virtually impossible to understand the intuition and decision-making process of someone who has thousands of hours of "practice," so again, you may find yourself relying on formulas rather than assimilating a level of knowledge and intelligence in order to act.

Perhaps the biggest obstacle toward growth and intelligence in modeling yourself after another is that your own direct experience and the learning process can be truncated if you don't start where you actually are rather than where you'd like to be or think you should be. Life's big questions and inherent elegance are invitations to release preconceptions and wake up day by day along a path of understanding and action—a cycle of learning, unlearning, learning, and letting go again ad infinitum.

As any of us who practice yoga, or any contemplative or fine art know, the central root of becoming more skilled in a chosen form is that we practice consistently and over a very long period of time. The art deepens and evolves by embracing the joys and difficulties of the practices themselves, as well as the residue from them, and doing so *without* an iron-gripped attachment to the outcome or fruits of the practice. This is how any practice matures to become a reflection of wisdom.

Developing a mature practice is dependent on *abhyāsa*, or practicing in the context of real life, during good times and bad times, focused periods and times of great distraction, blissful mind states and hell zones of thought and circumstance. Equally important is *vairāgyam*, or setting it all down before beginning again. A painter learns perspective, color theory, and brush techniques and moves paint around on the canvas for years while also observing the world, looking at other art, and eventually dissolving into the process of putting their individual essence onto the canvas in the form of an image. And then, when the painting is done, they let it go. It's framed, sold, or stacked in their studio alongside hundreds of others to collect dust. Just as classical theory aids the artist in creating works of art, philosophical theories that shape form and structure help the yogī assimilate the practices. But in yoga, as in any art form, if you wait until you think you've mastered every aspect of theory and technique before you engage in the physical form of the art, you're missing out because a considerable amount of insight comes not from the mind but from an intuitive, embodied experience available only through practicing the art itself.

We begin where we are. For example, we're stressed out, and we've heard meditation can help relieve stress. So we find a meditation teacher, read a couple of books about meditation, or take a class. Then we set up the cushion, have a seat, and sit still, in a sense "pretending to meditate." We take on the form by keeping our eyes steady, releasing tension in the jaw and face, noticing our breath when we remember to do so, and hoping that someday our mind and thoughts will catch on and begin to slow down so we can relax and actually meditate. In the meantime, we just hope nobody else in the room realizes what a bad meditator we are.

If we refuse to experiment by sitting still with the intention of meditating until we have passed some arbitrary, self-imposed standard of what it means to meditate, we will likely never meditate at all. It takes practice. By the same token, if we set up the scaffolding of a meditation practice with the perfect cushion and ideal timer to release us at the end and then glide through the motions of meditating in a dogmatic or ritualistic way, never for even an instant putting our preconceptions and techniques down, or if we practice for eons without continually inviting inquiry and context, then we short-circuit any deeper benefits we might find in the practice.

At the beginning of chapter 5 of the Gītā, Arjuna, who almost surrenders enough to let go and trust the process of life that Kṛṣṇa is laying out before him, suddenly flips back into needing to know with certainty and asks whether renunciation of work or nonattachment to outcome is better. Kṛṣṇa responds that both are honorable and can lead to liberation, but he explains that they are intrinsically intertwined paths. Fully experiencing one leads to the other and to a state of equanimity in which we are not swayed by whether something is perceived as pleasant or unpleasant. At that point we can focus on the space between our concepts of mind to fully embody a visceral connection to the circumstances of the moment. This is when a sense of equality and interconnectedness naturally arises and gradually leads us to a feeling of inner strength and peace of mind. Kṛṣṇa describes this as a union with the True Self, which today we might experience as a connection to God, to nature, or to an embodied realization of the tenderness of being that is our own true nature and is common to all sentient forms of life. It is experiencing commonality rather than focusing on differences that reveals the path of skillful action that each of us must take moment by moment if we are to see clearly what is arising and thereby see others.

Finally, after having laid important groundwork for understanding the subtleties of practice, Kṛṣṇa answers more directly Arjuna's inquiries about what it means to be wise. Describing some of the specifics about yogīs and yoga practice, he says, "The wise paṇḍits see equally a wise well-practiced Brāhman, a cow, an elephant, a dog, or an outcast" (5.18).

In this teaching we are instructed, alongside Arjuna, in the underlying truth that all beings are divine manifestations, and that it is paramount to cultivate sincerity and stillness of mind in order to fully comprehend that nothing, not even other beings, can be removed from the background of others. The teaching is one of equality rather than exclusivity. Kṛṣṇa reveals that it is our actions and our work, not our theories or our position in life, that are the means toward happiness and liberation for those inclined to search for meaning and to attain yoga. For those of us who study and practice yoga, the message is clear: We have to work not only for our own advancement but for the good of the whole. We should not just "go with the flow" in a detached bliss state or force our ideals and theories upon others. Instead, we must work intelligently, with discriminating awareness and within the context of our present circumstances. Work is where you get rooted down to earth, and yoga, in a sense, *is* work, where action, counteraction, and counter-counteraction are simple and straightforward, not contrived, not theoretical, but absolutely practical.

Work is not something that makes one person superior to another, nor is it something special, mystical, or predetermined by fate. It is just the activity of showing up and meeting life with an open mind and an attitude of sincerity that can lead to pure awareness even if you are just putting on your shoes or filing your taxes. Work, which is one aspect of karma, requires action and so an honest look at work is a means of understanding the integrative quality that defines the karmic chain of being. Work highlights the importance of causal relationships—all relationships—and brings an appreciation for karma back to ordinary, everyday activities both subtle and gross.

From a contemporary point of view, karma is often not considered work but is reduced to mean only destiny; short- or long-term consequences of our actions. A woman falls off a cliff and dies, and her New Age friend says, "Oh, it was her karma." But this is a cop-out. From this formulaic view of karma our intricate role in the story of here and now, the mystery of interconnectedness and our potential to make a difference by sincerely serving others, is totally ignored. Yes, in understanding karma we comprehend that every action we take, every emotion we feel, every thought we have leaves residue and as such has an impact and consequences. From the traditional Indian and Buddhist perspectives, which include a belief in transmigration from life to life, the karmic chain of events can even be carried from lifetime to lifetime.

The cop-out comes when we use the theory as an avoidance mechanism and thereby avoid truly engaging with life. When confronted by difficult (or comfortable) situations we turn up our hands in a pious gesture of sanctity, declaring that whatever happened was predetermined by karma. If we rationalize that karma caused the woman to fall off the cliff, there is an insidious dismissal of not only the unfortunate woman who fell but the value of knowing we all choose our actions and must take responsibility for them. Our understanding of karma to be predetermined destiny is laced with problems. First, seeing it as payment for sins or good deeds is not only an oversimplification, it is an invitation to inject a superiority/inferiority dichotomy into the mix. Such a limiting view of karma also implies that only the force of nature, or what we see as God (in the case of the Gītā, the guṇas acting on the guṇas or Kṛṣṇa), has the power, freedom, or responsibility to impact what is happening. Although we understand "our" actions to be a result of the guṇas acting on the guṇas, there is, nonetheless, within the process of every action as it unfolds, the opportunity and the obligation to stay awake and contribute skillfully to the situation, as circumstances unfold. Karma is a creative process when we stay awake moment by moment.

Disengaging from our own circumstance with an attitude that life is pre- or divinely determined is particularly troubling when attempting to understand the concept of supreme intelligence or Kṛṣṇa. If we see Kṛṣṇa as a separate entity, as God, it raises all sorts of questions and could be called the omnipotence paradox. Can our God make a mountain so heavy that he or she can't pick it up? If every detail of existence has been set in motion from some vague or sacred time billions of years ago, then there is no freedom for any creature to make a difference, at which point life devolves into a disturbing horror show. Within some traditional schools of Indian thought, such as Sāṁkhya, there are naïve factions who use this very interpretation of predetermination to restrict their thinking when speaking of karma. From such a limited perspective, you have no choice because it's all predetermined. You are not responsible for your sins (or your virtues), they are not actually yours, and it all becomes a meaningless show.

Karma becomes a far more profound and useful concept when considered as a creative process rather than payback or destiny. It is the nature and unfolding of work, residue, engagement, feedback, action, and responsibility, all of which is grounded in love. If everything is predestined, then even your thoughts are predetermined, as are your actions and your capacity to wake up to circumstances and to see through your own mind into the clear light of pure awareness where the deepest insights thrive.

Karma is the inescapable historical situation and the circumstances that you find yourself in and have to deal with. You are in New York City and the rents are high. You live on a farm and have to milk the cows. You had a party last night and wake up to a sink full of dishes that need washing. Karma as work is daily life, interactions with others, a step-by-step opportunity to wake up, interface with the world, and express one's lot in life. If we see work, or karma, simply as destiny, drudgery, or duty it has a nonparticipatory quality—I'm a victim of my karma. From the very start of the Gītā Kṛṣṇa tells Arjuna to let go of his tamasic instinct toward predetermination and victimization and instead get up, show up, and act. This advice does not deny that there are difficulties in many circumstances. Instead, it points out that if you act intelligently, you are free from the imaginary dictates of circumstance. The same law that seems to oppress and trap you is profoundly liberating when exposed to intelligence. It *is* freedom.

Karma as work and residue can be interfaced with the idea of dharma, or the law to be followed within a particular circumstance—one's duty expressed within context. Dharma dictates actions, and karma is the creative principle of action and reaction (feedback and knowledge) that allows you to transcend your circumstances and to skillfully improve everyone's situation. Therefore the teachings of the Gītā and Kṛṣṇa's guidance to Arjuna insist that one must wake up to the irreducible particulars of the situation at hand and then give up all personal or cultural dharmas that are defined through thought process. Instead of blindly following your perceived dharma or becoming a victim of your karma, you are encouraged to find your *svadharma*, your personal dharma or true nature. By doing so you can find a path to freedom, joyousness, and compassion. This important point is driven home in chapter 3 when Kṛṣṇa says, "One's own dharma (duty) done imperfectly is better than another's dharma done perfectly" (3.35).

This famous verse encourages us to look much more deeply at ourselves, others, society, and the whole big picture of life, so that we can find who we truly are and what our karmic and dharmic responsibilities are within the context of our given circumstances. In this verse, Kṛṣṇa is instructing Arjuna to actually *see* others and to know them as sacred so that he can realize that his dharma in this moment as he stands on the battlefield is not necessarily to engage in battle and to kill, but that his true nature, his svadharma (like everyone's svadharma) is actually to lovingly serve all beings. The verse encourages Arjuna to put in the effort and the necessary work to discover what his day-to-day dharma as a warrior is within the context of his own ever-changing circumstances. It is encouragement to all of us to pause within our unique circumstances and do the same.

The sentiment and value in doing one's dharma imperfectly rather than another's well are echoed in later sections of the text as well, underscoring its importance. By the end of the text the importance of authenticity as an expression of one's true nature has been revealed.

Each of us has a unique purpose for being here, and those who are wise are said to be fortunate enough to aspire to their purpose. The imperfections in the expression of our dharma are to be expected. As Kṛṣṇa says, "all undertakings have some faults just as fire is enveloped by smoke" (18.48). The teaching is that those of us who wish to serve the whole by releasing the distractions of the senses and the ego should work diligently and in so doing naturally transcend, or let go of the fruits of, our actions.

Those who practice yoga work to cultivate steadiness of mind to develop the capacity to look deeply, again and again, and to see through the seemingly infinite layers of distraction, expectation, and preconception that invariably ensnare relationships and interactions. The world, which is never in a steady state, appears not as chaos but instead as an interesting manifestation of phenomenon to those with a mind stable enough to personally disengage so that carefully considered, beneficial, and skillful action is revealed. Kṛṣṇa explains to Arjuna that cultivating a steady, clear mind is a process. It is a byproduct of working intelligently, following one's svadharma in the context of whatever is arising without seeking fruits from our actions, and at the same time training the mind to be stable as the world and the mind remain in flux.

Embodied contemplative practices such as meditation, prāṇāyāma, āsana, chi gong, tai chi, and so on are methods for consciously steadying the mind in the face of flux. In all of them a specific form, space, and ground for practice is chosen or defined, and the practitioner sets an intention to polish their attention skills through the practice. They then move the body and/or breath while steadying the gaze and observing the internal feelings, thoughts, and sensations that present themselves. When the mind wanders, the practitioner gently but decisively brings the attention back to the chosen field of attention. By practicing in this manner on a regular basis and over an extended period of time, patiently focusing and refocusing the mind on a chosen field without attachment to the fruits of the practice, the mind becomes comfortable, relaxed, and, very importantly, *alert* in a state of stillness. With regular practice, reaching this attentive state becomes simpler, until one day when you're least expecting it, you find that stillness, stability, and a taste of clarity have arisen when you're in the midst of something other than trying to find balance or attempting to rein in the mind.

Abstractly this stillness of mind may seem unreachable; however, we all have spontaneous moments in life when the mind becomes steady, stable, and clear, just like the mind of a well-practiced yogī, and no matter how we get there, it is these three qualities—steadiness, stability, and clarity—all working together that still the mind. The mind must be trained to be comfortable in a state of stillness within chaos. For instance, spontaneous moments of clarity may occur in the face of emergency such as a young baby falling into a swimming pool and someone in the crowd jumping in to scoop him out. Yet that same person might easily, unknowingly, check out mentally or emotionally during intensely demanding interactions with friends, colleagues, or loved ones. Others might find it easy to stay fully focused while interacting with other people or to be absolutely clear when faced with an impossible mental puzzle like repairing an intricate machine.

If we have an untrained mind, however, these states of clarity are infrequent and often not within our grasp or control or something we can call on at will. We might freeze by the poolside when the child falls in even though we cherish life, and we are able to be present and clear by the bedside of our dying friend. Teasing the thread of focus of mind out into longer and longer strands of attention is what meditation, prāṇāyāma, and internally focused āsana practice achieve. In so doing while feeling grounded, as if our feet are firmly rooted into the earth, there is the opportunity to sink into the knowledge that we really cannot know for sure what is the best action to take, yet knowing we are all deeply connected, we can begin to consciously still the mind and wake up to see more clearly and perhaps act more skillfully moment by moment.

In chapter 6 of the Gītā, after numerous requests from Arjuna to just tell him what to do as if there were a formula he could follow for his actions, Kṛṣṇa begins finally to weave together layers of theory with tangible, practical actions that Arjuna, or any one of us, might take in search of insight. He begins to teach the specifics of how to actually cultivate clear thinking and intelligence—what it is to be a yogī—and Arjuna heaves a huge sigh of relief: As a preliminary reminder, Kṛṣṇa says that a yogī is one who does the work (the karma) that is *kāryam*—the work that is to be done—and then offers it as a sacrifice into the fire of awareness. He says too that those who work attached to the fruits of their actions are not actually working. This is perhaps a comment on some of the yoga practices that were going on around greater India at the time the Gītā was composed, and it reflects the message of the Mahābhārata. Then, as now, it's likely that there were some identifying themselves as yogīs who weren't "lighting any fires," and who were engaging in ego-directed work or who'd imagined that an even easier path was to do no work at all. The message here is that yoga is the joy of correct action rather than a fear or avoidance of action—of saṃsāra.

Still, while teaching about the actions of a yogī, Kṛṣṇa reminds us again and again to let go because, even for well-trained minds, letting go is almost impossible. We are encouraged to liberate the activity of mind without buying into our ego and its byproducts in the form of illusion and imagination. Imagination, or *saṅkalpa*, is important as it allows us to visualize, dream, and bring interesting light to the process of reasoning. However, discernment within the process of thought—seeing through our very own imagination—is imperative. Even the best of intentions are conceptual constructions, sometimes used to describe intention, and they too must be placed down. Using imagination we all construct fantasies about ourselves, others, and our interactions in the world. You can have good fantasies and bad fantasies, and they are all stories that assign order to things as a means of making sense of what we encounter.

The art is being able to use the imagination intelligently and with the well-being of others in mind to create fantasies that are as accurate as possible, and then to eagerly set down those stories along with everything else. In the case of action, one common saṅkalpa is that there is some specific benefit that will result from our work. Even for the "advanced yogī," who knows not to be attached to the fruits of their actions, it's still easy to get tripped up by the illusion of the benefit one's actions will deliver to others: "I'm only helping my friend through her grief so she can feel better" or "I'm recycling because I want to save the earth." But you have to give it *all* up, even your noble desires of beneficial outcomes for others or the greater good. Maybe your friend, for reasons unknown, can't (or isn't ready) to feel better or maybe no matter how many bottles you diligently recycle, it's not going to help the earth in the long run because an asteroid is right on track to hit the planet and blow the whole thing to bits. So not being attached to the fruits of your actions actually becomes a chain of dovetailing good intentions, which can repeatedly be upgraded to allow skillful action that can lead to genuine happiness. This, of course, does not mean we stop our personal efforts to save the planet, but that we remain ever awake, considering whether there are more or different actions we can take that will be of service. We follow the natural instinct to dive deeply into that which we find fascinating, to symbolically light fires with inquisitiveness and to offer everything—even our own imaginations and concepts of self—into the fire.

Kṛṣṇa essentially summarizes yoga as exactly that: lighting the fire of the practice and offering it along with absolutely everything else to the fire. You begin tossing your bodily experience, your senses, your mind, and your thoughts into the fire as sacrifice rather than practicing with an outcome in mind, such as "I'll become happy, enlightened, and healthy." No, a true yogī merely gets into the process of the practice itself because as long as there's a saṅkalpa about the fruit, you're not paying attention to the process. The whole thing is a process, and that's very beautiful and relates to esoteric, or hatha, yoga. When the central channel is opened and the prāṇa (inhale) and apāna (exhale) are linked, the motions in the yoga are self-manifesting, self-fulfilling. There is no one in them because they are internally linked and then interface totally out into their environment. There's nobody there!

Perhaps the trickiest part of this process for most of us is that it takes a lot of practice (maybe even lifetimes), and you have to be patient and wait. Just like Arjuna wanted to collapse on the battlefield rather than face the process of life unfolding before him, we all have to show up, do the work required, and wait for insight to arise. The ego may want to disappear or to be the special one, making you the enlightened student that alone "gets it." But that isn't the message here. As the ego becomes stronger, you become weaker, more and more removed from actual yoga even though you might imagine your ego is dissolving, and you are doing well with your practice. That's the function that a teacher or outside feedback from others serves. It pops your egotistical bubbles of illusion! You say, "Roshi, I just saw the light," and the teacher says, "Nice. Now keep practicing."

Yoga, like life (and death for that matter), is a process of becoming integrated in body, mind, action, and spirit while being helpful to others. First we viscerally experience interconnectedness—the sense of the beginningless and endless process of life, the guṇas acting on the guṇas. We recognize the futility of being trapped in states of isolation by the mind's incessant urge to create a separate "self" and the "other" while ignoring a connection to everything else. Experiencing our self as part of a harmonized whole vividly reveals that interconnectedness is the glue that holds it all together. This visceral understanding of interconnectedness might arise as a luminous flash of insight, or we might simply know on some vague, unspeakable, intuitive level that the idea of union just seems right. This insight is the incentive to begin and sustain a practice—training so that the perception of interpenetration moves from the realm of theory into lasting embodied form that supports surrender into not knowing. So when throughout the text Kṛṣṇa says, "Come to Me," he means find the natural intelligence which is trust, surrender, and letting go in a way that facilitates insight. Without the multidimensional experience of intelligent surrender, yoga and other contemplative practices can be just a waste of time.

Yoga practices provide a direct path to this embodied experience of interconnectedness, yet as Kṛṣṇa points out, it isn't easy; yoga isn't for everyone. He says, "Among thousands of people maybe one reaches for perfection; of those endeavoring and even of those perfected, scarcely one knows Me in truth" (7.3). This verse could be taken to mean that yoga is exclusive, that only the ultraspecial and superior ones among us should try the path of yoga, but that is absolutely not what it means. The message is that yoga is a profound subject and cannot be rushed. While entering the deepest states of yoga, constructions of any separate individual self disappear into the present moment. When Kṛṣṇa says,

"Come to Me," he is hinting at a state of intimate union with the beloved where all of space-time, all "selfs," disappear as empty radiance.

Without a foundation of patience and trust, without a dedicated practice and the comprehension that yoga reflects life and is a process of interdependent arising—a demonstration that we are all profoundly interconnected—a yoga practice can be at best a distraction and at worst harmful to others. Just sitting on a cushion or doing poses on a yoga mat or holding your breath for five minutes at a time in prāṇāyāma will not guarantee that you move any closer at all toward kindness, compassion, and tasting a drop of the nectar of waking up. Yoga *is* difficult yet attainable by virtually anyone with time, practice, patience, and a persistent letting go, or restructuring, in light of observation and feedback from others. In our practice we may aspire to insight that reflects the power of infinity—and this is good—yet Kṛṣṇa reminds us that we can only start where we are. So in chapter 6 of the text he describes the classical method of yoga as follows: "The yogī should continuously focus on the true ātman established privately and alone, with the mind and body concentrated, free of aspiration and without grasping anything in any direction" (6.10).

The instructions continue, explaining that one should find a clean, solitary place that is neither too high nor too low and then lay down some *kuśa* grass with a deerskin on top. The mind is then brought into focus on whatever is arising, with the body, head, and neck held straight, lifted, and still. The eyes are steady, gazing at the tip of the nose. The work of the practice is then to sustain—or to learn techniques for returning to—a sense of stillness and equanimity. This practice is then carried out consistently in a spirit of devotion and without grasping at the illusory fruits of the practice.

Finding a solitary place eliminates a fraction of inevitable outside distractions, which is helpful since one's own mind, imagination, and body will easily come up with an infinite number of creative distractions. The kuśa, a long, ornamental grass, functions to make the seat soft but also is offered ritualistically to align correctly with the four directions—north, south, east, and west—and is a reminder that the practice is offered as a sacrifice rather than as a means to an end. The deerskin is a traditional top layer for a yogī's seat—connecting the practitioner to another sentient being and also, on a practical level, providing some protection against the bugs and thorns of the jungle where the seat is likely arranged.

The setup is relatively easy to achieve compared to the next request—to simply sit. Wherever the mind goes—it goes here, it goes there—you invite it back into the present moment, into the context of the ātman, which is to bring it into the context of mindfulness. This is what it means to observe without grasping onto or pushing away. Observing the arisings of mind exactly as they are. Kṛṣṇa describes to Arjuna a well-practiced yogī as follows: "peaceful, with fear gone, observing a vow of celibacy, with the mind collected and thinking of Me" (6.14). With practice, the yogī is calm and steady, able to face what arises even when it is unpleasant, without the aversion and fear that result from pulling our perceptions out of the background context. It is gradually revealed that the background context from which we separate ourselves when we imagine our perceptions to be our own separate experience, something absolute and real, is actually what Kṛṣṇa is referring to as "me," or himself: "One who sees Me everywhere, who sees all in Me; I am not lost to that one and that one is not lost to Me" (6.30).

The use of the term *Me* can be off-putting or misleading to those with an overly dogmatic perspective who are either rigidly religious or offended by religion. Kṛṣṇa's message is not to turn one's mind to Kṛṣṇa himself as the only manifestation of God but rather to focus on what he represents, which is whatever is immediately arising in our consciousness and sense fields within the context of the background of everything else. He represents unity, wholeness, and oneness. By practicing yoga in this way, with focus, stability, and calm in the midst of a world that is constantly in flux, there is potential for insight using as a focus, an anchor, whatever it is we are experiencing. Given that we practice in the "real world," Kṛṣṇa warns Arjuna that even the sincere yogī can encounter obstacles, and he encourages Arjuna to beware of distractions and that a considerable amount of the work of yoga is discipline. He then gives practical examples of habits and patterns of avoidance that Arjuna or any of us encounter, the obstacles that can sabotage a healthy yoga practice. "Yoga is not eating too much and it is certainly not fasting too much; not the practice of oversleeping and not staying awake too much, Arjuna" (6.16).

It makes perfect sense that if we are to find a harmonized, balanced state of body and mind there is a need for self-discipline that corrals the distractions of mind, body, and emotion and that we must behave in harmonious ways, noticing when we veer off in fragmented directions and returning time and again to the middle path. Discipline is not a punishment, but a sustaining, insightful practice in and of itself. It leads to stillness, concentration, and a form of intelligence that reaches far beyond the realm of the senses. "When the intelligence is precisely applied and one is abiding in the true ātman, free from all craving arising from desire, then they are said to be linked up (in yoga)" (6.18).

Yoga then can be seen as the ability to act with conscious attention to whatever is arising, one's response to the arising of phenomena, the ability to see the impact of one's actions, and the willingness to correct course due to feedback from the bigger picture. A disciplined practice in which you are neither led astray by your sense perceptions nor attached to the fruits of your actions fosters the ability to trust in truth. Kṛṣṇa speaks of the impact of this sort of mature practice as a source for supreme delight. "Knowing this endless delight held by the intelligence (buddhi) and beyond the senses, this one knows and, so grounded, does not waiver from the truth" (6.21). These are the types of practical steps one can take toward a sustained practice.

The simple instructions are that wherever the mind goes, you usher it back to the defined structure of the practice and into the present moment, a full-spectrum view of the here and now. This is a space where foreground and background merge into what could be considered the ātman. You see the mind—everything really—as it is. Ātman, in this case, could be considered to represent the context of contexts, or the present moment. Though as he requested, Arjuna has gotten some practical advice on the specifics of how to approach yoga, when he actually hears the details of what it takes to achieve a state of harmony through yoga, knowing too that it takes a long time and requires dedication, work, sacrifice, and surrender, he realizes it isn't quite as easy as he'd hoped and suddenly finds himself at another point of crisis. He'd wanted to go to the forest to escape his present circumstances—being a compassionate, inquisitive warrior in the center of a war that is destined to cause great suffering. Now he sees that yoga is not an escape at all but instead an endless pursuit and can be incredibly demanding and difficult. So again he's confounded and just as he did when he dropped his bow and fell to his knees in the very beginning of the story, here at the end of chapter 6, he hesitates, wrought with doubt and confusion. Filled with dismay, Arjuna says to Kṛṣṇa, "This yoga of even mind taught by you, O Slayer of Madhu, I see no lasting foundation for it because mind is so unstable. The mind is certainly always wavering, O Kṛṣṇa, troubling, strong and stubborn. I think it is as difficult to control as the wind"(6.33–34).

As anyone who's attempted meditation can attest, controlling the mind is indeed at least as difficult as controlling the weather. When you look closely, you see that in much of the Gītā Kṛṣṇa is convincingly telling us we should practice yoga and equally emphasizing how difficult this yoga—the process of waking up—actually is. Sure, as we develop our practices, sometimes, maybe five minutes every few months, it seems things are going pretty well. But then emotion or some other distraction comes up and we find ourselves, as did Arjuna, all the way back at square one, firmly planted in the very center of a state of crisis.

This cyclical pattern of difficulty, which can be relieved through work before more difficulty presents itself, is deliberately brought out in the Gītā because one of the most important messages within the text is that due to the nature of life as constant change, one must stay discerning, vigilant, and alert and at the same time learn to surrender to the truth and stillness beneath the tumultuous surface of endless fluctuations. Rather than blindly practicing and identifying with any specific technique, perhaps that of sitting placidly on a pile of kuśa grass staring into your navel, and instead of determinedly following any ritualistic dogma, the true bliss of practice is attained through *repeating* the practice, always coming home to the present moment and the point of safety that facilitates surrender.

Kṛṣṇa reassures Arjuna that although yoga is difficult, it is possible with abhyāsa and vairāgyam—which happen to be the very same teachings that are central to the Yoga Sūtras. Abhyāsa means to repeat form—almost like a copy machine makes copies. When performing its job well, the machine doesn't get creative or emotionally tied up in making copies that are special, distinct, or unique. In fact we've probably all experienced what happens when the copy machine's toner malfunctions and gets "overly inspired" so that things go haywire and copies are a mess. But a good machine just churns out the same exact thing over and over and over. In yoga practice, repeating the same form continually is how you create the sacred container of the practice that allows room for pure, noninterfering observation at the center of the practice.

However, you can easily become caught in abhyāsa. The ego can identify with the technique, the mantras, and the axioms and language of the system so that the ego actually inflates and becomes more separate, rather than dissolving into a state of trust that is imperative if we are to surrender into the glorious sense of being an essential yet fully integrated part of the whole. So to correct for this, we have vairāgyam, which means to "let it go, let it dissolve, let it be." Vairāgyam breaks the ego's identity with the process. In vairāgyam there is no need to get rid of form or to create form. It is simply letting things be. In our formal contemplative practices we are always letting go of techniques, dissolving mind, body, ego, and all of our theories, emotions, and habitual patterns of behavior into a brilliantly lit, open field of curiosity and not knowing. Yoga then becomes the art of surrender in action rather than an attempt to control.

Arjuna does not think he is up to the task of yoga (just as we might think we are not up to meeting the world head on) and that maybe he should forget the whole thing. But he's thinking this because he's seeing yoga as a sense object rather than a process—which is a trap we can all easily fall into. In Arjuna's mind enlightenment has become an object that his ego must attain, and attachment to this huge, glittery object called enlightenment is a setup for major disappointment because enlightenment is not a static, solid state and cannot be reached by grasping.

In response to Arjuna's fears, Kṛṣṇa begins to teach the doctrine of yogīc *saṃskāras*—the idea that through yoga you can reprogram negative habitual patterns of mind, action, and emotion that lead to suffering because they keep us stuck in saṃsāra, or conditioned existence. He also points out that in spite of the tendency to fall into saṃsāra, any little bit of insight is remarkably rare and good. Start very, very small and look into what is immediate without any hope of gaining anything. Right *here* you will get a glimpse of infinity, seeing things unfolding as a natural process and at precisely the optimal rate to support balance. In the Gītā this is referred to as *nirodha* or the suspension of thought processes. Nirodha leaves impressions, or liberating saṃskāras, in the deep mind. Through yoga, step-by-step, with no expectation, we offer everything we think, feel, do, learn, and imagine as sacrifice into the fire of awareness. This takes great *śrāddha*, or trust. The act of trusting while not knowing reveals infinity at your fingertips as it destroys negative saṃskāras.

Any minuscule amount of success in letting go and waking up to the present moment gives you a taste for something other than the misperception that there are objects in the senses. You get a taste of pure energy, pure vibration, and that is far more satisfying than the imagined world and storyline we each spin in response to input into the sense fields. Seeing things just as they are leaves an impression in the citta—a sort of memory—that ruins your taste for sense objects because reality, though not always as sweet, has a far more enticing and satisfying flavor. When you let go and trust, then sattvic, or harmonizing, saṃskāras arise allowing you to suspend the vṛttis, or distractions of the mind, rather than pulling or pushing them away. This is the process of a well-seasoned practice: Things arise without the mind habitually objectifying them into the old storylines. You're able to experience that same old thing almost as if it is unknown and utterly fresh. Gradually and with continued practice, nirodha saṃskāras or sattvic saṃskāras are reinforced while old, unhealthy habitual patterning and deep conditioning are transformed. This is why within your practice, and likewise within your habitual actions in and assumptions about the world, as well as your relationships to others or nature, it is *essential* to always look again. The moment you think, "Oh! I've got it. I'm going to cash in my chips now," you're on the verge of slipping into saṃsāra, or conditioned existence. So even if you think you've gotten everything there is to get out of the practice, or your life itself, the teaching is that you should look again as you keep practicing. Kṛṣṇa points out that even he continues to practice, which is one of the functions of the teacher: to show what practice is so others are drawn to it.

In summary, Kṛṣṇa says that if, when you die, you haven't completed the yogīc path (which, by the way, is highly likely), you will be reborn either into a family of yogīs or into a royal family. In other words, you'll get another chance. He reassures Arjuna that it's all going to work out. No matter how long it takes, it's not a problem. Yes, the practices per se are precise and difficult but just start where you are and start over again and again. In this central section of the Gītā, Kṛṣṇa convincingly tells all of us how difficult this work of yoga actually is, for it is the intention of waking up to our present circumstances. He doesn't give it a sugar coating. It is difficult because it requires that we surrender our theories, our patterns of avoidance, our stubbornness, and every single imaginable defense mechanism we manage to conjure up in order to avoid what is right before our eyes. In doing so Kṛṣṇa is attempting to crack open the core of Arjuna's heart where Kṛṣṇa himself, all of us really, happen to be living. He's demonstrating to Arjuna with great munificence and love that in the very center of his own heart he will find there is no difference between himself and Kṛṣṇa. They are not one, but they are not two. And as the story and teachings progress, we learn that it is there, in the core of our own heart—which turns out to be the core of the heart of all beings—where compassion and true happiness reside.

[6]

Climbing from Pedestals Down to Earth

MOST OF US will never have the distinct honor, as a handful of modern-day explorers have, of seeing the earth for what it is: a stunning blue sphere floating silently in space, swathed by swirls of white clouds, with rivers cutting through distinct patches of land, steadily moving sediment and delivering life to the sea. Our planet pulsates with energy—fiery volcanoes erupting from within, lightning striking on the surface—supporting and challenging all life-forms in myriad ways. Stepping back to look from afar we can see it is one organism, one mysterious, interacting system of being.

In reality, our own view of the world is likely to be that on a clear night we happen to find ourselves on a mountaintop or beach gazing up at the sky with millions of distant stars in pairs and intricate patterns shining down upon us. Out of two tiny pinholes we call eyes and from the single point on earth upon which we stand, we stare up and out into the vastness of the unknown. We might experience how intimately we are connected to everything around us, or instead we might feel small, alone, and how insignificant each one of us ultimately is. In a sense both of these views reflect the other turned inside out: we are at once powerfully and profoundly interconnected and simultaneously the seat of our own consciousness—a separate and unique bag of bones just trying to make sense of it all. Even if we never make it into outer space, experiencing an embodied sense of how we are at once fully part of a whole that is not "us" and also fiercely independent is possible if we look deeply within, if we can surrender to something bigger than our own perceivable self. The yogī who sits in the forest (or in a booming metropolis, for that matter) can experience this same sense of dissolution as boundaries of ego and mind soften through practice.

Insight into interconnectedness is one of the most important underlying messages that Kṛṣṇa has given Arjuna up to this point in the Gītā, and he's provided tools for understanding—through theory and practice. But he knows that until Arjuna fully surrenders, he (like all of us) will repeatedly slip into a mindset of doubt and dismay when the seemingly real, yet ultimately imaginary, feeling of separateness predominates. In chapter 7 of the text Kṛṣṇa begins again from a slightly new angle to explain the next step along a path of insight. We've learned that the wise ones (the yogīs) practice stabilizing and stilling the mind through meditation, which allows them to see through delusions of a separate self, and we have been introduced to the necessity of letting go, reframing, and looking again while working without attachment to the fruits of our actions. We recall we must act with an open mind for the sake of others, but when we think there's a chance that we'll finally get it all, Kṛṣṇa bursts the bubble of attachment to liberation with the strong precaution that the path of yoga and awakening isn't easy.

He tells Arjuna that out of the millions and millions of human beings, there is hardly one who is interested in reality or in yoga of any type or form. And of the thousands of those who do taste the nectar and become yogīs, hardly one of them knows him, meaning hardly any go beyond the ritualistic, ego-driven approach to truly experience within every cell of their body the inescapable truths of impermanence and interconnectedness. Though in the Gītā taking up the path of yoga is put forth as the means to attaining liberation, Kṛṣṇa is torturously slow in getting down to discussing the specifics of how to actually do it, how to practice yoga. And there is good reason for this. If we don't truly comprehend the potentially harmful effect of ill-timed attachment, and we prematurely begin a yoga practice, we are at great risk of either wasting our time because we just go through the motions without dropping deep into the internal experience of surrender, or worse, we become so dogmatic we form a cult. It could be relatively benign—the cult of "me," the great yogī. But it could also be devastating to others if our own delusion of self becomes infused with a taste for narcissism, and we form a cult that sucks in others. If we practice in a way that augments our need to feel special, superior, or enlightened, if we isolate ourselves and cut ourselves off from healthy evolution that is a byproduct of feedback, if we think we know and therefore need not question or study, we are likely to create more harm than good. This is why Kṛṣṇa waits until Arjuna sees the inescapable necessity of karma as creative work and has been exposed to the idea of separateness as ignorance and the taproot of suffering, before he begins to reveal the practice of yoga.

It is not uncommon for those brand new to yoga—meditation and āsana in particular—to immediately experience something quite profound: a feeling that part of them that has been lying dormant wakes up. In this moment a deep cord within us is struck and there is a sense that we've come home to a familiar, long-lost place of integrity. This awakening might be just a background taste or a full-bodied sense of harmony or even a mystical experience. Whatever form it takes, it happens when a free and internal approach to yoga taps into the truth of being, whether we're prepared for it or not.

As beginners in yoga, we're less likely to have a philosophy or theories about the practices than we are after having practiced for a while. So that's why so many people feel transformed or catapulted into a realm of bliss when first beginning to practice. As beginners we're likely to be caught off guard, without the protection and barriers our preconceptions and presuppositions about what yoga is and what we can gain from it can impose. Even though we may have come to yoga looking for a little distraction or to help with our sore back, we may find ourselves overcome by a sense of connection to something real. Usually the feeling doesn't last long. Some students then spend the next few classes (or decades) trying to recreate the same memorable feeling of wholeness experienced that first day. But if they're lucky they gradually realize that the sensation was the natural process of yoga beginning to wake them up. Others run away, frightened off by encountering the depth of who they really are. But a few of us run the danger of grasping onto that experience of truth, mistaking content for consciousness, as if it is ours to be had. "We" came to yoga and had a uniquely extraordinary experience that we later read about in the Yoga Sūtras, where there's reference to the few who don't have to do anything at all and are suddenly enlightened. And we're off and running, tempted to think we *are* one of the lucky chosen ones who doesn't have to work in this lifetime because we came into this life ready to be liberated. It's at that precise moment, with practice, we'll catch ourselves, smile, and look again. In other words, don't forget that this whole thing—life, death, insight, and waking up—is an endless process. Which is what makes it so nice!

This is why Kṛṣṇa tediously pounds home to his beloved student the complexities nestled within the ideas and theories about yoga; he wants Arjuna to flourish, rather than become a ritualistic drone or an inflated adolescent who thinks he's above others. Kṛṣṇa uses the word *kaścid,* meaning "scarcely one," when speaking of yogīs because he himself is always releasing any sense of separateness paving the way for all of us to see that anyone who experiences "Kṛṣṇa" (or insight into the divine quality of impermanence and interconnectedness) is actually no different from everything that Kṛṣṇa represents. Ultimately we are all the same being—each in the others' hearts. When you actually *feel* this, the pulsation of what is naturally occurring—an intimate connection between you and everything else—it just doesn't make sense any more to hold on tight evaluating your perceptions as separate (and perhaps superior or inferior) to the rest of the world. It almost seems silly to slip into the saṃsāric mindset through which we identify thoroughly with our feelings, thoughts, and sensations, while we cling with futile attachment to the fruits of our actions as if they are "our" solid objects and as if there's something to gain.

Looking down at the globe, as we might if we *were* to find ourselves in outer space, watching all of the energies and forms of the entire earth moving in graceful synchronization, we would see clearly that if even just one river decided to separate itself out from the process, to imagine itself as special or separate and to hold on tight to control the flow of waters running between its banks, the entire ecosystem would be impacted. And if enough rivers rose up to embrace their imaginary distinction, the entire system, the earth itself, could eventually be significantly changed or even destroyed.

If we can, even for a moment, step out of our own identity to see that we are part of this magnificently complex ecosystem, then it becomes clear that the freedom *and* responsibility of being born into this human form are utterly awesome. Our world is a strong yet delicate field of interpenetration made healthy through a balance of independent expression and dependent arising within a process of communication, cooperation, and surrender. When we look at the state of the world's ecosystems today, such as the destruction of rain forests and coral reefs, we see the physical manifestations of a world where ego has been given precedence over concern for other. Ecologically, politically, and in many cases interpersonally, we are confronted by the very real threat that our own species is manifesting in the world perpetuated by mindsets of divisiveness, intolerance, and disregard for others and the whole. It's not as though the self-absorption and destructive, self-centered foibles of humankind are a new phenomenon. They are part of our nature alongside our basic goodness. It is just that for now we seem to be at a tipping point where if we don't wake up to the truth of interpenetration, we as a species could potentially cause irreversible harm to the world as we know it.

Obviously, given the teachings within the text at the time of the writing of the Gītā, many of the same basic flaws of human nature were strongly evident. Now, as then, waking up is imperative in spite of the fact that it is a natural human tendency to resist insight by objectifying others and identifying with our ego and perceptions of the sense fields. However, by practicing mindfulness—watching the rise and fall of ego and sensation as a process—we can gradually surrender and begin to experience everything as sacred. Once this insight is deeply rooted in our embodied experience there is no turning back to a full-on life of narcissistic separateness at the expense of the whole. If we feel deeply connected to all aspects of life—seeing God in all beings (whatever God means to us) and all beings in God—then we will be eager to sincerely offer every action as a sacrifice with a sense of earnest generosity and nonattachment. Whatever thoughts are there are seen as being intrinsically without self, interlinked and sacred.

And *this* is what a healthy contemplative practice reveals: the capacity to question with openmindedness, to act with integrity, and to let go, to surrender. Healthy surrender is a step-by-step process. It requires trust, and to trust we must feel safe. Safety is nested in understanding, and the capacity to understand is facilitated by clarity, which comes from seeing through our preconceptions and predispositions—our ego—and then setting them aside. To set down the ego is the ultimate surrender. Important to this process of trust and safety is the desire to act with integrity and compassion along with the ability and willingness to forgive not only ourselves, but as importantly others, for honest mistakes made.

So where do you start in unraveling this process of insight? You start where you are and wherever you get the slightest foothold! And this is the pattern of teaching in the Gītā where Kṛṣṇa offers just enough theory to capture Arjuna's interest and quell his doubts. Then he offers a good dose of countertheory or practical examples that might inspire Arjuna to look again, more closely, while over and over again reminding him to surrender and trust.

The message he gives is "Come to Me" which, especially to non-Hindus, may sound quite theistic. But if you release religious preconceptions, you may be able to see that Kṛṣṇa uses his embodied human form, which represents all that there is in the world, as a nonthreatening, tangible form and expression of everything else, so that Arjuna (and perhaps others) can start to understand what it means to surrender to life. For those of us who are Jewish, Buddhist, Christian, Muslim, or of any other religious persuasion, and perhaps even more so for agnostics, secular humanists, or atheists, putting any specific God forth to whom we should surrender can feel uncomfortable if it isn't our God. But if we can put our religious biases aside momentarily, it might be possible to benefit from the powerful metaphorical message of the teachings: it is time *now* that we wake up and connect to everything around us as we work for the benefit of others if this world, and we along with it, are to thrive.

Interestingly, the problem of misunderstanding this central message of the Gītā is not so much one of theism but of lack of fearlessness, an open heart, and an endlessly discerning mind. So even for Hindus who revere Kṛṣṇa, if they become nontrusting and fearful, isolating themselves from other perspectives, the generous message of the Gītā can be overlooked. Seeing Kṛṣṇa as divine and supreme might make the initial surrender easier but could quickly lead to superficial, dogmatic, or fundamentalist views surfacing. In spite of the fact that in the story of the Gītā Kṛṣṇa *is* one of the Hindu gods, he is first and foremost Arjuna's friend. Indeed he makes it clear that as God, all emanates from him and returns to him, and that the wise ones think only of him and surrender to him. Yet Kṛṣṇa is also the servant, not only to Arjuna as his charioteer but to all of us as he returns lifetime after lifetime to help others awaken. As a pure demonstration of the teachings of interconnectedness itself, Kṛṣṇa appears as the embodiment of the Gītā's underlying message.

To bring Arjuna and all of us back into the practical realm, Kṛṣṇa next gives tangible examples of how he represents interconnectedness by pointing to everyday experience. He reveals what normally would be considered pantheism: that all of the things of the manifested world are considered sacred, including God or in this case Kṛṣṇa himself. He does this masterfully, in a way that does not separate him out as omnipotent and superior but rather as the link, the connection within, through, and surrounding all phenomena that compose this universe. He is everything: subtle phenomena, gross phenomena, phenomena that aren't obviously either subtle or gross; all phenomena are strung together like jewels on a thread, and Kṛṣṇa is the thread, the absolute common ground, the energetic link on a field of boundless pure consciousness that holds it all together as both origin and dissolution. "Earth, water, fire, air, space, mind, intelligence, and the ego function, this is the eightfold division of my prakṛti (creative energy)" (7.4).

Kṛṣṇa describes these manifestations of nature as his "lower nature." He also describes his "higher nature" or what he calls the nature of the subtle body, what would be described as prakṛti in Sāṁkhya. He points out that all beings originate from this higher nature (mind or subtle intelligence) and dissolve back into it. He says, "I am the taste of water, Son of Kuntī, I am the light of the moon and the sun. I am the syllable (Oṁ) in all the Vedas, the sacred sound of space and the virility in men" (7.8).

After connecting to the elements of nature, things such as sunlight or the taste of water, it is possible to then experience this same oneness, or Kṛṣṇa, as an extremely intimate experience, you're seeing it, you're swallowing it. It's a very familiar yet always wonderful experience. So the message here is that this sense of unity is no longer an abstraction or a theory, nor is it something that is 200,000 light-years away—a star on the horizon—so distant and subtle that your mind can't touch it. Instead, wholeness makes up the most familiar parts of your everyday experience that may not seem sacred at all—each of these is a source or thread of all that manifests.

For those who have studied yoga, the word, or seed mantra "Oṁ," represents the whole as the immediate vibratory experience. Starting with the sound of the letter *a*, Oṁ is said to contain the entire Sanskrit alphabet, ending in the universally satisfying sound of the *anusvāra*, or *mmm*. Oṁ is the generic name for sound as a phenomenon; the sacred sound appearing in space—all sound. For the esoteric yoga practitioner, this is Kuṇḍalinī. When the prāṇa and apāna (inhale and exhale) are united, and the central channel is unblocked, then all sound is Kuṇḍalinī. At this point you don't hear objects in the sound because there is no story; it is just vibration that unfolds as insight. This notion of insight made available through embodied vibratory sensation reflects back to the beginning of the Gītā, when Arjuna blew his conch and came back down to earth to his senses and began to wake up. Experiencing pure sound as a universal form of understanding is the immediate experience of connecting beyond ego, thought, emotion, and storyline into the direct experience of the moment. It is the process of waking up. So we can all experience the thread of interconnectedness if we are courageous enough to listen.

Kṛṣṇa then proceeds to give additional examples of the jewels along the thread of awareness and the connecting force uniting us all into one, describing himself in beautiful detail: "I am the sacred fragrance of the earth, the brilliant splendor of the sun, the individual life in all beings and the austerity of ascetics. Know Me to be the original, primeval seed of all beings, Son of Pṛthā. I am the intelligence of the intelligent and the radiance of the radiant. I am the power of the powerful, freed from lust and passion. In beings I am erotic love consistent with dharma (which does not oppose the dharma)" (7.9–11).

We are shown that all of this—everything—is Kṛṣṇa, even your grumpy mood. It isn't you. It's prakṛti. It is Śakti. It is the direct experience of the essence of interconnection; a recognition of the process of life as Kṛṣṇa. In this way yet again Kṛṣṇa gracefully reframes the teaching, always showing the process of nonseparation. In the microcosm of our own life experience, outside of the theoretical underpinnings and storyline of the Gītā, we've probably all had the experience of recognizing essence in this way, without even being fully aware that that is what was happening. If you bring to mind someone you love dearly—your child, your spouse, perhaps your dog—you can recognize them in countless ways both subtle and gross. Like Kṛṣṇa, who describes himself as the qualities of nature such as the taste of water, we too know those we hold dear not only by their clothes or their status in life but by the memory of the sound of their voice, the feeling of their heartbeat next to ours, or the scarcely discernible shift in their eyes when they're solving a puzzle. These intimate details are as fully them, if not more so, as is their full presence when they step into a room. *This* is our own individually wrapped and often overlooked gift of insight into what Kṛṣṇa is teaching when he begins to lay out the depth and diversity of his forms—demonstrating not only that he is everything but also that no one thing alone is him.

Kṛṣṇa then identifies four kinds of people who take up the path of yoga. "Of benevolent people four types adore Me, Arjuna; the distressed, the inquisitive seeker of knowledge, the seeker of wealth and the wise, O Bull of the Bharatas" (7.16).

We learn that first there are those who are afflicted, in other words those who suffer, which seems to be everyone. They try yoga because they are looking for something—anything—to alleviate their suffering. Then there are those who are curious, the inquisitive ones like scientists, who come to yoga because it seems interesting. Then there are those who work for *artha,* the first of the traditional four goals of life. They are those who have "grown up." They are more like adults who realize the importance of their estate, so they become worried about it: "I want to have a good roof and food, and something for my kids when I'm gone." This, by the way, is most people. They become religious or come to Kṛṣṇa because in the background there is a little bit of fear that they might end up living in a dumpster. Even though all three of these types of individuals are motivated by a self-concept, it's alright because at least they are looking in the right direction. The fourth type of seeker is the *jñānī*—the one who sees through the fiction of the separate self. Kṛṣṇa explains that these are the ones who are wise or who naturally feel interconnection in their body, heart, and mind. He describes them as *priya*, a Sanskrit term meaning "extreme love." "I am extraordinarily fond of the wise one (*jñānī*) and that one is fond of Me," he says (7.17).

The message here, the principle teaching of the entire Gītā, in fact, is that the path to happiness is love. It is not through Kṛṣṇa as a Hindu deity nor any other conceptual separate, egotistical story you might choose as God, and it is not as Jesus, the Buddha, or any particular god or absolute. The implication is that we surrender to pure love, pure bhakti—an utterly unbreakable link to all beings. The connection isn't theoretical; it is not arrived at by thinking at all but by an embodiment of love that is condensed and condensed until it produces nirodha, or a suspension of thought, which by definition is not what you think it is.

[7]

Steadiness within Love's Mutable Base

THE IDEA OF SURRENDERING to pure bhakti comes as such a relief at this point in the Gītā, given the buildup of intense storyline and dense teachings. Especially since it's all been topped off with the news that the method that will get you through crises and on a path toward lasting insight—yoga—is virtually impossible for most of us. Learning that all we really need to do is to trust bhakti, eager students may heave a deep sigh of relief and sink slowly back into that supportive nest only love makes available. Pure, unobstructed love is warm, rich, full, accommodating, and strong. It provides a time and place where you can feel safe enough to truly let go. Arjuna's relief too is palpable, but after only an instant of reflection on the blissful idea of bhakti and surrender, he—the wonderfully insatiable student—is troubled by the next logical step that again throws him into a moment of crisis. Given all the teachings that he's learned from Kṛṣṇa to this point, including insight into the absolute nature of life, the self, the process of elements unfolding, and embodiment and sacrifice, how ultimately does surrendering to bhakti help? How can we "know Kṛṣṇa," surrendering body, mind, emotion, and ego into the unknown at the time of death? So he asks, "What is this Brahman? What is the original self and what is action, O Best of Persons? And what is said to be the primordial domain of the elements, and who is the original divinity? How and what is the nature of sacrifice here in this body, O Slayer of Madhu? And how are you to be known at the time of death by the self-controlled" (8.1–2)?

Arjuna's question is often interpreted as a query into how, in the end, knowing Kṛṣṇa will improve the inevitable situation we all face that one day we, and everyone we know, will die. Confusion about and fear of death are common unspoken uncertainties. Even more insidious than the background worry of winding up in a dumpster that ushers some to yoga is the seed of fear of our impending death. It is buried deep in the fertile soil of the imagination and embodied experience for virtually everyone. We may *think* we know interconnectedness and nonattachment. We may be cavalier, speaking of change as the constant and of impermanence as a blessing, and we may even imagine we are prepared for death. But then the time of reckoning comes and we find ourselves face-to-face with death—our own or that of someone we cannot imagine the world without. Perhaps we fight or sink into despair, depression, or denial but hopefully at some point in the process we find that these methods of postponing the need to confront the inevitable do not serve us or those we love.

Death *is* unavoidable—we are all barreling along on a one-way, dead-end street to death from the moment we're born. The process of death is riveting, raw, the absolute invitation to show up, to get real, and to witness that everything is precious beyond description, transient beyond thought, and inherently intangible in its perceivable form. But truly facing these facts, surrendering to the present moment and, as Kṛṣṇa says to Arjuna, giving up our sense of separate self and coming to him and into the unknown takes tremendous courage. If we can quell our fears and avoidances, then the reality of death rips open our illusions to expose connections into the heart, the essence of existence, where we find that love is the only thing that sets us free. Without death there is no life, there is no true bhakti, there is only imagination.

Yet again, Arjuna is filled with doubt and finds himself in crisis. How does surrendering to Kṛṣṇa at the time of death actually help him or others he might encounter on the battlefield? Should he surrender to love or stand up as a good warrior and forget ahiṁsā in order to fight? Are fighting and ahiṁsā mutually exclusive? Kṛṣṇa reminds Arjuna that the way to see through the doubts, confusion, and fears is through yoga, the practice of focusing the mind and refining the capacity to let go into the vastness that is all manner of manifestations from subtle to gross. In chapters 8 and 9 of the Gītā, Kṛṣṇa offers a wider range of examples of who he is—which is everything—so that Arjuna can gradually start to experience the wholeness of manifestation and see that it is the surrender of self into this vastness with the knowledge that one's self is actually part of the whole that helps at the time of death or any crisis. Kṛṣṇa advised Arjuna at the very start of the Gītā to stand up and fight—to meet his crisis head on, as a practice for that moment of death. Here too, in the middle of the story, he underscores the importance of facing our fears and crises by standing up with love, strength, and integrity, surrendering not out of duty or despair but out of devotion, courage, curiosity, and trust for the process. This is the most effective way to meet not only death but the full spectrum of life that leads us there.

His message is that to surrender, especially at the time of death, takes practice. This is what yoga is; the step-by-step practice of quieting the mind in a way that increases the capacity to let go and to surrender into the circumstances within any given nanosecond. Practicing the art of surrender *before* we meet the big one—death—is training to stay focused, and it prepares the ground for presence within a multiplicity of circumstances while we're still alive and in this body. In this way the act of intelligent surrender facilitates the ability to let go and trust the unknown in a healthy, natural way. We are not so easily tossed into emotional imbalance and confusion when faced with complexities, dilemmas, or disillusionment in times of upheaval. Contemplative practices give us some experience in finding our way back to the present moment. Most importantly, with practice we're more prepared to cope with whatever particular circumstances we face—including death. No guarantees of course, for at the time of death many factors converge to set the stage for the exit from this lifetime. Maybe it will be within our capacity to be conscious and "awake" as we release that final breath, and maybe not. Either way, as Kṛṣṇa teaches, for those who practice letting go and focusing on him in *this* lifetime—for those with the right intensions—death is a path (short or long) toward liberation. Even within the process of death we are encouraged to not be attached to the fruits of our actions. In other words, the message is that we aim to meet death exactly as it manifests, setting down our ideas of a good, bad, scary, enlightened, or chaotic death. We practice yoga and letting go as sincere offerings and sacrifices and out of devotion rather than as a means toward salvation or mastery in any way. By repeatedly and consciously rekindling a taste for focusing on and experiencing the divine nature of all manifestation, we prepare for and meet death in just the correct manner appropriate for each one of us in this particular lifetime.

Kṛṣṇa reminds Arjuna of what we see with the clarity of mind that we cultivate through practice: "The primordial domain of elements (*adhibhūta*) is the perishable existence. The puruṣa (the witness) is the basis of the divine creations. And I myself am all the sacrifices here in the body, O Best of the Embodied. And at the end of time, remembering Me, having released the body, the one who goes forth comes to my state of being. Here, there is no doubt" (8.4–5).

An important part of this teaching is the unquestionable truth that we do not know the circumstances or time of our death. We could die at any moment. Therefore we should be ready for death by consistently and under all manner of circumstance within the context of the ever-changing landscape of life focus on the interconnected nature of things. This section of the Gītā offers beautiful images through which we can recognize the process of death as well as practices, like chanting, that might be helpful in keeping us tethered to the present moment and the process that emerges when death presents itself. Kṛṣṇa explains that "Attending to all of the gates (of the body) and suspending the mind in the heart, having placed one's own prāṇa in the head, established in yogīc concentration and saying "Oṁ," the one syllable Brahman, meditating continuously on Me, the one who comes forth while releasing the body goes to the highest path" (8.12–13).

But he warns that all the worlds other than this imperishable realm (revealed and explained later in the text) are subject to rebirth. Kṛṣṇa calls the manifested realm as day and the unmanifested as night and says that all things come from the process of manifestation. Next he describes the "unmanifested," the "eternal or imperishable being," which is what he represents, what he is. Kṛṣṇa is "fire, light, day, the bright lunar fortnight, and the six months of the northern path of the sun are when Brahman-knowing people go to Brahman. Smoke, night, the dark lunar fortnight (*kṛṣṇaḥ*) and the six months of the southern path of the sun are when the yogī returns giving the lunar light. These two paths, the light and the dark, are thought to be perpetual in the world. By the first, one goes to not return, by the other, one returns again" (8.24–26).

In the context of the Gītā, in which reincarnation is a foundational belief, these practices prepare one for understanding the fabricating nature of mind and for touching into insights that can be helpful in the process of moving through death and into the next incarnation. Yet you need not believe in reincarnation to apply and benefit from the teachings. The idea, in part, is that if we have repeatedly practiced the process of letting go of attachments and have focused on all manifestation as an interpenetrating matrix of the divine, then at the time of death—at least in the background of our awareness—we may instinctively do the same. By not clinging to the body, the emotions, the life—even others we love dearly—we may be able to truly let go and, if circumstances permit, show up during the process of death. Those who do accept reincarnation would also be practicing not clinging to or coveting past or future lives. Envisioning the dissolution of our own corporeal and mental boundaries into a state of unification with our world, with the universe, and out to infinity, we may find moments of liberation, seeing death as a metaphorical concept for all transitions from moment to moment rather than just the end of a particular life.

As a means of understanding this, Kṛṣṇa then spends considerable time in chapters 8 through 11 describing and eventually displaying in vivid, sometimes spine-chilling detail the layers buried within layers of mutable manifestation that he is. We've reached a point in the story where Kṛṣṇa can do so because finally Arjuna has begun to settle down, to be less distracted and far less immobilized by his pending dilemma of whether or not to go into battle. Arjuna's mind is beginning to soften its grip on its presuppositions, and he is eager to hear more. By now he is taking delight in the words of Kṛṣṇa—"they are like nectar," he says, and he begs Kṛṣṇa to tell him more. Arjuna has reached a point of voracious curiosity, like any of us might if we'd stumbled upon something that touches us so deeply that our sense of truth, meaning, and aesthetics is roused beyond thought. When this happens, no matter how often you hear about this thing that has awakened your essence, it is still new; not for lack of understanding, but because it is powerful, compelling, and infinitely interesting to the point you cannot get enough. This is now where Arjuna finds himself, and this is why the Gītā is sometimes referred to as nectar, or Gītāmṛta, as it is in the Gītā Dhyānam.

The Gītā emphasizes that understanding these concepts is a process of attaining knowledge, then letting go of the knowledge in a spirit of trust and surrender. Essentially Kṛṣṇa teaches the prerequisite of understanding, which is the ability to trust the unknown, the unknowable. Kṛṣṇa is saying that *he* is whole and unknowable by most, even by the gods and equally by those who are awakened. "Neither the hosts of gods nor the great seers know my source. Indeed I am the origin of the gods and the great seers in every way. One who knows Me who is birthless and the beginningless, knows the great lord of all worlds. Among mortals that one is undeluded and is released from all evils. Intelligence, knowledge, freedom from delusion, patience, truthfulness, self-control, calm equanimity, happiness and suffering, existence and nonexistence, fear and fearlessness. Nonviolence, impartiality, contentment, austerity, generosity, fame and ill repute—these many varieties of conditions of all beings arise from Me alone" (10.2–5).

Kṛṣṇa then reflects on the profoundly internal nature of true knowledge and again draws attention and refers back to the intimate direct experience of what is immediately before us at all times. Everything radiates directly out of Kṛṣṇa: understanding, knowledge, freedom from bewilderment, patience, truth, self-control and calmness, pleasure, pain, existence and nonexistence, fear and fearlessness, nonviolence, equal mindedness, contentment, austerity, charity, fame. These are all desirable qualities that we might like to think we possess; however, the Gītā has taught us that they are not ours, they are part of the infinite interpenetrating scope of things—all of the states proceed out of the whole, out of Kṛṣṇa. With this glimpse of the whole, we are then given four verses that many people consider the most precious gems of the Gītā as essence for those who seek freedom: "With all their thoughts in Me, with the prāṇas (vital breaths and all sensations) flowing to Me, awakening each other, always conversing about Me, they are content and delighted. To those who are continuously devoted and adoring the adoring, filled with joyous love, I give this yoga of intelligence by which they come to Me. Out of compassion for them I, dwelling in their hearts, destroy with the shining lamp of wisdom, the darkness born of ignorance" (10.9–12).

Kṛṣṇa explains that he is the source of *all* things and that the awakened ones (the buddhas among us) know this and are content in this knowledge. Rather than struggling, overthinking, conjecturing, controlling, and misperceiving, those who understand become content, wise in the knowledge that they can simply offer devotion to the divine, to Kṛṣṇa—Bhāvasamanvitāḥ. We are reminded that those who really know and surrender to the unknown often chant devotional songs, not only as an act of devotion but as a practice that is helpful in focusing and clarifying the mind by stabilizing the breath. This is true in cultures around the world.

Prāṇa (or breath, sensation, and the connection of mind and breath) is the substratum of sensation and thought for all sentient beings, and this biosubstratum of experience flows and flowers in and out as Kṛṣṇa and as all manifestation. This is all wonderful and potentially filled with insight, and it is made even more so when shared with others. Speaking in the plural, Kṛṣṇa reminds Arjuna that the buddhas help to wake each other up (*bodhayantaḥ parasparam*) just as he has patiently carved space in the very center of the battlefield for Arjuna himself to take hold of his inclination to wake up. Kṛṣṇa chooses to explain this with the words *kathayantaśca māṁ nityaṁ*. *Katha* means talking but not ordinary talking. It describes the sense of a clear discussion of truth. The telling of a myth is katha if it is soaked in bhakti. Katha is not just talking mindlessly or gossiping to someone, it has to be enlightened talk—or at least sincere talk of the truth. This type of talking is delightful, and it lasts eternally—like when you really get into a profound conversation with someone and it goes on and on and suddenly you realize it's gone on all night. Your lotus seat starts to ache, but you are still so happy! This is the key to katha: it is so delightful that it is thrilling to share; you *must* share the truth. It turns out that it's the sharing or the linking between—in this case linking together of—buddhas that is beautiful beyond words. If you have an insight or exciting experience that reveals a glimpse into the nature of reality, it is much nicer to share it than to hoard it as if it's all yours and there isn't enough to go around. It's as if you're out hiking and you discover an immaculately crafted den full of foxes with four tiny innocent baby foxes staring out, waiting for their mother to return. You come to a standstill and watch, barely breathing in order to not disturb—you're so excited that, just like Arjuna, your hair stands on end! You turn to your companion, if you're lucky enough to be hiking with a friend, and exchange looks of awe. It is much nicer if there's someone there with you to share it with and better still if they too are on a path to awakening. Sharing is a central characteristic of bhakti, and it is how bhakti or pure, unadulterated devotion unfolds.

This is spoken of in many classical Indian texts, the idea of *sadhu saṅgha*, or hanging out with people who are waking up, knowing there's a lot of waking up to do. It's thrilling to find yourself on that delicate edge where you're caught off guard from your beliefs and the center of gravity shifts away from self-obsession toward other. With that little bit of tipping of the center—with awareness of and respect for saṅgha or other—the whole thing moves into a new, significant realm of reality. The best part of it all is that it is spontaneous—you don't *do* anything at all. In fact, if you *try* to make community or friendship happen you're destined to fail miserably until you let go and trust the process of meeting the other authentically and without an agenda—the true meaning of community, or saṅgha. The sharing and insights come because it is a spontaneous process, not one done out of obligation or theory or in order to get something but one offered with sincerity, love, and in a spirit of kindness without knowing where it will lead. That's when you actually start to wake up.

It turns out that those who embrace this sense of bhakti—sharing with others and welcoming insight without clinging to it—are those to whom Kṛṣṇa gives buddhi yoga, or the yoga of discernment. Buddhi yoga is considered the yoga of intelligence and just like the sharing of love and freedom, it isn't something you do or take; it is not a function of the ego because intelligence is a gift. And from the perspective of the Gītā, intelligence is a gift only to those who are absorbed in *bhajatāṁ prītipūrvakam*, or devotion filled with joy. In this sense we are seeing buddhi as the context maker, that which, within the Sāṁkhya system, envelops the I-making principle, the ego, or the *ahaṁkāra*. When the ego is contextualized it effortlessly dissolves into intelligence. Buddhi yoga is considered a gift because it is given out of compassion as the process of shining the lamp of observation and ultimately wisdom into everything experienced.

Again, for those philosophers among us who do not resonate with the storyline of Kṛṣṇa, or possibly any deity, as the all manifesting and all knowing, the metaphor of a deity representing wholeness can still be very helpful, unless we are so self-absorbed—as unfortunately some are—that we are unable to let go of our theories and to experience interconnectedness in nature, relationships, or even in birth and death. Even staunch atheists or brilliant agnostic philosophers have bodies. They experience breath entering and exiting the body and the vibratory quality of all sensations. So for spiritual seekers and deep thinkers alike the direct perception of even simple moments of daily life can plant seeds for insight and awakening. This is especially so when, having merged with sensation and emerged on the other side with theories or stories, we can remember to give it back, to surrender to the truth that even our most brilliant insight and knowledge must be poured back into the fire of awareness if we are to dive deeper still.

People seldom do the sacrifice of prāṇa—of breath or sensations—because they're off in the thought patterns. We start by offering the two ends of the breath, the prāṇa pattern (inhaling) and the apāna pattern (exhaling) to one another, pouring them back and forth. It is easy to think about but not always so easy to do because to really pour prāṇa into apāna requires good alignment, and good alignment is scary because you must be undefended, vulnerable with your emotions revealed. Once you've connected with the prāṇa it is so beautiful you might be reluctant to sacrifice it. Yet the message of the Gītā is that we must give the whole thing up. "Come to Me," Kṛṣṇa says repeatedly, knowing this is the path into his true nature. The essence of yoga practices, it turns out, is as much the practices themselves as it is putting the whole thing down. It is the act of sacrificing the breath, and along with it sincerely sacrificing sensations, fears, stories, and so on into the fire of awareness. It is observing the embodied experience that is constantly transforming to inform you that you are indeed the sensations themselves—everything, even the sensations of fire, but not only the thought that fire could burn you, but the air, the ashes, the shape, and even the moisture in the fire. The whole thing, we put down and offer it into the sacrificial fire of awareness.

This is not done just at the time of death, but at all times, and this is Kṛṣṇa's consistent and final teaching when he says, "Come to Me," because all times are the time of death, and metaphorically we are constantly placing things down into the eternal fire of awareness. Even the moments between what you conceptualize as reality—right there is where space, the uncategorized, nondifferentiated connection to all else, resides. And you put that down too. If you're doing this at all times, then when the actual time of death comes, at the very least you'll be familiar with the practice and the feeling of putting things down. Having practiced putting down things—from the insignificant to the insightful—you may already have found in that release the wonder of letting go into the process of life, which is really what waking up to the present moment, waking up to life itself, is all about. By practicing the ongoing art of letting go during life, when death arrives at your door perhaps there will be an opportunity to experience and to express—offer to others—the compassion of interconnected awareness. This is an essential aspect of the buddhi or imagination.

It's interesting that in the text the word *anukampā* is used to describe this process of giving buddhi. *Anukampā* is often translated as "compassion," but literally it means "trembling along with." Within the story, Kṛṣṇa expresses this as a connection on an embodied level with Arjuna and his experience of truth, saying that he is trembling along with—

or utterly empathic to—the experience of others with whom he shares this wisdom. Basic ignorance, known as avidyā, or the sense of separateness, is considered to be the root of all suffering, and it is the polar opposite of anukampā. By explaining to Arjuna the fundamental problem with the "ignorance" of seeing oneself as separate, Kṛṣṇa shows him a path toward liberation. Avidyā leads to *asmitā* (ego), which leads to *raja* and *dveṣa* (attraction and hatred, respectively), and eventually to *abhiniveśa*, or the fear of death.

These are said to be the causes of suffering because within them lie an absolute obstruction of pure relationship and insight into the interconnected nature of life. They also contain food for ego embellishment and fear. By eliminating the root cause of suffering (avidyā) even if we do so only theoretically while still feeling separate and alone on tangible levels, we begin to chip away at the natural human obliviousness to the fact that all life is absolutely divine so that we may begin to see whatever it is we imagine to be "God" everywhere. In this way, at the time of death we may have the good fortune to surrender to the process of life, resting in the strength of being surrounded by the divine.

With this teaching Kṛṣṇa has given Arjuna yet another potent building block to balance upon in his step-by-step process along a path toward waking up. Arjuna gains a newfound sense of freedom and begins to feel stable and happy, and this is when he hears Kṛṣṇa's words as nectar and longs for more. Kṛṣṇa is delighted and offers images for an even more intimate layer of his manifestations—deeper than Arjuna's personal experience of water, others, or his own fears or joys. Kṛṣṇa next moves into the realm of myth saying that of snakes, he is Ananta (the serpent of infinity), and of collators, he is time. He is the wind, all-destroying death, and the origin of those things that are yet to be. He goes on to say that there is nothing that could exist without existing through him. But then he asks Arjuna why he needs to know all this, and this question leads into chapter 11 of the Gītā, one of the most intimate, beautiful, and profound—almost psychedelic in its imagery—pieces of writing within the whole text.

[8]

The Unfolding of Time and Devotion

As chapter 11 of the Gītā opens, Arjuna is not only inspired but at last confident with the sense that he is fully prepared to meet the world head on. The petrifying fears and doubts that arose and immobilized him on the battlefield have subsided through trust in his teacher—his friend—and he has begun to comprehend the foundational teachings that initially overwhelmed and threw him off. Seeing Kṛṣṇa as the manifestation of everything he encounters—and trusting Kṛṣṇa with his life as both friend and teacher—he is confident that he is beginning to have insight into the nature of reality and an understanding of the karmic chain of events that define and support birth, life, duty, and death. So he asks Kṛṣṇa to continue unveiling the truth, passionately urging him to reveal his "imperishable self." The idea of the imperishable self, briefly mentioned earlier in the story, before Kṛṣṇa detailed the multiplicity of his worldly manifestations, is then elaborated upon.

Kṛṣṇa explains that the yogī, or the wise one, kindles the fire of intelligence by stilling the mind, meditating without distraction on the supreme, and chanting the syllable Oṁ while embodying the interconnected nature of being. He then goes on to explain that those who remember this multifaceted practice of folding and refolding intelligence into the embodied experience *at the time of death* do not have to take rebirth because they have insight into what is described as the imperishable realm—the same realm of realization as Kṛṣṇa himself. Others, he explains, work through lifetimes of birth and death, some coming back quickly into the manifest realm, some of whom pause in the unmanifest realm, before returning to life once again. The imperishable realm is described in the Vedas as beyond that of the unmanifest and it is said that those who reach this realm need not return. Yet Kṛṣṇa, like anyone who truly understands the process of life, death, suffering, and enlightenment and, by that definition reaches the imperishable realm, *chooses* to return—to continue to work—out of compassion for others. This is similar to the Buddhist idea of the Bodhisattva vow; a vow taken by those who pledge to strive not only to liberate themselves, but to return to life—even after reaching enlightenment for as long as it takes—until all sentient beings are enlightened. Kṛṣṇa, like the Bodhisattva, has vowed to offer his work for the benefit of others until everyone is set free. The imperishable realm is not defined as the "ultimate realm" which would establish a hierarchical order of insight into enlightenment where if you're really cool and extraordinarily devoted, you achieve the grand prize of reaching the one realm where you can forget about the other feeble seekers and nonbelievers who just "don't get it" and from which you won't have to return to a life of saṃsāra (conditioned existence). Quite the contrary, Kṛṣṇa explains that the ultimate freedom of body, mind, and spirit is revealed through the embodied experience of the boundless realm of existence where there is no beginning, no middle, and no end; a realm that by this very definition is imperishable. The imperishable realm, therefore, is a nonexclusive state of being in which everything—good, bad, ugly, divine, and so on—manifests in a clear light of equanimity. It *is* interconnectedness and more importantly it is why those who experience a taste of it feel compelled to return for the sake of others. We learn that there is yet another realm in which Kṛṣṇa, who himself is timeless, eternal, and all encompassing, resides. Beyond this unmanifest there is said to be yet another layer, an unmanifested "Eternal Being" who does not perish even when all existence perishes. "But there is higher than this unmanifest, primeval unmanifest, which does not perish when all manifestations perish. This unmanifest they declare as the supreme goal, arriving there they do not return. This is my supreme abode" (8.20–21). This is the real yoga.

Kṛṣṇa also makes it clear to Arjuna that though he is referred to as this very being, the unmanifest, supreme goal is not only him. Instead, it encompasses everyone and everything. In other words, by imagining and experiencing this all-pervasive, interpenetrating nature of life, any one of us may become "imperishable," just as Kṛṣṇa himself is because in truth we are united and one with Kṛṣṇa. Through this teaching Kṛṣṇa steps down from the perceived role as a separate almighty to demonstrate that seeing him with a distinct status is merely a theoretical projection by those not ready or willing to wake up. Experiencing the imperishable is possible if we are willing look again more closely at what is arising before us as if looking through a new set of eyes.

Kṛṣṇa agrees to reveal this realm to Arjuna by showing him his universal forms, but he cautions Arjuna that this vision is not one he will be able to see with his normal human eyes. The vision is available only through a special eye, an eye that must be given from one who has access to it. This special, divine eye does not look out to focus on the world as do our ordinary eyes, but instead looks inward, into the depths of existence, where ego is as irrelevant as a grain of sand on an infinitely wide beach. The seeming paradox of the magic eye is that it does not make the one with the eye, who is looking inward, irrelevant. Instead, combined with our own circumstances, perceptions, comprehensions, and a sincere longing to know, the special eye provides a sort of "tri-ocular" vision that accesses an instantaneous embodied experience of the process of life in vivid, multidimensional Technicolor. Every presentation is the infinite, divine form. With this extraordinary eye there is a direct experience of being an intricately interwoven, essential element within the fabric of life with no distinction between our individual experience and the entirety of existence.

Swooning at the thought of this, Arjuna, who is still intoxicated by the nectar of Kṛṣṇa's words, is eager to see Kṛṣṇa's full form—his imperishable self—with this seemingly magical eye. If Arjuna had worn socks—they didn't wear socks in those days, but if they *had*—his socks would have flown right off his feet. Yet still he's feeling pretty good now, having forgotten his immediate crisis and dilemma and thinking he's had full insight into the teachings. He's getting a little "practice pride," and his ego is directing the show, which is a wonderful and endearing stage many reach, and hopefully move through, while on a path to waking up. So he asks for it. Kṛṣṇa agrees to reveal the mystery of his full and countless forms—hundreds of thousands of forms of infinite variety; endless divine forms arising of various shapes, colors, and hues with no two alike. In a unique yet perfectly natural way, his manifestation interconnects to everything else and opens up endless realms; and if you look closely you'll see it's already happening all over the place.

Kṛṣṇa begins by detailing his form as various gods—the Ādityas, the Vasus, the Rudras, the two Aśvins, and the Maruts—and he says that everything is here in his body. In the story, Arjuna sees this and realizes that because he is feeling as one with Kṛṣṇa, these forms are *his* own body as well. And, by the way, the message is that these forms are reflected in all of us too, in our individual body because all bodies belong to this realm. When Arjuna experiences this in his body—or you do in yours—it is impossible to continue to reduce the body to a theory of "the body" or worse yet, "my body." The body becomes *divya*, or divine, and you start to instinctively experience the endless field of *cit*, of consciousness, in which each point in the body is experienced as *cintāmaṇi*, or a jewel of pure joy.

Having granted the divine eye to Arjuna so he can have a direct experience, Kṛṣṇa continues to reveal layer upon layer of form, what is called his *paraṁ rūpam aiśvaram*, or his supreme, opulent, majestic forms. He unfolds not one mouth or one eye but an infinite number of mouths and endless chains of eyeballs, implying that the multiplicity of manifestations is not that useless forms or eyeballs line up, but that there are eyes within eyes, perspectives within perspectives, all shifting and wrapping endlessly around one another. Each is a unique, irreducible, divine whole. The message is not that there is one ultimate universal form, but that the multiplicity of endless forms is the "universal form," or the Viśvarūpa. Seeing into the vastness is experiencing the universal form, and it is a full-bodied expression of how the mind opens up. Kṛṣṇa says, "Not of one, but many mouths and eyes, many wondrous visions, many divine ornaments, many raised divine weapons. Wearing divine garlands and apparel with divine fragrances and ointments and composed of all wonders, the Lord infinite with faces turned everywhere" (11.10–11).

It is important to note the extensive range of experience that is covered by contemplating the meaning of every small detail of each of Kṛṣṇa's forms. The task is not to fixate on one form alone as sacred but to always look again and to dive deeply into a process of visualizing the form at any point that catches your interest. This results in the broadest, most complete vision and potential for insight. For example, citing "the many divine ornaments," as Kṛṣṇa does in verse 11.11, may seem like an insignificant or poetic detail, but these ornaments become revealing, if not profound, when you consider their implications. Ornamentation implies playfulness and beauty, which open the mind to the possibility that there is so much more to consider. If this idea catches your attention, you dive into it. Life is not all stiff upper lip and seriousness; the whole thing is exquisite beauty that is going on all around us all of the time, some of which does not have a "purpose" or cause in and of itself. But all of it is an unfolding into an aesthetic experience where there is no need for a self to function, in which the beauty would make an observing "self" unbearable.

Kṛṣṇa goes on to describe the powerfully moving prospect of truly seeing interconnectedness as follows: "If a thousand suns rose at once in the sky, such a brilliance might be the splendor of this great being" (11.12). We are invited to imagine an infinite number of suns simultaneously rising up as an expression of the overwhelming power and brightness of Kṛṣṇa's unfolding. It is interesting to note that Robert Oppenheimer, who invented the atomic bomb, quoted the Gītā when the first bomb went off. Some scholars believe this "brightness of the sun" verse is the one he quoted. Others think it was a later verse (11.32) in which Kṛṣṇa describes himself as time, the mighty destroyer of the worlds. Regardless, both are chillingly accurate of what Oppenheimer and others were witnessing and equally on target for the visceral experience one has when deeply contemplating and embodying insight into the interpenetrating nature of all things.

Considering the image of a thousand suns rising all at once is a metaphor for the entire universe standing at once in *samastitiḥi* (equal standing). It is the idea of seeing the whole world as being suddenly perfectly balanced, which, incidentally, it happens already to be if only we could see it. Too often, trapped in our own chaotic corner of mind and the world, we are unaware of the counterchaos someplace else that brings overall balance. This is the natural order of things. Given how selfish and greedy some world leaders and their followers have become in the last few decades, disrespectfully treating others and the world at large, we can only hope that this natural resilience toward balance will not be completely toppled. The good news is that through callous behavior toward others we are shown firsthand how destructive the attachment to sense objects—the self-centered materialistic drive—can be and perhaps compassion will arise. For those who see the injustice, imbalances, and devastation that occur when we abandon others for the sake of our own egos and attachments, there is plenty of loving work and service to be done.

This very insight makes Arjuna's hair stand on end again, which is considered to be one of the classic signs of the arising of bhakti or *samādhi*. It's one of the initial signs that your prāṇa is starting to get oriented, so we know Arjuna is waking up, and he tells Kṛṣṇa what he sees: "I see in your body all of the gods and all of the distinct variegated families of beings, the beloved god Brahmā sitting in a lotus flower, and all the true seers and all the divine water serpents. O Lord, Beloved of the Universe, O Form of the Universe, I do not see your end, your middle, or your beginning. I see you with endless form on all sides, with endless arms, bellies, faces, and eyes. Wearing a crown, holding a club, spinning a discus, a massive radiance shining in all directions, I see you who are difficult to see completely and who are the immeasurable radiance of fire and the sun" (11.15–17).

Bathed in the splendor of this magnificent vision, Arjuna is ecstatic and completely enthralled because he has gotten a tangible taste of what it feels like to merge with absolute insight into the true nature of things—interconnectedness. But then the unexpected happens; Kṛṣṇa reveals aspects that are less effulgent, beautiful, and uplifting, and Arjuna is forced to realize that he was seeing only the uplifting aspects of Kṛṣṇa. His ego was sugarcoating the notion of interpenetration so that he could avoid the truth that everything—even the most vile and disturbing aspects of existence—are also Kṛṣṇa. This is something that is so tempting for any of us to do: to see what we like and ignore what distresses, confuses, or disturbs us. Midthought, Arjuna shifts from being delighted and in awe of his vision of infinity, to seeing beyond his beautified concept of what infinity is. His exhilaration waivers as he must let go of his limited perceptual overlay to wake up even more deeply, and he says, "I see you without beginning, middle, or end, unlimited, infinitely powerful with endless arms, with the moon and the sun as eyes, with your oblation consuming mouth as blazing fire, whose brilliance burns up this world. Between heaven and earth in all directions, this is filled by you alone. O Great One, seeing this awesome and horrible form of yours, the three worlds tremble. Over there communities of gods are entering into you; some terrified, they sing praises with reverent gestures. Calling out 'svastī' the hosts of great seers and perfected being praise you with abundant, splendorous songs" (11.19–21).

Not only does Arjuna see the gods in Kṛṣṇa's embodied form along with every imaginable being, he also sees infinite forms, not the beginning and not the end. And he sees that the lord of all—every individual's perception of God or ultimate truth and pure consciousness—is the universe. He has this insight *because* these images of Kṛṣṇa's universal form are not breathtakingly beautiful and inspiring, like the thought of tuning in to the subtle taste of water as one of his forms, but instead some are of total destruction, far worse than Arjuna could ever have imagined. Not only is everything marching forward into the jaws of destruction, but Arjuna sees that some gods are cheerfully going into Kṛṣṇa's mouth and to their own ruin. They're being friendly, familiar, saying "svastī" or "How're you doing? Good health. Nice day!" Arjuna is terrified by the thought that they're marching into the mouth unaware of their impending demise. (It turns out that these are the ones who've realized the imperishable realm, and they're delighted to be part of the process, so it's not quite as bad as it appears to Arjuna's untrained eye.)

Within just a few verses Arjuna is catapulted from the bliss of thinking he has realized infinite wisdom and form, back into fear, doubt, and confusion. He starts to see the death of all creatures as *this* universal form, and he suddenly understands that impermanence isn't just something to give lip service to, but that it is the core around which everything is organized and revolves. The powerful, unavoidable conclusion from his vision is that there is no escaping death—nobody evades the fate of death, and there is no place in the conceivable universe where this is not happening. Arjuna sees an infinite number of mouths, so if someone has dodged one of death's mouths, they enter into another. He sees warriors, teachers, relatives, and friends from the impending battle. Some have had their head crushed, and their shabby remains stick between Kṛṣṇa's teeth—like specks of spinach that get stuck in your teeth after a meal. And suddenly not only does Arjuna face the nature of life as one of impermanence, but also this becomes an immediate reminder of the horrible reality of his current situation, what he is actually facing on the battlefield, today. His bravado is shaken to the core, and he starts to succumb to fear once again—even backing away from Kṛṣṇa as his longtime friend and seeing him only as the all-powerful, fierce manifestation of God, or Viṣṇu. He begs Kṛṣṇa to help him understand all of this and says, "As many torrents of water, rivers, and streams flow to the ocean, so too these heroes of the human world flow into your flaming mouths. Just as moths into a bright light with such speed fly to their destruction, so these worlds quickly enter your mouths to their destruction. You lick and swallow from all directions all of the worlds with flaming mouths. O Viṣṇu, your fierce and terrible brilliance fills and consumes the whole universe with splendor. Tell me who you are, O Terrible Form. Salutation to you, Finest of Gods. Be kind, merciful. I want to understand you, O Original Being" (11.28–31).

As Arjuna pleads for mercy and attempts to understand, Kṛṣṇa is relentless, partly because Arjuna asked to truly see in full. Perhaps too it seemed to Kṛṣṇa that Arjuna had learned from previous teachings and was ready to wake up to a new level of insight. Since Kṛṣṇa gave Arjuna access to the special eye, they both have a responsibility to ensure that Arjuna looks deeply. Instead of softening up, Kṛṣṇa goes on to say he is here to annihilate the worlds, which is enough to give anyone who imagines his wrathfulness as callous and violent good reason to become terrified and back down (as Arjuna does) or to dismiss Kṛṣṇa with utter disdain as a teacher of senseless killing (as many scholars who read the

Gītā do). Of course, if you just examine history, this vision of ultimate destruction and death does actually seem to be happening everywhere. Look around. Sometimes it's due to unfair or evil deeds, but even when people are caring and civilized it seems to be the path; every single one of the kings and heroes of the past, right up until now, are all dead. So any of us contemplating this profound teaching are forced to see the unavoidable process of life and death and the seemingly permanent nature of death. We are obliged to meet the uncomfortable reality that our own perceivable existence is finite. Even if we've gotten very comfortable and philosophical, and we see how tiny our reality is in the big picture, we *are* all marching with resistance, blindly or with glee, into the jaws of death, which is ultimately where theory meets reality and where there is no turning back and no benefit to anyone—especially oneself—in putting on an act, in not embracing the process that is life.

And just like Arjuna, we find ourselves in the midst of the well-scripted narrative of "our life." The dramas and boring moments, the heroes and villains, the conflicts and solutions; such an interesting story we spin! But faced with this image we, again like Arjuna, may panic when contemplating our death or the death of our loved ones. After all, usually when death raises its fearsome head it hasn't been written into our script yet. We may choose to ignore or hide from the truth of impermanence for many more lifetimes—and really, that's okay; we each must face death when the time is right. Or perhaps we're seasoned enough to find a thread of trust through which we can pause to look again.

The crisis gripping Arjuna on the battlefield pales in comparison to his terror at seeing Kṛṣṇa's universal forms, yet having built some understanding of the underlying philosophical doctrine that Kṛṣṇa is trying to teach him, and more importantly, relying on the love and trust he feels for Kṛṣṇa—his friend and teacher—this time Arjuna does not collapse into an immobilized state as he did at the onset of the story. He now intuitively knows that there will be action in this sort of inaction and that he must "stand up" to meet his circumstances head on. Instead of collapsing, with utter sincerity he pleads with Kṛṣṇa to return to his familiar four-armed form. In other words, Arjuna needs a breather to recover from the intensity of insight bestowed upon him through the gift of inner vision he experienced by way of the special eye.

His desire to connect again to his friend is also fueled by fear that perhaps in the past when he thought of Kṛṣṇa only as his best friend, hanging out with him in many stories prior to the Gītā, somehow he offended Kṛṣṇa by treating him without enough respect. He now realizes that Kṛṣṇa is the ultimate manifestation of everything from subtle to gross—he is "God." Arjuna begs Kṛṣṇa for mercy and forgiveness. But because Kṛṣṇa does encompass all, he knows that one of his manifest forms is Arjuna himself, so Arjuna is just as important to him as everything else: the forms in nature, his demonic or fierce forms, even the realization of pure consciousness. All of this Kṛṣṇa knows to be one and equally sacred. Of course he is not at all offended and returns again to his normal everyday form, his intoxicatingly wonderful appearance, *saumyavapus*, or gentle, mild, and pleasant form. In fact, rather than being insulted by Arjuna, Kṛṣṇa is delighted. Arjuna's intense reaction to the fullness of Kṛṣṇa's multiplicity of forms and his ability to stand up to meet his current crisis are testaments to the fact that he truly *is* waking up, which is actually all that Kṛṣṇa hopes to facilitate. Once Arjuna sees Kṛṣṇa in his familiar form and as his friend, he can relax and begin to feel composed and that his mind has been restored to normal.

Kṛṣṇa explains that the universal form is always right in front of our eyes, yet it is difficult for anyone, even the gods, to see. This is because we are prone to reduce what is immediately arising to concepts and stories about it. If you are living in a manifested form (a human body) it is challenging to see beyond the boundaries of your imagination. Due to the nature of mind, when we perceive a particular form before us, our theories and ideas about what that form—what we believe we are seeing—tend to make us unable to see it as an integral part of the divine whole. It's like when you're doing your sitting meditation practice and decide you are going to meditate only on God. It's not so difficult to spin a tale of what God looks like, what God does, what God means, and what your relationship to God is. It's pretty easy as you sit there to develop a story around God and follow the story into all sorts of alleys and corners of mind. But this is not practicing the skill of surrendering to the present circumstances and observing what actually arises in the moment, which is ultimately what leads to stilling and stabilizing the mind. Patiently practicing sitting down, sitting upright, and sitting still, watching thoughts, sensations, and feelings come and go while always coming back to a chosen field of attention, such as the breath, are powerful forms of being able to rest with the unknown. If you *have* decided to meditate on a particular question or problem, when a thought about something else—dinner or the sensation of pain in your knee—arises, you ignore it as irrelevant to "solving your problem" or "giving you insight." This is usually what happens if you're steadfast in your aim to meditate on "God" or anything specific. Other thoughts or sensations arise, and you either spin off into a new storyline, or you push them aside and look behind, beneath, or around them to find the thing that you've decided to think about; what's "really important." If you contemplate a particular topic in this exclusive manner, it is impossible to focus on what is right before your eyes. Still, you examine what arises without latching on to it. It is also important to know that focusing on what arises as it comes up does not diminish or negate the importance of your chosen topic, not at all. In fact, by allowing your chosen topic to rest in the back of your mind as you meditate, you are giving it a context in which to reveal itself fully so that new perspectives and solutions to whatever it is you're wrestling with spontaneously present themselves. This approach to meditating—contemplation on a particular chosen field—is a good start to open presence and is by no means inherently harmful. However, it is less likely to directly "solve" deeper problems. Meditating in this way is good in that it polishes the skill of focusing the mind, but it does not necessarily refine the ability to stay fully engaged and unattached to outcome.

Mindfulness is the practice of trusting the process of dependent arising without attachment to either the act of observation or to whatever part of the process manifests. A common mistake is to try to turn mindfulness practice into a formula that can control and direct thought. This is especially true if we have an ulterior motive for the practice—even if that motive is noble, like "I want to meditate so I can understand my relationship, so I can be a better person and save the world." In mindfulness practice we greet whatever is arising with kindness and compassion, holding it with great care in a space of pure awareness, as if it were of immeasurable, inherent value but not an *object* of extraordinary value. We greet it without becoming trapped within the storyline that is being concocted about whatever it is that is arising: "Poor me, my knee always hurts, maybe I need surgery, maybe I should just quit meditating." Mindfulness practice is curiosity without a motive to solve, observation without an impulse to fix, and acceptance with no underlying dogma or judgment directing the flow. There is discipline too as we gently remind the mind to let go. By bringing focus back to the breath, for example, again and again and again, we can slowly see more and more clearly—without our overlays of perception, mind, and emotion—exactly what is arising as it manifests. Misinterpreting mindfulness practice as something from which we expect an outcome is common. It is not inherently bad and, in fact, sometimes arranging a situation that allows us to still the mind can be helpful in solving problems or at least calming the mind, but it is also a way to short-circuit the deeper benefits the practice may reveal.

If we interpret whatever is arising as a problem, or we see it as getting in the way of what we "should be focusing on," then we've split things apart again; we've created a problem where one doesn't exist. Yet the instinct to split things apart is quite normal, since whatever we perceive in the world is just a teeny, tiny fragment of the whole. It is a sliver, something exceedingly small because we are looking from the singular perspective of our own embodied form. No wonder the mind almost automatically creates a dualism between what is "real" or right before our eyes, and the unmanifest. From this limited view, the unmanifest is clearly something else.

This holds true until, as a side effect of continued practice or, if we're lucky by chance, we connect to look more deeply inside and glimpse through our own "tri-ocular" vision into the nature of life. We see it as being endlessly manifested in every form we encounter, as well as those we've yet to see as part of the interconnected net of perceivable forms. This vision supports the honest letting go required to experience the limitless, vibratory true nature of life. Through the experience of yoga practice, we get tastes of this compelling view of the world. Then again in the midst of practice, even as experienced practitioners, we find we're striving to make our direct experience reveal to us corners of what Arjuna experienced when he saw Kṛṣṇa's universal forms. Suddenly we realize we are desperately wanting something specific out of our practice, perhaps thinking, "I'm going to practice *nirvikalpa* samādhi (samādhi that arises without focus on a single, separate object) until I'm enlightened." But with patience and more practice we notice even our own commentary is part of the process, and we can see it as an object of meditation. When we notice something like this happening as we practice, we smile, observe the process going on within the practice, and then we can let go of even that noble urge to control in the name of enlightenment. Contemplative practice is just that: a practice rather than a finished, static entity. It takes time and patience, and with continued practice we slowly polish a path toward deeper understanding. We gradually learn to embrace and support the process of mind by bringing the light of awareness to everything, and then letting it go.

Kṛṣṇa explains that insight into the true nature of things is not accessible only through study of the Veda (philosophy, mythology), nor is it possible through *tapas* (work) or as a gift alone. He says that one cannot even see the universal forms by pure sacrifice alone either. In other words, no *one* technique or single method can take you to the final step. They will potentially all get you close, he says, but the key—the final little ingredient needed—is the ability to truly surrender into the vastness of the unknown that is rooted in relationship, letting go into the field of devotion, bhakti, or love. In a sense when Kṛṣṇa asks us to meditate on him he is asking for something very, very difficult: not surrender to a power-hungry God or tyrant but surrender to the process of life. He suggests we meditate on him in both his personal *and* his impersonal forms. It is really Viśvarūpa, or the form of the universe or the world, that Kṛṣṇa is asking us to pay closest attention to. Looked at in this light, the Gītā is a nondual text and the normal, everyday form of Kṛṣṇa is also Viśvarūpa. But in Arjuna's mind there is a difference between his friend Kṛṣṇa and his universal forms. He thinks Kṛṣṇa is his charioteer and friend and then there is this Viśvarūpa, this big, scary, infinite form Arjuna cannot comprehend. "I'd prefer to take my nice, normal friend," he thinks. Of course we know that this is a misperception on his part—he does not see these two types of manifestation as linked. Yet it was within the perception and vision of Kṛṣṇa's tangible embodied form that Arjuna began to wake up, where he started to see the universal forms interlinked and interpenetrating with Kṛṣṇa's normal form—his familiar, blissful face, his strong arms, and his powerful chest. So the vision, the insight, is right before Arjuna, but his preconceptions and fears deny him access to it. On a practical level he saw that the forms were not separate, yet the notion of interpenetration and the process of life and death are so profound that Arjuna's mind had to make them into two separate things so that he could hold on to the thread of insight arising within him.

Each of us has moments—maybe only a split second here and there—where we experience this union of manifest with the unmanifest, and it is stunning. As a newborn, when we see no separation between our self and the rest of the world, there is a natural insight into interconnectedness. We are all born out of the womb of another, developing cell by cell within the physical structure of a "separate" embodied being. It is true that we are not one, yet neither are we two completely unrelated, independent beings. We are all born with this inherent knowledge on an intimate, cellular level—the direct experience of interdependence. As life unfolds and our storyline becomes "real," however, we develop a sort of amnesia. If we're lucky we have a memory-refreshing experience, often it happens within a contemplative practice, yoga, or meditation, for example, when we feel connected in an unspeakable way to everything, everyone else. It can happen spontaneously too when watching a beautiful sunset, encountering art that hits us just so, through the use of certain psychoactive substances, or for no apparent reason at all. When it happens we feel safe in the process of life, truth, kindness, and the ability to let all of our preconceptions go into the field of not knowing because viscerally and deep in our core we are experiencing the truth of interconnectedness and the beauty of impermanence. The benefit of reaching this state through contemplative practices is that they train, strengthen, and embody mental stability. Through focused attention the state becomes increasingly easy to return to consistently and at will without any outside prompting. This experience of interconnectedness is the embodiment of true love, and it is what fuels the insight that helps us to see that our attachments, misunderstandings, and perception of separate self that lead to suffering are just minor inconveniences. With this insight, we see that saṃsāra is like a puddle rather than an ocean, and we are happy to do whatever it takes—even living another lifetime or thousands of lifetimes—until we wake up to the process of experiencing boundless bhakti.

[9]
The Ultimate Surrender

SURRENDERING TO BHAKTI, or love, makes our quest for enlightenment sound so simple and trouble free. And in some ways it is, until ego, manifesting as confident misperception, enters the scene. We know what love is. It's that feeling of union, the deep sense of connection to another that allows us to let go and reveal ourselves without fear of rejection. Oops, here we go! In just three short fragments of thought we're off and running toward a dualistic view of things that will keep us suffering for lifetimes. Yes, love *is* union, connection, and freedom to express oneself, but it is not something we can ever truly know. It is visceral, intuitive, interdependent, and ever changing.

The form of bhakti that becomes a catalyst for insight carries with it the distinguishing characteristic that it starts from the inside out rather than the outside in. Bhakti is integrally interwoven with everyone and everything else, but it is absolutely not dependent on the other. When, on a cellular level, we experience the nature of all things as unification rather than separateness, then we have touched into bhakti, and in fact we have found yoga. At that point it becomes obvious that things do not come together in union, they are *already* unified (while retaining individual uniqueness), and it is only our misperceptions that separate them.

Once we latch on to a foundational belief in and attachment to our separateness, we can then spend lifetimes working to bring together things that are already unified. It is so easy to be confounded by the instinctual trap of separating things into a dualistic view, but when we can see through our resistance to letting go of our concept of a separate self—separateness altogether—we are no longer blinded by an inability to embody the feeling that all forms, even our own unmanifest forms, are sacred and real. When the root of understanding is that all manifest forms are substrates of unified patterns, then on a multifaceted, intuitive level we experience the dependent arising of all things. Kṛṣṇa explains that this simple yet profound insight is attained by cultivating trust and bhakti and through the practice of stilling the mind. He says, "Always, a completely content yogī, who is self-controlled, unwavering in resolve, with the mind and the intelligence merged with Me, one who is devoted to Me, is beloved to Me" (12.14).

Kṛṣṇa's recommendation to fix the mind and intelligence "on him," meaning meditate on a relationship with all beings, is another way of revealing that he is in the heart of all beings, that in fact, he *is* all beings. The instruction is to meditate on interconnectedness, not to meditate on a fanciful image of a beautiful blue god playing the flute. This verse implies that once the yoga, or the bhakti, is very deep there is an inner juice called *prema* or priya that automatically bubbles up as a seamless exchange of self with the other. It starts to flow like a strong, mysterious, magnetic core and is ignited in a way that is verbally indescribable; it must be understood through direct experience of the thing itself. *This* is bhakti, and it is the final catalyst that allows dissolution into a state of enlightenment.

From this starting point of unification, Kṛṣṇa then contextualizes and clarifies some of the earlier teachings in the story, explaining that for those who do not shrink from the world and from whom the world does not shrink nonattachment and equanimity quite easily occur saying, "One who has no hatred for any and all beings, who is friendly and compassionate, free from possessiveness and egotism, equal to pain and pleasure, who is patient. . . . From whom the world does not pull back and who does not pull back from the world, who is free of pleasures, impatience, fear, and misery, is also dear to Me. One who is impartial, pure, dexterous, unprejudiced, untroubled, who has let go of all undertakings and who is devoted to Me, is beloved to Me. One who neither rejoices nor hates, who neither grieves nor lusts, who has let go of good and evil, who is filled with love, is dear to Me. One who is the same to enemy and to friend and also to their own honor and disgrace, who is alike to cold and heat, happiness and distress, and who is free of attachment. Who is equal to blame and praise, who observes silence, content with anything, who is without a house, with steady judgment, filled with love, this person is dear to Me" (12.13; 12.15–19).

These are very important teachings for any of us who practice yoga or decide we want to wake up and evolve. You find a nice quiet place to do your practices, or you have insight into the idea of Indra's net or some other foundational teaching of interconnectedness, and you feel fantastic. But then you step outside, you go into the street and you think, "Eeew, traffic! And look at all these people." You shrink away from the world. Or you isolate yourself in the ivory tower of your ideals and insights rather than walking down the street with pure open presence, embodying the experience of the sometimes-messy state of the world. People see you and they run away, annoyed by your demeanor and egotism or hurt by your inability to reach out first with mercy and to embody compassion. You're too busy building your fantasy of what it means to be a yogī, a mystic, a parent, a teacher, a guru, or a philosopher, separating yourself out from what is actually arising. We practice meditating on what is arising so that when the dualistic mind pops up, we notice just that: the dualistic mind. And we see that state of mind as sacred. It's fine when the misperception of separateness occurs, if we notice it because we're meditating on the current pattern rather than on an idea of what we should be meditating on. The true yogī notices the arising of a dualistic mind, then notices the noticing of that arising, and so on. As we learned in verse 12.13 of the Gītā, yogīs have "no hatred for any and all beings" or any manifestation. They are only perfect in their imperfections—not always able to control the mind, the emotions, their runaway dualistic tendencies but able to see and learn from their mistakes, and this happens either spontaneously from looking deeply inside or through external feedback.

This is what is being taught as bhakti. Through it we learn not to go off on any extreme. Instead, with an extreme perspective we consciously include its complementary opposite as we take the middle path to bhakti. This is very difficult and it is why, earlier in the story of the Gītā, we learned how rare it is to find someone ready for yoga. The nature of mind is to make philosophical propositions that tend to be extreme. So usually we end up with a position of thought that is unconscious of its complementary or opposite position. We hate or fear our shadows and immediately we've missed the mark, ending up unable to see the natural process and evolution of things as that of relationship, bhakti, love.

Arjuna, having calmed down from, but also having stood up to, the fear that arose in him when he saw Kṛṣṇa's full universal form, again becomes inquisitive. This is an interesting and important part of his character: the desire to know and the willingness to look again. He is never satisfied that he *knows* for certain, although he persists in asking which of two things is better because he imagines that he *can* know for certain. Kṛṣṇa loves and encourages this part of Arjuna's spirit—his need to always look again. This is the sign of a great student, and it is why at the start of chapter 12 of the Gītā, Kṛṣṇa is pleased that Arjuna asks, "Of those continuously engaged, who worship you with love everywhere, and of those who worship the imperishable unmanifest; which of these has the better knowledge of yoga" (12.1)? In verse 12.2, Kṛṣṇa answers that it is the ones who fix the mind on and worship him while continuously practicing yoga, that those who possess the highest faith, are considered the most devoted to him and, therefore by definition have better knowledge of yoga. The word *śraddhā* is used here in the text. It can be translated as "faith," but not blind faith. Instead, it is the ability to rest in the unknown; a very deep trust in the process of life and an ability to surrender to the way things are. As Kṛṣṇa points out, śraddhā is in accordance with the truth or the nature of each being when he says, "Śraddhā closely follows the form of one's nature. Humans are composed of their trust in their metaphysical assumptions. What one's śraddhā is, *that* one is" (17.3).

This reflects back to an early teaching where Kṛṣṇa explains that puruṣa (often translated as "pure consciousness," but also means "man," or "all of us") is made of faith. It is our faith and what we trust that results ultimately in our happiness. Even those whom he refers to as the demonic, who are possessed by ego and pride, lust, anger, and greed, still have faith and that's what keeps them alive and what makes them what they are. It is important to discern that faith surfacing as divisive, constricting, and harmful aspects of nature, such as ego or pride, drives wedges of doubt and hatred into relationships and causes all involved unhappiness rather than joy. Faith in a healthy sense is the softening of ego boundaries into a balanced and intuitive connection to another, a connection to the unknown. Finding faith, trust in the other that opens the gate to love, is a core teaching of the Gītā. In a very practical sense, it is this level of pure faith that allows you to breathe. It would be impossible to breathe if your ego actually succeeded in paving over space, separating you out from everything else, which is the impulse of a healthy ego. The separatist impulses of the ego are countered by complementary aspects of nature—the dissolution of ego and trust of and surrender to the other, all of which sprout from roots of faith that enable the capacity to truly let go. This is bhakti, and it is a process that automatically leads to a spontaneous, authentic desire to serve others, the whole, and it is when love comes to light. The arising of ego, pride, lust, anger, greed, and other divisive qualities is balanced in a state of harmony and equanimity in healthy individuals, healthy relationships. Pride is balanced by humility, lust by contentment, anger by forgiveness, and greed by generosity. Only in a state of harmony, where qualities of destruction are brought into rich balance by their complementary opposite, is deep trust and faith in interconnection possible.

Whatever faith one has, that is what one is, and it is how bhakti works. In this spirit we think, "I am a servant of a servant." And then, "I am a servant of a servant of a servant." The traditional understanding of this is that, "My teacher is a servant." Which any good teacher must be. Not a dictator or tyrant, not a know-it-all or a callous egotistical show-off wanting everyone to know how gifted *they* are. No, a good teacher is someone who, like Kṛṣṇa himself, loves their student—sees the student as residing in the core of their own heart and with great tenderness offers to the student whatever it is they actually need: knowledge, support, feedback, direction, and so on. Just like a servant would support their master, a teacher meets the student exactly where they are. But this is very tricky and demands a lot from the teacher, who must quell their own ego and presuppositions and pay very close attention in order to discern details of the student who stands before them. The teacher too must look closely to find new angles of observation while welcoming feedback in a sincere attempt to perceive as clearly as possible moment by moment. The traditional teaching begins with the idea that my teacher is a servant, and I am a servant of my teacher. Both teacher and student consider themselves to be the servant of a blade of grass that touched the foot of a servant who was carrying water to a great servant. In other words, we all do things for one another out of devotion and bhakti when we realize the nature of interconnectedness.

Of course the mind will turn anything into a farce. The ungrounded teacher might think their students are indeed their servants (forgetting they themselves are a servant first and foremost) and might inflate themselves and deflate others in their own personal mythology. Unseasoned students can also become confounded by this instruction, confusing blind trust—a surrender of integrity and intelligence—with healthy surrender, which is a kind of grounded, inquisitive trust, rooted in mutual respect and compassion. The kind of surrender that is called for in the Gītā, and that is beneficial to both student and teacher, as well as to any relationship, tradition, or lineage, is one that is filled with an enthusiasm to explore the subject matter in full context. Then the flaws of the system and the individual are revealed so that both individuals and systems can evolve within a setting of mutual support. Everyone is happy because insight into the subject matter is becoming more clear and enriched by the multiplicity of perspectives that are being shared and considered from all sides in a spirit of support and selflessness.

This kind of trust is not a formulaic interpretation of things as they appear to be; it is not a giving away of intelligence and integrity within an unhealthy power dynamic. It is an interchange within which both parties are awake, communicating, and giving and taking feedback, as well as continuously questioning and offering their actions and knowledge freely and honestly into the sacrificial fire of pure awareness. When a beginning or "innocent" student falls under the spell of a manipulative or power-hungry leader—be it a teacher, a religious leader, a family member, or a work acquaintance—then abusive behavior or even cults can arise and cause great and lasting harm. In true bhakti, healthy surrender is founded in respect and an honoring of relationship. Bhakti is where two things meet, and at that point of conjunction, the ātman, or reality, is revealed. A good teacher is one who is skilled in sacrifice, particularly in *jñāna yajña*, the sacrifice of wisdom, along with the sacrifice of ātman or their own whole being. They give it up, all of it, freely and with a spirit of service to others.

In the beginning of chapter 17 of the Gītā, Arjuna has become intrigued by this idea of sacrifice as bhakti and asks an interesting question of Kṛṣṇa, which leads to the final teaching of the book in the last chapter. Kṛṣṇa invites Arjuna to question more deeply the motivation and intention of those who imagine themselves to be on a path toward awakening. Arjuna asks, "What is the position (situation) of those who, throwing aside the injunctions of the scriptures, yet filled with śraddhā, offer sacrifices, O Kṛṣṇa? Is it sattvic, rajasic, or tamasic" (17.1)?

This would cover people who are ignorant of the teachings but have good intention in their actions. It would also apply to others who, knowing the scriptures, decide to dismiss them. For many who attempt to understand the teachings of the Gītā, there is an urge to abandon them. In fact, throughout the story we see moments of confusion for Arjuna when he experiences this urge to toss it all away. Much of the time he can't even figure out what the teachings are advising him to do because they seem to be contradictory, so time and again Arjuna asks for certainty or he longs to know which is better, this or that? Each time, consumed by doubt, he is about to abandon the teachings out of frustration and confusion. It would simplify things so much if there were just one straightforward teaching, one way, one dogma to be followed.

As sincere students studying the Gītā we too may be tempted by the human instinct to follow one path dogmatically or to dismiss the subtle yet complex teachings of the text altogether. Just doing "our" practice, following "our" dharma, or forfeiting relationships to do "our sacrificial rituals" may sound good, but that attitude toward practice, dharma, ritual, or sacrifice—that it is ours and by definition separate from the rest of the world—derails us completely. The Gītā teaches the mandate to find the middle path, not to become rigid or righteous. It teaches that relationship—love—is at the core of all practices and is central to understanding life and finding happiness.

But we must be careful because even one's concept of love, just like anything else, can become a cop-out. We hear bhakti is the key, and we give up everything to travel around the world to practice bhakti, chanting songs of devotion day and night. At first we're devoted and sincere, chanting for the sake of all beings. But unless we balance that practice with other contemplative forms or, even better, by taking on real-life responsibilities and relationships, like raising a family or serving the poor, we may become ungrounded. We run the risk of becoming caught up in and distracted by the superfluous details of the scene, like what we should wear as we sit piously onstage next to our chanting guru, rather than recalling the intention and meaning behind the chants. If we are intoxicated by the sound and vibration of chanting all day every day, the idea of standing up to face our circumstances and the responsibility of being part of something far bigger than our own tiny little corner of perception can slip out of our awareness so easily. Then suddenly one day (if we're lucky) we wake up to find we've morphed into practicing "Look-at-me bhakti" rather than any form of devotion at all. True bhakti—our relationship to all beings, which indeed *can* be expressed beautifully through chant—has evaporated. What began as sincere devotion became swallowed up by our attachments to the trappings and outcome of our activity, having fallen under the influence of rajas and tamas guṇas. Instead of chanting as an expression of interconnectedness, we've surrendered to our own ego. It happens all the time!

This is just one example of how love, devotion, and faith can erode; when the ego—always looking for ways to survive—captures a thread of flattery or a corner of superficial teachings. If it remains unchecked it will exploit that seed of delusion in order to make sure it is securely positioned within our perception of "self" as separate from the other. A feedback loop with others provides communication and perspective from all directions and safeguards against losing integrity within the teachings. This is perhaps the most important and unifying global theme of the Gītā, a teaching that is also central to Buddhism as the idea of the three jewels: the buddha (the teacher or fully enlightened one), the dharma (the teachings or scriptures), and the saṅgha (other sincere students, the community). All these together support one's path toward liberation.

With trust and open communication, it is safe and a source of lasting happiness to surrender intelligently. So when Arjuna asks this question about those who ignore or discard the teachings, Kṛṣṇa reviews a number of the ideas and philosophical underpinnings discussed much earlier in the text. He speaks of the characteristics of the guṇas—rajas, tamas, and sattva. He speaks of sacrifice, reminds Arjuna of what it means to act without attachment to the outcome, and underscores that practicing yoga (steadying the mind) makes nonattachment easier. Then he introduces the idea of doing one's work and ending with the chant, "Oṁ tat sat."

Oṁ is of course, Oṁ—familiar to all beginning yoga students, though it's not always uttered with an understanding of what it actually means. Oṁ traditionally refers to Brahman, or everything. It is one full, vibrational sound intended to encompass every imaginable form, sensation, thought, vibration, emotion, manifestation—everything. *Tat* means "just that" or "that's it," implying we're doing whatever we are doing for no other reason than to simply do it. This is how Kṛṣṇa wants Arjuna to perform his practice, how he is advising him to act. Not to get anything else but to just purely perform the action itself without any sense of ahaṁkāra, mineness, ego, greed, hope, or anything else. *Sat* means "truth, in reality." Kṛṣṇa is instructing all of us through Arjuna to practice without any strings attached, as if practicing the truth—which is what a real yoga practice is.

Of course, this defines *śuddha* bhakti, or purified bhakti, which is understood to reside outside of the three guṇas—not separate from the guṇas, but outside of them. When practicing śuddha bhakti you see that whatever you do is composed of the three guṇas—nothing arises or manifests that is not a braiding of these three. However, with practice the intelligence, the double-edged sword of discriminating awareness, gives you the ability to see through the layering of mind, to slice right through everything, including your own perceptions, to reveal the truth that everything—including your self-concept—is in a process of dependent arising.

When we are able to stay wide awake and alert while letting go into the stream of pure consciousness, then activity can be carried out in an intelligent manner—manifesting outside of the guṇas. We can then observe the patterns of the guṇas as divine forms. When this type of discernment or discriminating awareness is accessible, there is no residue from our work because there is no motivation to change the pattern of manifestation for our own separate benefit. Therefore, the action is always revealing its final goal, which is bhakti itself. In other words, the bhakti is practiced only for the sake of the bhakti. Bhakti is interactive, not passive, and this ability to let go while being vigilant is absolutely different from an unengaged, passive letting go, as if it's all good and no responsibility for action or attentiveness to detail is required. So bhakti, just like the other approaches to liberation that are laid out in the Gītā, is paradoxical; it takes work, but is all about letting go. It is finding stability in the midst of constant change and flux. Bhakti is a blossoming of unequivocally knowing and trusting in the face of the unknown.

This form of bhakti is not necessarily easy. It takes courage, trust, surrender, openmindedness, and openheartedness, as well as the ability to roll with the punches by letting go of our preconceptions and plans when circumstances demand a different course. It requires embracing change. These are capacities we cultivate through contemplative practices. To complicate matters more, for most of us there is an inherent resistance to change that almost seems to be hardwired into being a human. Even if on an intuitive level we know things are always in flux, and we can theorize about them as the process of the guṇas acting on the guṇas, we are still prone to fall into habitual patterns of our own in which change is not part of the equation. Habits like ego or ahaṁkāra are not inherently bad; in fact they are important functions and are divine weavings of the guṇas. We define our corner of the story through ego and then rely on habits to streamline our actions but in the long run this alone is not sustainable. Just as ego becomes a hindrance when we believe its subtexts of self-importance and separateness, so too are our habits, or saṃskāras, ineffectual when they blind us and make us resistant to the ever-changing nature of the present moment.

We may also resist change, not so much out of a sort of rajasic ego-driven approach to things, or the more tamasic approach that mindless habitual actions have, but because of another tamasic tendency—fear of the unknown. If things are always changing, how can we be sure that we're making the right choices as we act? Since we can never have a full picture because something is always in flux, then we never have all the information (of course, it's an illusion that this is even possible because we see things only from our limited perspective), so our perception is never guaranteed to be accurate a moment later. This uncertainty can drive us mad. "Just tell me for *certain*," we hear Arjuna ask again and again. He, like many of us, longs to know so that he doesn't have to stay on the edge, constantly waking up.

Resistance to change is a sort of layered phenomenon that starts on an inner, personal level, as it does for Arjuna. When we are not operating from a perspective that is in concert with our circumstances, engaged in the effort of paying attention to the most minuscule level of perception we are capable of, then change appears to be a threat to our very balance and stability. Change and *in*stability can become confused as being the same thing when, in fact, they are complementary and interpenetrating aspects of balance. Yet our identity and perceived proficiency may rest in an illusion of stagnant, tamasic stability—the misperception that we need to control or avoid change. If this happens we are likely to avoid changes and the delightful unknowns that they inject into our limited storyline. Just as it took thousands of years for architects to figure out how to construct strong, stable buildings in earthquake zones—allowing for the shifting elements around the building rather than fortifying against them—it can take many crumbled walls of ego structure and holding on too tightly for us as individuals to learn to trust and work with the process of change as well.

To complicate matters, regardless of whether we as individuals begin to welcome the changing nature of things, the moment we walk outside the walls of our tiny mind, we encounter an even stronger resistance to change. We run into resistance from the culture we find ourselves within, be it the culture of our family, our work environment, our place of worship, or the society we are part of. If too many members of any one culture start to wake up to interconnectedness, to soften societal ego boundaries and begin to accept the fact that we are all connected and interdependent, then the identity structure—the caste system in India, the prejudices between races in America, lineages in yoga, the royal families all over the world—and many, many more aspects of the established societal infrastructure could be challenged. So cultures resist change too if those in charge refuse to wake up. Change in certain aspects of culture might be good for the masses or in the long run for everyone, but for those in power, change is usually equated with instability and certain destruction, even though change is the nature of healthy evolution.

As individuals, learning to keep our personal resistance to change in check is an accessible and practical way of becoming balanced and free. It is also a means of supporting and perpetuating stability within our circumstances and culture. A trust of change and of other, a determined commitment to waking up layer by layer—personally, interpersonally, culturally, and globally—would be of great benefit on so many levels and might even shift consciousness to a point that we could finally move on from the fear of change that keeps us chained to our identities, differences, and separateness.

[10]

The Middle Path of Love

IN THE FINAL CHAPTERS of the Gītā, Kṛṣṇa is fully revealed, not only as tangible manifestations like the taste of water or the brilliance of the sun and not strictly as the terrifying wheel of time manifesting as monstrous heads crushing others in their jaws nor the warmonger we may have written him off to be as the story began. But here in the end, having offered sometimes direct, often subtle, and always profound teachings on the nature of life, Kṛṣṇa is represented in his purest and most sweet form as love itself; the capacity that exists within each and every one of us to endure and to flourish. Love is the ultimate expression of interconnectedness. It is an act of open reciprocity. Our ability to thrive is therefore rooted in relationships, so it is no wonder that most of us feel happiest when we have healthy relationships with others and are connected to the world around us. The funny thing is, though, that our ideas about love or relationships are often a cause of suffering. This happens when our image of what it means to be in love, what a relationship looks like, or how another "should" be in "our" relationship doesn't match what is unfolding. Instead of trusting the limitless shared reservoir of love that is within us, the truth that we are all interconnected is obscured by our mind states, illusions, and attachments to sense objects and outcomes.

If we are to begin to wake up, we don't have to believe that Kṛṣṇa is a historical figure or that the story of the Gītā should be taken literally as an unchangeable dogma in order to begin to experience the visceral sense of the vastness of what Kṛṣṇa signifies. Kṛṣṇa, who is considered to be everything that manifests and who holds all beings in the core of his heart, symbolizes interconnectedness and our inherent capacity to love boundlessly. He, and therefore we, are pure consciousness itself interlinked through our true nature, which is this basic goodness and tenderness of heart—compassion. When we put aside preconceptions, habituations, and prejudices, we automatically experience this deep sense of interconnectedness and on a gut, visceral level we find we have connected to who we have always been and who we will always really be; it's like coming home.

This is what frequently happens for people when they first begin practicing yoga because their curiosity about yoga has opened them up to see what's actually before them without the shadows and shadings of their presuppositions and habitual behaviors. Reconnecting to this primordial understanding we find the familiar territory of self—in both the personal and global sense. This is our natural state and is where we find true, lasting happiness. Happiness is our birthright, yet for so many, whether in crisis or not, it can seem unattainable. The teachings put forth in the Gītā show us that even though goodness, happiness, and compassion, just like love, are natural states for us, we must work with integrity, in a spirit of generosity and kindness, if we are to find them. Lasting happiness requires that we, like Arjuna when he woke up on the field of action and dharma, stand up and meet the circumstances and difficulties of life. This takes work, steadiness, and alertness during the continual cycle of waking up to the present moment. Defining and inquiring, holding on and letting go, we take decisive actions based on a trust in the nature of change and the power of relationships.

In chapters 16 and 17 of the Gītā, Kṛṣṇa reinforces the notion that critical to this process of waking up is the art of discriminating awareness—the ability to see through illusions of mind (both one's own and those of others). Until this point in the text Kṛṣṇa has offered Arjuna endless details about how the world works, and he has pointed out pitfalls and given Arjuna advice on to how to proceed. Seeing that Arjuna is progressing on the path, in chapter 16 Kṛṣṇa broaches the subject of intention gone awry, something that can obscure clear vision like nothing else. He details the characteristics of those who are of "divine" nature and those whom he calls "demonic." Truly divine beings hold all others in the very center of their heart. They are the very few who've achieved enlightenment. Others who have consciously and sincerely chosen to pursue a selfless path toward enlightenment but aren't quite there yet (which is true of most spiritual seekers) are also considered very dear to Kṛṣṇa and on their way to becoming divine. Throughout the Gītā, the importance of good intention is underscored, and here too we are reminded that selfless, sincere intention is key and more important than outward gestures of piousness or of following dogma.

But now, for the first time in the text, Kṛṣṇa emphasizes the fact that there are those who are evil by nature, who absolutely lack good intentions. Still, he does not reject these beings. He does not remove them from the tender embrace of his heart, nor does he support their misguided and destructive means and actions. Instead, he offers them compassion, knowing they live in a state of confusion and personal suffering. In this teaching he is clear with Arjuna that waking up to reality means to exercise intelligence and discernment, especially when encountering this sort of being. We must see them for who they really are: though they are evil, they are also divine manifestations and Kṛṣṇa teaches that one should practice *upekṣānam*, or equanimity, when encountering this type of being. This means we should not buy into their delusion or act in ways that perpetuate their ill will or harm they may cause. Using discriminating awareness, we should, when the opportunity arises, do what needs to be done to prevent them from causing harm, but at the same time, we must keep even those who are evil in our hearts.

The practice of upekṣānam may seem impossible, especially when we encounter a truly vile individual who causes great harm to others, such as some politicians, murderers, or slick-talking tricksters, to name a few. How can we keep them in our hearts? There are tricks like visualizing in vivid detail a deity, such as an image of Viṣṇu or whatever realized being speaks to us, and then imagining we hold *them* in our heart. They, being divine, have all beings in their heart so, by default, when we embrace them, everyone in their heart is now also in ours! Or we might practice *metta*—offering loving-kindness—to the one who is evil and in so doing get a glimpse of their suffering, which can create space for them within our core.

Like everything else we've encountered in the Gītā, there is no one technique that will always work, but what *is* always true is the question, "What do we risk if we do *not* hold all beings in our hearts?" The instant any individual (or any part of the world) is pulled out of our hearts we create separateness—avidyā, or the foundation of ignorance and the root cause of suffering—and our action contributes to an inevitable karmic cascade of misery. Finding some way of holding even evil beings within our heart with a sense of compassion and equanimity is the only path toward healing and lasting happiness. For beginners perhaps we contemplate the teaching from the Gītā that we are one with Kṛṣṇa and that he has an infinitely large heart. Like Kṛṣṇa, we hold even those who are difficult, even demonic, in our hearts, but we see them as clearly as possible in the light of love, always looking again and asking what actions we can take that will best serve the whole. We are careful to remain grounded and not be overwhelmed by them by overly empathizing with them to the point that we lose sight of our own core values, intention, and ability to act with compassion. Yet we hold all others tenderly in our heart in a spirit of kindness and compassion. Easier said than done, but it becomes easier with practice and with support from others. Importantly we must remember that, while holding all beings in our heart, we always practice discernment—seeing everything as clearly as possible.

Kṛṣṇa explains that we can recognize the demonic because not only are they absolutely rajasic or bound by a knotted mess of tamasic and rajasic drives, but because they are filled with ill intent and deceptiveness. Those who are demonic have a self-serving, self-absorbed, destructive nature that is fueled by lust, anger, and greed. In modern terms, these individuals would be labeled narcissists, sociopaths, and psychopaths.

For those who are driven by demonic delusions there is little chance of change because there is no desire to change. They see flaws in the system, in others, and in patterns of nature but are incapable of considering that something might be wrong with them, so why should they change? It's helpful to remember that this demonic form is not something relegated to the dark corners of abnormal psychology that only a few may brush up against but rather something that most of us will encounter at the very least once in our life, so it is very important to be able to recognize it. Those with ill intent have been around forever, and the potential to express the demonic manifestation is something we all have seeds for and could potentially fall prey to as well.

Perhaps Kṛṣṇa left this teaching until the end because without first familiarizing ourselves with the classic patterns of human nature that may create obstacles on the path of enlightenment, such as becoming trapped in our beliefs about our dharma or attached to the rituals we imagine will bring us something of value, we could not differentiate between innocent confusion and deep-seated bad intention. Ill intention is where self-serving, demonic tendencies arise and, if left unchecked or ignored, as in the case of narcissists or psychopaths, things deteriorate quickly, as these people drive wedges of divisiveness between themselves and others and within systems so that an impending sense of separateness, fear, and contracted defensive behaviors in themselves and finally, in others, arise.

This is what happens in cults, when a leader becomes carried away by their own greed and delusions of grandeur and convinces followers to "drink the Kool-Aid" even at their own expense. It happens in business deals or politics where an ill-intentioned yet charismatic leader, using all the right words while tossing confusion onto the path of unsuspecting others, turns out to be a con artist ripping their friends off for great sums of money or causing other irreparable harm to the world. Even in the yoga world, or on other spiritual paths, this pattern arises far too often. You find your way to yoga and have a profound experience that after some time of study and practice (hopefully more than a couple of years), you feel compelled to share with the world. Suddenly you're teaching others who are saying, "Wow! You know so much. You healed my aching back. Please, let me touch your lotus feet." And even though secretly you know it was the yoga itself and not you that healed them, and that you don't know much at all, you start to believe what the students are telling you. From being completely neurotic and impoverished, you've become practically a billionaire with limousines taking you everywhere—helicopters, if you're in a hurry. But, of course, you're not attached to it at all. Right! The teacher buys into their own fabricated story, and what seemed years and years ago to be a sincere yoga practice has transformed into a closed narcissistic loop in which the teacher believes the praises and flattery the students are giving. It's a loop so tight that when the words of the students don't reflect the teacher's illusion of their own greatness, there is no room in the fold for those naysayers: "Get rid of all the mirrors that reflect my demonic face and the curled lip of insidious greed for power. Instead, I want only the injured or confused students who've come to join my cult."

This has not happened once in history, or even twice; it's happened millions of times and is a potential inherent in all of us. The fierce forms of demons represented in Indian and Buddhist art show this potential, as do characters such as Shakespeare's Lady Macbeth, who commits herself to evil and is driven by extreme greed and envy, or certain twenty-first-century moguls and politicians whose entire drive in life is the pursuit of their own power, wealth, and glory with total disregard for others and the planet. Kṛṣṇa emphasizes the importance of learning to recognize this type of person and warns that without the ability to discern fully and recognize evil, there is potential to be profoundly harmed by the abuse and disregard perpetuated by a demonic leader, teacher, or businessman (to name just a few manifestations) who becomes infatuated by their own glory at the expense of those around them.

If we don't recognize the lack of moral integrity that leads to this when it presents itself in others or in our own private thoughts, the outcome is always disastrous. It is a temptation to all of us that is kept in check when we sincerely inquire and study and find and maintain a healthy relationship with a good teacher and participate in a healthy saṅgha that gives clear feedback. Refraining from constantly seeking people who agree with our perspective or garnering praise from our teacher that we're the best student ever and maintaining a practice that requires looking ever more closely at the teachings and at ourselves are imperative if we are to avoid our own demonic potential. This is perhaps the most important impact of a healthy yoga practice; it keeps us embodied and grounded in our own experience and within the context of our relationships to others. We then remain steady rather than being swept away by emotions, thoughts, sensations, and desires within the ever-present churning of change that is life and time.

Having warned Arjuna of the demonic downfall of those who allow ego to rule, Kṛṣṇa then reiterates that everything that arises is a function of the guṇas acting on the guṇas, including our own experience of the world. To see clearly and cultivate the ability to recognize the contextual, dependent, relational, and interpenetrating pattern of the guṇas (even demonic tendencies), we need a clear picture by which to distinguish and differentiate between the guṇas—the sattvic (good), rajasic (passionate), and tamasic (dull) characteristics. Of course nothing is composed of only one aspect of the guṇas—only sattva, for example—but rather manifests in a unique ever-changing pattern as a combination of the three qualities. However, because one characteristic is usually most prominent, we can begin to learn about the guṇas by observing whether something is predominantly sattvic, rajasic, or tamasic, and this gives us a foothold to clearly assess and perceive what we encounter. With this we then refine our inquiry.

Noticing the moment-by-moment pattern of the guṇas unfolding within whatever it is we are observing, we can hone the skill of releasing our overlays of mind and ego to look more closely and to see ever more clearly. We notice the pattern: tamas, fixedness, is booted into action through rajas, or opposition. This stimulates the unfolding of sattva, synthesis, which eventually becomes stuck and stagnant, turning into tamas once again. Close observation reveals that everything—including the guṇas—is in constant flux and exists in an atmosphere of relationship or context; even the guṇas are in an endless relationship with each other. So here, toward the end of the text, Kṛṣṇa offers list upon list of specifics as to how the nature of the guṇas is revealed in objects, individuals, actions, and thoughts. Familiar with the characteristics of tamas, rajas, and sattva we are equipped with specifics that facilitate our ability to assess things quickly and with more accuracy, so we can act skillfully, not with the motivation to gain something from our actions, but with trust, intelligence, and openness, seeing the background and the foreground of our experience more clearly. When we see everything, including ourselves, as an integral part of the process—the symphony—of the guṇas, we can enjoy the moments we meet and this magnificent orchestra of life unfolding within the circumstances at hand.

Returning to the story of the Gītā we see that now Arjuna has the necessary building blocks of discernment. He can finally "stand up and fight," face his crisis by weighing the pros and cons of different actions he might choose to take. He could follow his dharma as a warrior, he could run away from the battle out of fear and confusion, he could avoid the situation through ungrounded bhakti or blind ritual, or he could assess the situation clearly and act with intelligence and integrity. He knows that every action, counteraction, nonaction—even every thought—has karmic consequences and that attachment to the rewards he may imagine to be associated with his actions (even altruistic desires) is poisonous. He has come to understand that discernment does not stop with simply seeing the pattern of the guṇas, and he knows he must release his preconceptions about everything, even about the nature of the guṇas themselves and the illusion of what and who he imagines himself and others to be. Only with this level of self-reflection will he be able to navigate intelligently through the impossible dilemma he faces. He sees, as we should too, that maintaining this level of trust and honesty is not easy, nor should it be. It is a vulnerable process of placing down the boundaries of ego that keep us "protected" and then stepping willingly to dissolve into the paradoxical experience of being at once completely independent and absolutely interdependent.

Here, by the end of the text as Arjuna inches closer to insight, we watch him waking up to meet his own unique strengths and predispositions that will guide him through difficulties moment by moment. We may begin to see that his situation belongs to all of us, that the way through his or any crisis is an ongoing process of awakening, holding on and letting go, over and over again on more and more subtle levels with the aim of acting responsibly, intelligently, openly, and with compassion—keeping all others in the center of our hearts—even in the face of uncertainty. Just as Arjuna will finally decide the best course of action to take on the battlefield, we too are invited to pause, to get grounded in an embodied sense of the present moment, to recall that our true nature is one of happiness and love, nested in relationships. We are encouraged to inquire deeply into our self and our service to others as we face with courage and clarity the present moment, along with the inevitable difficulties and dilemmas that will be tossed onto our path.

Ever since the beginning of the story, when Arjuna felt the vibrations throughout his body from blowing the conch shell, an experience that brought him to his senses and snapped him into an embodied understanding of what it meant to step onto the battlefield, he has been waking up. Slowly he has been realizing that he is something far bigger than his own perceptions and conclusions. He has learned to suspend his impulse to act reflexively and instead to pause and inquire when faced with difficulty. He does so again here at the end, yet this time something is very different: he does not ask for certainty—to know which of two things is better. Instead, this time Arjuna wants to know the *difference* between the two forms of nonattachment *saṁnyāsa* and *tyāga*. He is beginning to let go of the need to know. This is a vitally important skill that is cultivated through contemplative practices, the ability to quell the ego's need to know for certain. When we practice yoga or meditation we learn to observe the process of change that is always unfolding before us to reveal the present moment. The more closely we watch this pattern of change the easier it becomes to be comfortable with the fact that we can never know anything with 100 percent certainty. And this need to know without a doubt has troubled Arjuna since the story began. Yet now, he is shifting his grip on certainty, asking Kṛṣṇa to help him juxtapose concepts by looking more deeply at what it means to let go of attachments. This demonstrates to Kṛṣṇa that Arjuna is not only maturing and releasing attachments to his ideas, but that he is starting to trust on a profoundly deep level the process of truth unfolding that is revealed when one watches the present moment closely. He is finally beginning to experience the virtue of unhindered inquiry, which leads to discernment and, at the same time, he has been contemplating the difficulty of putting things down. It is so challenging to truly set things down, yet if we cannot release our feelings, thoughts, emotions, and sensations—even our ideas about these things and what it means to set them down—then we are incapable of deeply, innocently trusting life. Without release and trust, lasting happiness is impossible.

One of the things we learn from a healthy yoga practice is that putting things down, or vairāgyam, is the essential final step in every action we take. From the outset of the Gītā, Kṛṣṇa has emphasized the importance of letting things go, nonattachment, the *nyāsa* in *vinyāsa*. Every modern-day yoga student can chime in with the platitude that they are not attached, but we've all experienced the very same hesitation Arjuna has felt at the thought of truly letting go. Within our yoga practice perhaps the most important part is the end, when we set it all free, when we put down and completely release the practice no matter how it unfolded. Perhaps it was a phenomenal practice where every pose flowed effortlessly and angels chimed in as we followed the wave of the breath. Or maybe it was a tangled mess of mind, body, emotion, sensation, and resistance that started the moment we thought about rolling out the mat or setting up the cushion. Nonetheless we set it down, we offer it into the fire of pure awareness. The offering is a gesture of insight into the fact that "we" didn't practice. Just as we didn't actually turn on the light in the kitchen when we flipped the switch, our very own practice was a manifestation of the guṇas acting on the guṇas.

If we hold on to the residue from the practice, or cling to the illusion that the practice is healing us or how our practice will catapult us into yoga stardom (which we find out when we get there is just one of the rings of Dante's Inferno where lust, greed, anger, fraud, and so on rule our so-called yogic existence), then we aren't actually practicing at all. If we cannot set the entirety of our practice down, including self-concepts and their background, then we are practicing with attachment to the fruits of our actions. Attachment to any aspect of the practice means the practice is essentially useless and will eventually cause suffering as it transforms into just another means of separating ourselves out from the world. At the end of practice we sincerely offer the good that has come from the practice that it may be of benefit to others. We give it away;

all of it. *This* is joy. This is what it means to let things go without attachment. Arjuna is beginning to see this, but still he needs clarification between terms used to describe this act of nonattachment—*saṁnyāsa* and *tyāga*.

Ultimately both terms are quite similar and in the Gītā are used somewhat interchangeably because they both mean putting things down. But there is a subtle important difference. One who has taken the vows to be a *saṁnyāsīn* consciously gives up all worldly attachments. In the context of Indian culture, being a saṁnyāsīn is part of the ashram system and is very ritualistic, pointing to one's status in the culture. Being a saṁnyāsīn is an order in life, like *gṛhastha* (householder), brahmacarya (a monk or student), *vānaprastha* (one who retires at the end of a long life to the woods to do yoga and reflect on the meaning of life), and so on. When the vow of saṁnyāsa is taken you give up your name and all of your possessions. If you're a Brahman, you even take off your sacred thread. Basically you're acting as if you were dead. With the release of all worldly trappings, including your own personal and cultural identity, there is a focus on reflecting deeply both on the traditional teachings and the embodied experience in order to release habits of mind and ego. As with everything, sometimes becoming a saṁnyāsīn goes terribly wrong, interpreted not as a way of enriching the background of life but instead as the opportunity to do nothing at all and to distance oneself from the world or to enjoy the high status it gives. These types of wayward saṁnyāsīn do nothing to support others yet rely entirely on generosity for their own existence. This one-sided approach is a complete misunderstanding of karma, or work, and confusion about what is intended in taking the vow of saṁnyāsa. It is a waste of time and quickly turns into an empty, ritualistic gesture of ego.

What Kṛṣṇa encourages is not the ceremonial saṁnyāsīn, who only theorizes about putting things down, but instead a giving up of actions that is motivated by the intention to release everything completely—and *this* is tyāga. The subtle distinction between tyāga and saṁnyāsīn, therefore, is that with tyāga one gives up of the fruits of *all* actions for the benefit of and in service *to* others. It is a refinement of saṁnyāsa, a high state of continuous mindful giving up of fruits. Giving up actions prompted by desire, duty, standing in life, theory, or training or putting things considered to be distractions aside would be called saṁnyāsa. Kṛṣṇa, who is enlightened, but chooses to come back again and again in order to help others, is the epitome of what it is to be a tyāgi.

This most transformative form of tyāga is a malleable approach of responding to circumstance. It is letting go, then observing closely to let go more deeply again and again in a continuous wave pattern. Residue from this type of release resides in every corner of our experience, in our nervous system and awareness, as a fully embodied experience. Thinking that nonattachment is a good thing to strive for is one thing, but living with nonattachment embedded in one's approach to life is something completely different because it is anything but an idea or a calculated act of release. Like so many of the aspects of practice and understanding discussed throughout the Gītā, tyāga is an unfolding, a process of responding skillfully to circumstances, and at its root is that tyāga is initiated from a heartfelt desire to act for the benefit of the others.

Tyāga *is* release, but it is important to remember that tyāga is rooted in action, so sometimes while practicing tyāga we are consciously holding on to things—otherwise how could we set them down? The nature of the untrained mind is to unconsciously latch on to anything it happens to perceive as solid or catchable. Not only could this mean grasping onto sense objects but also holding on to ideas, conceptual understandings, and so on. When we hold on to things instinctively rather than consciously choosing to pause within an unending process of change, we become trapped by familiar patterns of body, speech, and mind that draw us into a world of conditioned existence. Trapped on the wheel of saṃsāra and suffering we hold on desperately until something more attractive comes along or until an outside force causes us to release our grip. But if we are practicing tyāga, even though we may hold on at certain points, at just the right moment, we let go. Like the tide entering a shallow cave by the seashore, rolling in to fill every obscure corner and crevasse of the complex landscape then flowing evenly back out as the water subsides, our ability to let go of attachments is in a perpetual rhythm of ebb and flow. Tyāga in this way is a full-bodied experience responsive to the guṇas acting on the guṇas, and it has a feeling of receptive stability and compassion without resistance. When practicing transformative tyāga "we" disappear, integrating fully with whatever is arising almost as if we *were* that cave by the shore with welcomed tides of change washing through every corner of awareness.

Here at the end of the Gītā, having given Arjuna the tools he needs to take skillful action no matter what the circumstances, Kṛṣṇa's final teaching is simple and subtly sublime. It is the elegant directive to find strength in one's true nature by staying awake and standing up to meet circumstances as they arise, the same advice he gave to Arjuna when the story began. We've learned by now, however, that *what* he means by standing up and fighting isn't the unilateral advice to stand up and kill, but instead to stand up and identify the seeds of the demonic that Arjuna (all of us) has within; the potential for greed, anger, lust, jealousy, and so on. Instead of discerning that his dharma as a Kṣatriya should solely inform his actions and that he should engage in battle and killing, Kṛṣṇa is advising Arjuna to wake up to the moment and act with intelligence, conscious of his full circumstances with an awareness of the fact that his actions (or inactions) will impact the whole. This final teaching from Kṛṣṇa is to release *all* dharmas and become absorbed by the truth of love.

So far in the Gītā, surrender has been used in the sense of not becoming stuck in one's identity or ideas, attachments, beliefs, actions, or motives for action. We've seen that surrender is a type of karma, or work. It is not a complete collapse or helpless release but a directed, skillful action that sets aside egotistical illusions that keep us stuck, separate, and suffering. Now here, in the final teachings, Kṛṣṇa refines the idea of surrender to mean "to take refuge." This is significant because it insinuates that the type of surrender required is not only an act of release but also the process of letting go in the context of deep mutual respect and trust. *Refuge* means "to take shelter"; it is a place or person providing sanctuary and protection from danger, trouble, or unhappiness. Like surrender, refuge requires letting go, but it also involves letting *in.* Refuge infers a relationship and that there is interaction, communication, and respect between the one taking shelter and the place or person in whom one finds safety. Refuge is only possible when we allow others in and embrace the fact that everything is interconnected. In other words, when Kṛṣṇa says "Come to Me" he means surrender to—trust and take refuge in—the seat of our shared true nature, that of open-hearted compassion.

The space for this connection already exists within all of us and is nourished by relationships that are built upon good intention, motivation directed toward the benefit of the whole rather than the individual, and honest, open communication. This final teaching is not only essential if we are to find happiness but carries with it a huge responsibility—to trust, to be trustworthy, and to be able to discern if trust in another is merited, so we know when and where to find and share safe refuge in the form of unobstructed love.

As the Gītā opened we found Arjuna on the battlefield, in a crisis of conscience, faced with the seemingly impossible dilemma of taking one of two courses of action, each of which seemed flawed: to fight for a cause he believes in, knowing great harm will come to many he loves and respects, or to collapse in dismay, sidestepping the problem, his responsibilities, and his integrity. In the beginning these are the only two options he can imagine. As the story progresses and he rides waves of thought and emotion while allowing himself to trust his beloved teacher and friend, he starts to see that the picture is not as completely black and white as he first imagined. Perhaps there is a middle path.

This same confusion of seeing only extreme views when encountering any crisis or dilemma is common to most of us. We may initially feel isolated, ineffectual, and alone and that our options are extreme and limited. Access to our internal resources, such as creativity and compassion, begins to dry up and there's likely to be a pervasive feeling of panic and a sense of being so overwhelmed that we must protect or separate ourselves if we are to survive. This inclination to cling to ideas and emotions as if they are a matter of life and death, especially in times of change, is not Arjuna's alone. It is a natural response that the uncertainty inherent in change can trigger. We might feel in crisis at the end of one phase of life as we move into another, the end of a career or a relationship, for example. We could be engulfed by feelings of fear when one of our well-worn patterns of behavior transforms into another, even if the transformation is healthy, such as finding a path out of depression or breaking an addictive substance abuse pattern we've used to cope with stress.

Crises, by definition, are times of change that mandate letting go and trusting the unknown. They are times where the well-established, functional (and ill-functioning) aspects of the ego must take a back seat to the context of the situation and, as such, crises can pose a threat to a strong ego. This is why many begin practicing yoga but just as the practice starts to work, they abandon it. When yoga is practiced well there is a letting go of everything, including our ego, which can lead to an identity crisis. And this is one reason Kṛṣṇa repeatedly reminds Arjuna that yoga isn't for everyone. But if we persevere with a yoga practice we become familiar with the feeling of finding a sense of balance while not really knowing for sure what will come next. We learn to trust the process of change. We can release illusions of "knowing" and "control" so that as our concocted pictures of a stable reality shift, we do not find ourselves in a state of crisis. This is important because when we feel we are in crisis, rather than in transformation or transition, there is a tendency to feel alone and contracted to the point that our vision of possibilities becomes extraordinarily limited, and our actions become directed from a place of fear, self-doubt, and the perception of separateness. In this state ego identification and inflation, anger, lust, greed, attachment to dogma, rigidity, and all sorts of isolating and destructive qualities prevail. However, if we suspend our theories and take refuge in the process of life unfolding moment by moment, then we have the possibility to tap into the intelligence of interconnectedness. From this point of steadiness we can then access the sort of tri-ocular vision that Arjuna experienced when seeing Kṛṣṇa's universal forms, so that we too can see into the core of existence and the meaning of life. From *this* perspective we may see that, though change may be uncomfortable, within it—even if it feels like a crisis—there is opportunity for courage, attentiveness, release, love, and above all, evolution. Crisis is a call to remember that we are strong and unique but not separate and alone. It is an opportunity for communication and relationships to flourish and intelligence to blossom and a time to trust the strength found in compassion. This is bhakti. This is what it means to set everything down, to fully surrender, acting with nonattachment to personal gain as we take refuge in the power of compassion so that we may sincerely work together for the benefit of others.

Kṛṣṇa's teaching "Come to Me" is often considered the final teaching of the Gītā. It's a beautiful message, yet if you stop there it could lead to a superficial or dogmatic interpretation of the entire text: "I surrender to the deity Kṛṣṇa and will, at all costs stand up and fight!" Or the New Age counterpart to that, which is equally dogmatic: "It's all love, it's all one, and I'm just surrendering to bliss—riding the wave of love." However, if you read on just a little further, there are two strong reminders that these sorts of approaches miss the underlying point of the text altogether.

After inviting Arjuna to take refuge in him, Kṛṣṇa, says, "And so this wisdom, the ultimate secret of secrets, has been revealed by Me to you. Contemplate it deeply so there is no residue and act as you choose" (18.63). In other words, when he suggests that Arjuna take refuge in him as love, instead of setting up a power dynamic (*you* are surrendering to *me*) he offers trust and freedom of choice in return. He implies that Arjuna knows all he needs to know and is now trustworthy; he is ready to use his intelligence to act skillfully. Kṛṣṇa shows Arjuna that he trusts him but then just as a worried parent might say, "Have a great time and call if you need anything!" when they send their child off to university for the first time, Kṛṣṇa too qualifies his statement to his beloved student with the reminder, "Fill your mind with Me, loving Me, sacrificing to Me, make salutations to Me. In this very way you will really, *truly* come to Me. I declare this, for you are precious to Me. Give up all dharmas and take refuge in Me alone. I will set you free from all evils. Do not worry" (18.65–66).

So here at the end of the text Kṛṣṇa, who has revealed himself to be everything that manifests, becomes very, very human once again. In doing so he demonstrates the importance of fully expressing oneself while carrying no pretenses of power or superiority into our relationships with others. This teaching about relationships is vital. It is especially relevant in a world where it is becoming increasingly common for superficial platitudes and clever sound bites to be tossed out in a spirit of self-promotion or self-gain and where working for the good of others often plays second fiddle to karma aimed strictly toward one's own imagined advancement or fame.

Kṛṣṇa's ultimate teaching is an invitation into the insight one gains from the direct experience of our commonality. Yet he warns that this teaching, just like the practice of yoga, is not for everyone; it is "secret." In doing so he is not saying that the knowledge of interconnectedness should be confidential. Instead, he cautions that the information might be misinterpreted, in which case it could do more harm than good. So the teachings should be shared prudently. He adores those who teach the truth he expounds upon in the book and is happy when the wisdom is openly offered, but still, he points out, it will remain hidden—a secret—because it will not be understood.

Like many truths of life, this deep wisdom is likely to remain hidden before our very eyes until we are ready to see it. Kṛṣṇa advises us that although insight into the meaning of life is founded in relationships, it is rooted to earth through the context of a sincere pursuit of truth. Flaunting devotion or speaking of this to others who resist, who have no desire to do the work necessary to listen and connect deeply outside of their own egocentric perspective, is therefore ill-advised. This is a final reminder to any of us who are sincerely pursuing an understanding of the truth. We must be willing to be honest enough with ourselves and to cut through our own illusory game of separateness and survival to admit we have our own pesky ego hovering in the background, forever looking for a way around even the most pure teaching such as this. We must always give up knowledge—our egocentric perspective—and look again.

With this final teaching Kṛṣṇa, again like the worried parent, asks Arjuna, "Listen to this, O Son of Pṛthā. Have you heard this with one-pointed concentration of mind? Has your delusion caused by ignorance been dispelled, O Conqueror of Wealth" (18.72)? In the next verse, Arjuna replies that his delusion *has* been destroyed. He adds that by Kṛṣṇa's grace, what we can see is Kṛṣṇa's supportive, careful, and respectful teaching, he has gained *smṛti*, and he no longer has doubts. Doubt, of course, is what struck Arjuna down when he first arrived on the battlefield, and uncertainty has plagued him throughout most of the rest of the story, so this is a huge sign of Arjuna's evolution.

Smṛti is often translated to mean "memory," but here it means "the mindfulness that is accessed through meditation." In meditation we examine things moment by moment. Smṛti infers that we re-*cognize*, or rethink, everything. With practice, meditation not only enhances memory but other aspects of perception such as focus, insight, and inquisitiveness as well. This is the power of a contemplative practice. Its impact is to, on a subconscious level, gradually build clarity, fostering dissolution of delusion (misperception) so that seeds of doubt are naturally resolved.

When our minds are delusional, we are like those in Plato's cave who were chained so that their heads could not turn and who saw only the shadows of forms on the wall projected from behind. But once we begin to see things more clearly, we can never go back to our previous delusions of mind. It is this level of life-changing, paradigm-shifting perception that the Gītā offers us, and that Arjuna has finally experienced through the teachings laid out before him in the text. Being able to use the double-edged sword of discriminating awareness to look more closely at our perceptions and conclusions so that we can discern with increased levels of clarity and therefore choose to act skillfully with integrity and intelligence is the path through *any* crisis. This capacity for discernment is the essential fertile ground upon which a sense of the truth of interconnectedness can flourish. Once we begin to really truly see—to embody—this insight we can then let everything go. Trusting the process unfolding around us, we can safely take refuge in the vast spaciousness of kindness, love, and compassion that is the actual interpenetrating order of the world.

This then is the official conclusion of the teachings put forward in the Gītā. Yet there is an interesting twist in the telling of the Gītā that appears even after the formal story ends. When Arjuna says he can take action with confidence, Sañjaya, the one narrating the story, mirrors Arjuna's statement. Sañjaya tells Dhṛtarāṣṭra (the blind king to whom he is speaking) that he is completely enthralled by the detailed telling of the story, the profound teachings and the step-by-step instructions Kṛṣṇa has presented in the text. Sañjaya says, "In this way I have listened to this wondrous dialogue of Kṛṣṇa and the Son of Vāsudeva and the Son of Pṛthā, the great being, making my hair stand on end. By the grace of the poet Vyāsa I have heard this ultimate secret yoga from Kṛṣṇa, the lord of yoga, narrating it himself right before our eyes. O King, as I contemplate again and again this amazing and sacred dialogue of Keśava and Arjuna I am thrilled every moment, again and again. And mindfully recollecting again and yet again the extremely amazing form (*rūpa*) of Hari, my astonishment is huge and I am thrilled again and yet again. It is my thought that wherever there is the lord of yoga, Kṛṣṇa, and the Son of Pṛthā, the archer, there is beauty, victory, well-being and certainly morality" (18.74–78).

It is no coincidence here that Sañjaya also describes the idea of smṛti (using the term *saṁsmṛti*, which literally means "complete mindfulness") when he says that he will look again and again, just as in any yoga practice we watch closely what is arising, then look again. This is so we may not only see the surface of what is "before our eyes" but so that we look with the quality of discriminating awareness and an intention of discerning what will best serve the whole.

So rather than Sañjaya's message being one of surface adoration for Kṛṣṇa and the story of the Gītā, the use of the word saṁsmṛti here implies that the intention of the original poet in telling the story of the Gītā was that the one listening to the story—be it Sañjaya or any one of us—should always look again at *everything* that arises in life: our crises, our joys, our complexities, and simple everyday wonder. We should see as clearly as possible, draw conclusions based on our understanding of the context of the situation, which is understood through cultural, personal, and theoretical fragments of the story that is before us, and then put it all down. We should offer our precious conclusions and our most skillfully crafted knowledge, along with everything else, into the fire of pure awareness as we look again. In this way, we contemplate what is before us openly and honestly, in context of relationship, keeping all beings in our hearts and with a spirit of setting things free. As such there is no residue, and we can fully embody a dissolution into the limitless spectrum of love's light so that the ultimate secret of secrets—wisdom—is born.

This is the teaching of the Gītā that can serve us as we travel our unique and auspicious path through this lifetime, knowing we are intimately intertwined with everything else in search of a mutual awakening. Changes come, emotions bubble up, insights arise, habits slow us down, deaths arrive, sorrow and joys abound. And life goes on. We are faced with crises along the way. They are always part of every journey, yet it is in the moments of crisis that we find opportunities to wake up to deeper, more connected, kinder, and more compassionate levels of awareness and behavior. Step-by-step, action-by-action, thought by counterthought, and breath-by-breath there is always the possibility of waking up; coming home to the truth of who we are and what it is we are truly here to do. It is at this point, when we take refuge in the profound interconnectedness of life and embrace the freedom of releasing concepts and constructs—our ego—that transformation is nourished. It is here too that the brilliance shining out as love, as bhakti, resides.

divi sūryasahasrasya bhaved yugapadutthitā |
yadi bhāḥ sadṛśī sā syād bhāsastasya mahātmanaḥ ||

If a thousand suns rose at once in the sky, such a brilliance might be the splendor of this great being (11.12).

PART TWO

The Bhagavad Gītā

Chapter 1

dhṛtarāṣṭra uvāca

1. *dharmakṣetre kurukṣetre samavetā yuyutsavaḥ* |
māmakāḥ pāṇḍavāś cai va kim akurvata sañjaya ||

Dhṛtarāṣṭra said (to Sañjaya):
What did my people (army) and the Sons of Pāṇḍu do, gathered together eager to fight on the field of dharma, on the field of action?

sañjaya uvāca

2. *dṛṣṭvā tu pāṇḍavānīkaṁ vyūḍhaṁ duryodhanas tadā* |
ācāryam upasaṅgamya rājā vacanam abravīt ||

Sañjaya said:
Then Duryodhana, the prince, seeing the army of the Sons of Pāṇḍu arrayed for battle, went up to his teacher (Droṇa) and spoke these words.

3. *paśyai tāṁ pāṇḍuputrāṇām ācārya mahatīṁ camūm* |
vyūḍhām drupadaputreṇa tava śiṣyeṇa dhīmatā ||

Behold this great army of the Sons of Pāṇḍu, O Teacher, arrayed by your wise student, the Son of Drupada.

4. *atra śūrā maheṣvāsā bhīmārjunasamā yudhi* |
yuyudhāno virāṭaś ca drupadaś ca mahārathaḥ ||

Here are heroes, great archers, as good as Bhīma and Arjuna, Yuyudhāna, Virāta, and Drupada, whose chariot is great.

5. *dhṛṣṭaketuś cekitānaḥ kāśirājaś ca vīryavān* |
purujit kuntībhojaś ca śaibyaś ca narapuṅgavaḥ ||

Dhṛṣṭaketu, Cekitāna, and the brave king of Kāśi; Purujit, Kuntībhoja, and the bull among men, Śaibya.

6. *yudhāmanyuś ca vikrānta uttamaujāś ca vīryavān* |
saubhadro draupadeyāś ca sarva eva mahārathāḥ ||

The bold Yudhāmanyu and the brave Uttamaujas, the Son of Subhadrā, and Sons of Draupadī, all of them great warriors.

7. *asmākaṁ tu viśiṣṭā ye tān nibodha dvijottama* |
nāyakā mama sainyasya saṁjnārthaṁ tān bravīmi te ||

Now know leaders of our army, O highest of the Twice Born (Droṇa), the most preeminent among us. I will properly name them for you.

8. *bhavān bhīṣmaś ca karṇaś ca kṛpaś ca samitiñjayaḥ* |
aśvatthāmā vikarṇaś ca saumadattis tathaiva ca ||

You, yourself (Droṇa), and Bhīṣma and Karṇa and Kṛpa, always victorious in battle, and also Aśvatthāma, Vikarṇa, and the Son of Somadatta.

9. *anye ca bahavaḥ śūrā madarthe tyaktajīvitāḥ* |
nānāśastrapraharaṇāḥ sarve yuddhaviśāradāḥ ||

And many other heroes who give up their lives for my purposes, using all kinds of weapons and all of them skilled in battle.

10. *aparyāptaṁ tad asmākaṁ balaṁ bhīṣmābhirakṣitam* |
paryāptaṁ tv idam eteṣāṁ balaṁbhīmābhirakṣitam ||

This force of ours, though protected by Bhīṣma, is not sufficient. *Their* force, protected by Bhīma, *is* sufficient.

11. *ayaneṣu ca sarveṣu yathābhāgam avasthitāḥ* |
bhīṣmam evābhirakṣantu bhavantaḥ sarva eva hi ||

Indeed all of you protect Bhīṣma in all your actions stationed in your respective positions.

12. *tasya saṁjanayan harṣaṁ kuruvṛddhaḥ pitāmahaḥ* |
siṁhanādaṁ vinadyoccaiḥ śaṅkhaṁ dadhmau pratāpavān ||

To bring out good cheer in him (Duryodhana) the elderly grandfather of the Kurus (Droṇa) bellowed loudly like a lion and blew his conch shell powerfully.

13. *tataḥ śaṇkhāś ca bheryaś ca paṇavānakagomukhāḥ* |
sahasaivābhyahanyanta sa śabdas tumulo 'bhavat ||

Then conch shells, kettledrums, cymbals, drums, and trumpets (*gomukhās*) quickly were struck or blown and the uproar was tumultuous.

14. *tataḥ śvetair hayair yukte mahati syandane sthitau* |
mādhavaḥ pāṇḍavaś caiva divyau śaṅkhau pradadhmatuḥ ||

Then standing grounded in the great chariot yoked with white horses the Descendant of Madhu (Kṛṣṇa), and the Son of Pāṇḍu (Arjuna), blew their divine conch shells.

15. *pāñcajanyaṁ hṛṣīkeśo dvadattaṁ dhanañjayaḥ* |
pauṇḍraṁ dadhmau mahāśaṅkhaṁ bhīmakarmā vṛkodaraḥ ||

Kṛṣṇa blew his Pāñcajanya, Arjuna blew Devadatta, while the Wolf bellied of terrific deeds, Bhīma blew the great conch shell Pāuṇḍra.

16. *anantavijayaṁ rājā kuntīputro yudhiṣṭhiraḥ* |
nakulaḥ sahadevaś ca sughoṣamaṇipuṣpakau ||

The king, Yudhiṣṭhira, the Son of Kuntī, blew Anantavijaya. Nakula and Sahadeva (Arjuna's youngest brothers) blew Sughoṣa and Maṇipuṣpaka.

17. *kāśyaś ca parameṣvāsaḥ śikhaṇḍī ca mahārathaḥ* |
dhṛṣtadyumno virāṭaś ca sātyakiś cāparajitaḥ ||

And the king of Kāśi, the supreme archer, and Śikhaṇḍī, the great warrior; Dhṛṣṭadyumna and Virāta and Sātyaki, the unconquered.

18. *drupado draupadeyāś ca sarvaśaḥ pṛthivīpate* |
saubhadraś cā mahābāhuḥ śaṅkhān dadhmuḥ pṛthak pṛthak ||

Drupada (the father of Draupadī) and the Sons of Draupadī, as well as Saubhadra, of mighty arms, all together blew their conch shells one by one.

19. *sa ghoṣo dhārtarāṣṭrānāṁ hṛdayāni vyadārayat* |
nabhaś ca pṛthivīñcaiva tumulo vyanunādayan ||

This tumultuous uproar caused the sky and even the earth to reverberate. The noise burst the hearts of the Sons of Dhṛtarāṣṭra.

20. *atha vyavasthitān dṛṣtvā dhārtarāṣṭrān kapidhvajaḥ* |
pravṛtte śastrasampāte dhanur udyamya pāṇḍavaḥ ||

Then Arjuna, whose chariot banner bore Hanuman, having seen the Sons of Dhṛtarāṣṭra in battle formation, raised his bow as the missiles were about to fly.

21. *hṛṣīkeśaṁ tadā vākyam idam āha mahīpate* |
senayorubhayormadhye rathaṁ sthāpaya me 'cyuta ||

O Master of the Earth, he (Arjuna) spoke these words to Hṛṣīkeśa: draw my chariot up the middle between the two armies, Imperishable One.

22. *yāvad etān nirīkṣe 'haṁ yoddhukāmānavasthitān* |
kairmayā saha yoddhavyam asmin raṇasamudyame ||

Until I see these men arrayed and lusting for battle, with whom in all this readiness for war I must fight.

23. *yotsyamānān avekṣe 'ham ya ete 'tra samāgatāḥ* |
dhārtarāṣṭrasya durbuddher yuddhe priyacikīrṣavaḥ ||

I want to see these who have come together here ready to fight and hoping to achieve in battle that which is wanted by the evil minded Son of Dhṛtarāṣṭra.

24. *evam ukto hṛṣīkeśo guḍākeśena bhārata* |
senayorubhayormadhye sthāpayitvā rathottamam ||

[Sañjaya says:]
O Bhārata (Dhṛtarāṣṭra), spoken to in this way by Arjuna of thick hair, Kṛṣṇa with bristling hair, drove the great chariot up to stand in the middle between the two armies.

25. *bhīṣmadroṇapramukhataḥ sarveṣāṁ ca mahīkṣiām* |
uvāca pārtha paśyaitān samavetān kurūniti ||

Right in front of the faces of Bhīṣma, Droṇa, and all the rulers of the earth he said, "Son of Pṛthā, behold these Kurus united together."

26. *tatrāpaśyat sthitān pārthaḥ pitṝn atha pitāmahān* |
ācāryān mātulān bhrātṝn putrān pautrān sakhīṁstathā ||

The Son of Pṛthā saw standing there fathers and then grandfathers, teachers, uncles, brothers, sons, grandsons, and even friends.

27. *śvaśurān suhṛdaś caiva senayorubhayor api* |
tānsamīkṣya sa kaunteyaḥ sarvān bandhūn avasthitān ||

And even fathers-in-law and beloved companions in both armies. The Son of Kuntī, contemplating them, all his relatives, standing arrayed.

28. *kṛpayā parayāviṣṭo viṣīdannidam abravīt* |
dṛṣṭvemaṁ svajanaṁ kṛṣṇa yuyutsuṁ samupasthitam ||

Despondent and filled with deep compassion he said this: Kṛṣṇa, seeing this, my own people coming near, eager to fight.

29. *sīdanti mama gātrāṇi mukhañca pariśuṣyati* |
vepathuśca śarīre me romaharṣaśca jāyate ||

My limbs sink down, my mouth dries up, my body trembles, and my hair stands up on end.

30. *gāṇḍīvaṁ sraṁsate hastāt tvak caiva paridahyate* |
na ca śaknomyavasthātuṁ bhramatīva ca me manaḥ ||

Gāṇḍīva (the bow) drops from my hand and my skin is burning all over. I am not able to stand steady, and my mind is flying about.

31. *nimittāni ca paśyāmi viparītāni keśava* |
na ca śreyo 'nupaśyāmi hatvā svajanamāhave ||

And I see inauspicious omens, O Keśava. And I do not see any good in killing my own people in war.

32. *na kāṅkṣe vijayaṁ kṛṣṇa na ca rājyaṁ sukhāni ca* |
kiṁ no rājyena govinda kiṁ bhogair jīvitena vā ||

I do not crave after victory, Kṛṣṇa, nor kingdom and enjoyments. What is a kingdom to us, O Govinda, Herder of Cows? Or pleasures, or even life?

33. *yeṣām arthe kāṅkṣitaṁ no rājyaṁ bhogāḥ sukhāni ca* |
ta ime 'vasthitāyuddhe prāṇāṁstyaktvā dhanāni ca ||

Those for whose sake we would yearn for kingdom, pleasures, and enjoyment, they stand assembled here in battle formation, letting go of their lives and riches.

34. *ācāryāḥ pitaraḥ putrās tathaiva ca pitāmahāḥ* |
mātulāḥ śvaśurāḥ pautrāḥ śyālāḥ sambandhinastathā ||

Teachers, fathers, sons, as well as grandfathers, uncles, fathers-in-law, grandsons, brothers-in-law, and other relatives.

35. *etān na hantum icchāmi ghnato 'pi madhusūdana* |
api trailokyarājyasya hetoḥ kiṁ nu mahīkṛte ||

I do not wish to slay them, even those who are killing, O Slayer of Madhu, even for sovereignty of the three worlds. Why then for just the earth?

36. *nihatya dhārtarāṣṭrān naḥ kā pṛtiḥ syājjanārdana* |
pāpamevāśrayedasmān hatvaitānātatāyinaḥ ||

What satisfaction would be ours, killing the Sons of Dhṛtarāṣṭra, O Janārdana? Only evil would consume us having slain these aggressors.

37. *tasmānnarhā vayaṁ hantuṁ dhārtarāṣṭrān svavāndhavān* |
svajanaṁ hi kathaṁ hatvā sukhinaḥ syāma mādhava ||

Thus it is not right that we will kill our own relatives, the sons of Dhṛtarāṣṭra. Having killed our own people, how indeed, would we be happy, O Mādhava?

38. *yadyapyete na paśyanti lobhopahatacetasaḥ* |
kulakṣayakṛtaṁ doṣaṁ mitradrohe ca pātakam ||

Even if these whose minds are overwhelmed with greed do not see the evil done by the destruction of the family and by betrayal of friends;

39. *kathaṁ na jñeyamasmābhiḥ pāpādasmānnivaritum* |
kulakṣaykṛtaṁ doṣaṁ prapaśyadbhirjanārdana ||

How could we not know to turn back from this sin by insight into the evil caused by destroying the family, O Janārdana?

40. *kulakṣaye praṇaśyanti kuladharmāḥ sanātanāḥ* |
dharme naṣṭe kulaṁ kṛtsnam adharmo 'bhibhavatyuta ||

In the destruction of the family, the ancient dharmas (customs, laws, and culture) of the family vanish. When the laws perish, the entire family is overwhelmed with lawlessness.

41. *adharmābhibhavāt kṛṣṇa praduṣyanti kulastriyaḥ* |
strīṣu duṣṭāsu vārṣṇeya jāyate varṇasaṇkaraḥ ||

When overwhelmed by lawlessness the women of the family are defiled, O Kṛṣṇa. When women are defiled the upheaval of castes arises.

42. *saṅkaro narakāyaiva kulaghnānāṁ kulasya ca* |
patanti pitaro hyeṣāṁ luptapiṇḍodakakriyāḥ ||

This confusion makes the destroyers of the family and the family itself fall to hell. Even their departed ancestors fall, deprived of their offerings of rice and water.

43. *doṣairetaiḥ kulaghnānām varṇasaṅkarakārakaiḥ* |
utsādyante jātidharmāḥ kuladharmāśca śāśvatāḥ ||

By the crimes done by the destroyers of family, creating a confused intermixing of castes; duties and laws of birth disappear and also the immemorial laws of the family.

44. *utsannakuladharmāṇāṁ manuṣyāṇāṁ janārdana* |
narake niyataṁ vāso bhavatītyanuśuśruma ||

We have heard again and again, O Janārdana, that the men of families whose laws are destroyed dwell perpetually in hell.

45. *aho bata mahat pāpaṁ kartuṁ vyavasitā vayam* |
yad rājyasukhalobhena hantuṁ svajanamudyatāḥ ||

Alas! We are determined to commit a great sin in resolving to kill our own people through greed for the pleasures of a royal kingdom.

46. *yadi māmapratīkāram aśastraṁ śastra pāṇayaḥ |*
dhārtarāṣṭrā raṇe hanyus tānme kṣemataraṁ bhavet ||

If the fully armed Sons of Dhṛtarāṣṭra should kill me, unarmed and unresisting in battle, it would be a greater happiness for me.

47. *evamuktvārjunaḥ saṁkhye rathopastha upāviśat |*
visṛjya saśaraṁ cāpaṁ śokasaṁvignamānasaḥ ||

Having spoken in this way on the battlefield, Arjuna sat down on the seat of the chariot, casting aside his bow and arrow, his heart overwhelmed by sorrow.

Chapter 2

sañjaya uvāca

1. *taṁ tathā kṛpayāviṣṭam aśrupūrṇākulekṣaṇam |*
viṣīdantam idaṁ vākyam uvāca madhusūdanaḥ ||

Sañjaya said:
To him who was overwhelmed by pity, whose downcast eyes were filled with despondent tears, Kṛṣṇa, the Slayer of Madhu, spoke these words.

śrībhagavān uvāca

2. *kutastvā kaśmalamidaṁ viṣame samupasthitam |*
anāryajuṣṭamasvargyam akīrtikaramarjuna ||

The Beautiful Lord said:
From where has this dejection of heart come at the approach of crisis? It is not befitting to an Aryan (noble); it leads not to heaven, but causes disgrace, Arjuna.

3. *klaibyaṁ māsma gamaḥ pārtha naitat tvayyupapadyate |*
kṣudraṁ hṛdayadaurbalyaṁ tyaktvottiṣṭha paraṁtapa ||

You should never yield to cowardice, O Pārtha, it does not suit you. Abandon this lowly faintness of heart. Stand up! Scorcher of the Foe.

arjuna uvāca

4. *kathaṁ bhīṣmam ahaṁ saṁkhye droṇañca madhusūdana |*
iṣubhiḥ pratiyotsyāmi pūjārhāvarisūdana ||

Arjuna said:
O Slayer of Madhu, how shall I, with arrows, attack in battle Bhīṣma and Droṇa, who are worthy of worship?

5. *gurūnahatvā hi mahānubhāvān śreyo bhoktuṁ bhaikṣyamapīha loke* |
hatvārthakāmāṁstu gurūnihaiva bhuñjīya bhogān rudhirapradigdhān ||

Indeed, it would be better in this world to live on alms from mendicant begging than to slay these great, noble gurus. Having, with a lust for worldly gain, killed these great teachers I would here on earth enjoy delights smeared with blood.

6. *na caitadvidmaḥ kataran no garīyo yadvā jayema yadi vā no jayeyuḥ* |
yāneva hatvā na jijīviṣāmas te 'vasthitāḥ pramukhe dhārtarāṣṭrāḥ ||

And we do not know which is better for us, whether we should conquer them or they should conquer us—the Sons of Dhṛtarāṣṭra standing before our face, whom having killed we would not want to live.

7. *kārpaṇyadoṣopahatasvabhāvaḥ pṛcchāmi tvāṁ dharmasaṁmūḍhacetāḥ* |
yacchreyaḥ syānniścitaṁ brūhi tan me śiṣyaste 'haṁ śādhi māṁ tvāṁ prapannam ||

My very being is overwhelmed with weakness and pity. Bewildered in heart about my duty (dharma), I ask you: tell me for certain which is better. I am your student. Teach me who is supplicant to you.

8. *na hi prapaśyāmi mamāpanudyād yacchokamucchoṣaṇamindriyāṇām* |
avāpya bhūmāvasapatnamṛddhaṁ rājyaṁ surāṇāmapi cādhipatyam ||

Truly, I do not see what could take away my sorrow which is drying up my senses, even if I attain our unrivaled prosperous kingdom here on earth or even sovereignty of the gods.

sañjaya uvāca

9. *evamuktvā hṛṣīkeśaṁ guḍākeśaḥ parantapaḥ* |
na yotsya iti govindam uktvā tūṣṇīṁ babhūva ha ||

Sañjaya said:
In this way Arjuna (the beautiful-haired burner of foes), having spoken to Kṛṣṇa (with vibrant hair), then said to Govinda, "I will not fight." And he became silent!

10. *tamuvāca hṛṣīkeśaḥ prahasanniva bhārata* |
senayorubhayormadhye viṣīdantamidaṁ vacaḥ ||

O Bhārata (King Dhṛtarāṣṭra), Kṛṣṇa (with vibrant hair) as if beginning to smile, spoke this word to him, the despondent one, in the middle between two armies.

śrībhagavān uvāca
11. *aśocyān anvaśocas tvaṁ prajñāvādāṁś ca bhāṣase* |
gatāsūn agatāsūṁś ca nā nuśocanti paṇḍitāḥ ||

The Beautiful Lord said:
You grieve for those for whom you should not grieve. And yet you speak about wisdom. The paṇḍits do not mourn for those who have gone or for those who have not yet gone.

12. *na tvevāhaṁ jātu nāsaṁ nā tvaṁ neme janādhipāḥ* |
na caiva na bhaviṣyāmaḥ sarve vayamataḥparam ||

There is certainly not ever a time I have not existed, nor you, nor these rulers (lords) of people. From now on there will never be a time we all will not be.

13. *dehino 'smin yathā dehe kaumāraṁ yauvanaṁ jarā* |
tathā dehāntaraprāptir dhīras tatra na muhyati ||

As this body passes from childhood, to youth, to old age, so the embodied (one) passes to another body. A wise one is not confused by this.

14. *mātrāsparśāstu kaunteya śītoṣṇasukhaduḥkhadāḥ* |
āgamāpāyino 'nityās tāṁs titikṣa sva bhārata ||

Sensual contact, O Son of Kuntī, gives rise to cold, heat, happiness, and suffering. Being impermanent, they come and they go. Patiently endure them, Arjuna.

15. *yaṁ hi na vyathayantyete puruṣaṁ puruṣarṣabha* |
samaduḥkhasukhaṁ dhīraṁ so 'mṛtatvāya kalpate ||

The one who is not tormented by these, O Leader of Men, the wise one who is the same in pain and pleasure is prepared for immortality.

16. *nāsato vidyate bhāvo nābhāvo vidyate sataḥ* |
ubhayorapi dṛṣṭo 'ntas tvanayostattvadarśibhiḥ ||

Of that which is nonexistent (*asat*) there is no becoming existent (*sat*); of that which is existent (sat) there is no becoming nonexistent (asat). The truth of both of these is clearly understood by seers of truth (thatness).

17. *avināśi tu tad viddhi yena sarvam idaṁ tatam* |
vināśam avyayasyāsya na kaścit kartuṁ arhati ||

Know, that that by which all this world is spread out is undecaying. No one is able to destroy this imperishable.

18. *antavanta ime dehā nityasyoktāḥ śarīriṇaḥ* |
anāśino 'prameyasya tasmād yudhyasva bhārata ||

These bodies of the eternal, indestructible, immeasurable embodied are said to have an end. Therefore, fight, O Bhārata!

19. *ya enaṁ vetti hantāraṁ yaścainaṁ manyate hatam* |
ubhau tau na vijānīto nāyaṁ hanti na hanyate ||

One who thinks that they kill and one who thinks that this is killed; they both do not understand. This neither kills nor is killed.

20. *na jāyate mriyate vā kadācin nāyaṁ bhūtvā bhavitā vā na bhuyaḥ* |
ajo nityaḥ śāśvato 'yaṁ purāṇo na hanyate hanyamāne śarīre ||

This is not born nor does it die at any time, nor does this having been, ever cease to be. It is unborn, timeless, continuous, and primeval. It is not killed when the body is slain.

21. *vedāvināśinaṁ nityaṁ ya enam ajam avyayam* |
kathaṁ sa puruṣaḥ pārtha kaṁ ghātayati hanti kam ||

One who knows this as indestructible and eternal, unborn and undecaying; how could such a person kill, causing whom to kill and killing whom?

22. *vāsāṁsi jīrṇāni yathā vihāya navāni gṛhṇāti naro 'parāṇi* |
tathā śarīrāṇi vihāya jīrṇāny anyāni saṁyāti navāni dehī ||

Just as when a person throws off worn-out clothing and puts on new clothing, so the embodied one casts off worn-out bodies and gets new ones.

23. *nainaṁ chindanti śastrāṇi nainaṁ dahati pāvakaḥ* |
na cainaṁ kledayantyāpo nā śoṣayati mārutaḥ ||

Weapons do not cut this, fire does not burn this, waters do not make it wet, nor does wind dry it up.

24. *acchedyo 'yamadāhyo 'yam akledyo 'śoṣya eva ca* |
nityaḥ sarvagataḥ sthāṇur acalo 'yaṁ sanātanaḥ ||

This is uncuttable, this is unburnable. It cannot be made wet or even dry. This is eternal, everywhere and stable, unwavering and primordial.

25. *avyakto 'yamacintyo 'yam avikāryo 'yam ucyate* |
tasmād evaṁ viditvainaṁ nānuśocitum arhasi ||

It is said that this is unmanifest, unthinkable, and without variations. Therefore, having understood this, you should not continue to grieve.

26. *atha cainaṁ nityajātaṁ nityaṁ vā manyase mṛtaṁ* |
tathāpi tvaṁ mahābāho nainaṁ śocitum arhasi ||

And furthermore, even if you imagine that this is always being born or is always dying, O Mighty Armed, you should not grieve for this.

27. *jātasya hi dhruvo mṛtyur dhruvaṁ janma mṛtasya ca* |
tasmādaparihārye 'rthe na tvaṁ śocitum arhasi ||

Truly, for one who is born, death is certain and for the dead, birth is certain. Therefore, for what is completely inevitable in its outcome, you should not grieve.

28. *avyaktādīni bhūtāni vyaktamadhyāni bhārata* |
avyaktanidhanānyeva tatra kā paridevanā ||

All beings are unmanifest in their beginning, manifest in the middle, and again unmanifest in their ends. Over this what is there to lament?

29. *āścaryavat paśyati kaścidenam āścaryavad vadati tathaiva cānyaḥ* |
āścaryavac cainam anyaḥ śṛṇoti śrutvā 'py enaṁ veda na caiva kaścit ||

Someone sees this as wondrous, another one declares this as wondrous, and even another hears this as wondrous; and even after hearing, no one at all knows this.

30. *dehī nityamavadhyo 'yaṁ dehe sarvasya bhārata* |
tasmāt sarvāni bhūtāni na tvaṁ śocitumarhasi ||

This, the dweller in the body of all, is eternally beyond harm, O Bhārata. Therefore you should not mourn for any being.

31. *svadharmam api cāvekṣya na vikampitum arhasi* |
dharmyāddhi yuddhācchreyo 'nyat kṣatriyasya na vidyate ||

And just looking at your own duty (svadharma) you should not waiver. There is nothing found to be better for a Kṣatriya (warrior) than a lawful fight.

32. *yadṛcchayā copapannaṁ svargadvāram apāvṛtam* |
sukhinaḥ kṣatriyāḥ pārtha labhante yuddham īdṛśam ||

And if by good luck the gate of heaven opens, the Kṣatriyas are happy, O Son of Pṛthā, finding such a fight.

33. *atha cet tvamimaṁ dharmyaṁ saṁgrāmaṁ na kariṣyasi* |
tataḥ svadharmaṁ kīrtiṁ ca hitvā pāpam avāpsyasi ||

Now, if you do not embark upon this proper lawful engagement, having avoided your own duty and fame, you will incur evil.

34. *akīrtiṁ cāpi bhūtāni kathayiṣyanti te 'vyayām* |
saṁbhāvitasya cākīrtir maraṇād atiricyate ||

And also people will tell the stories of your disgrace forever; and for the honored, disgrace is worse than dying.

35. *bhayād raṇād uparataṁ maṁsyante tvāṁ mahārathāḥ* |
yeṣāṁ ca tvaṁ bahumato bhūtvā yāsyasi lāghavam ||

The great warriors will think that you retreated from battle out of fear. Those who once held you in high esteem will make light of you.

36. *avācyavādāṁśca bahūn vadiṣyanti tavāhitāḥ* |
nindantastava sāmarthyaṁ tato duḥkhataraṁ nu kim ||

Your enemies will talk about you with many words not to be spoken, making fun of your capacity. What greater misery is there than that?

37. *hato vā prāpsyasi svargaṁ jitvā vā bhokṣyase mahīm* |
tasmād uttiṣṭha kaunteya yuddhāya kṛtaniścayaḥ ||

Either being killed you will go to heaven, or being victorious you will enjoy the earth. Therefore, stand up, Son of Kuntī, resolved to fight.

38. *sukhaduḥkhe same kṛtvā lābhālābhau jayājayau* |
tato yuddhāya yujyasva naivaṁ pāpamavāpsyasi ||

Making happiness and suffering the same, as well as gain and loss, victory and defeat, then yoke yourself to battle! In this way you will not incur evil.

39. *eṣā te 'bhihitā sāṁkhye buddhiryoge tvimaṁ śṛnu* |
buddhyā yukto yayā pārtha karmabandhaṁ prahāsyasi ||

This is the wisdom of Sāṁkhya given to you; however, now hear this wisdom as the practice of yoga. Yoked with this intelligence, Son of Pṛthā, you will throw off the bondage of karma.

40. *nehābhikramanāśo 'sti pratyavāyo na vidyate* |
svalpamapyasya dharmasya trāyate mahato bhayāt ||

Here no work is lost nor is there any reversal of progress. Even a small amount of this practice (dharma) protects from great fear.

41. *vyavasāyātmikā buddhir eke 'ha kurunandana* |
bahuśākhā hy anantāś ca buddhayo 'vyavasāyinām ||

In this the focused resolute nature of the intelligence is one, Joy of the Kurus, while the intelligence of the irresolute has many branches which are endless.

42. *yāmimāṁ puṣpitāṁ vācaṁ pravadantyavipaścitaḥ* |
vedavādaratāḥ pārtha nānyad astīti vādinaḥ ||

The undiscerning, delighting in the words of the Veda, proclaim its flowery discourse, saying that there is nothing else to it.

43. *kāmātmānaḥ svargaparā janmakarmaphalapradām* |
kriyāviśeṣabahulāṁ bhogaiśvaryagatiṁ prati ||

Their (the undiscerning's) very nature is desire, holding heaven as the highest object, while using many specific rituals for gaining enjoyment and power. The flowery Vedic discourse gives rebirth as the fruit of action.

44. *bhogaiśvaryaprasaktānāṁ tayāpahṛtacetasām* |
vyavasāytmikā buddhiḥ samādhau na vidhīyate ||

To them, attached to pleasure and power, whose minds have been stolen by these (words of the Vedas), the single-focused resolution of the intelligence in meditation is not given.

45. *traiguṇyaviṣayā vedā nistraiguṇyo bhavārjuna* |
nirdvandvo nityasattvastho niryogakṣema ātmavān ||

The activities of the three guṇas are the realm of the Vedas. Be free of the three guṇas, Arjuna. Always abiding in truth, free of the dualities, not concerned for acquisition and preservation, and holding the True Self.

46. *yāvān artha udapāne sarvataḥ saṁplutodake* |
tāvān sarveṣu vedeṣu brāhmaṇasya vijānataḥ ||

As is the use of a well in a place flooded with water on all sides, such is the value in all of the Vedas (rituals) for a Brāhman who truly understands.

47. *karmaṇyevādhikāraste mā phaleṣu kadācana* |
mā karmaphalahetur bhūr mā te saṅgo 'stvakarmaṇi ||

You have a right to action alone and never at any time to its fruits. The fruits of action should never be your motive. And never let there be any attachment to inaction.

48. *yogasthaḥ kuru karmāṇi saṅgaṁ tyaktvā dhanañjaya* |
siddhyasiddhyoḥ samo bhūtvā samatvaṁ yoga ucyate ||

Established in yoga perform actions, O Winner of Wealth, giving up attachment, having become equal to success or failure. It is said that yoga is equanimity.

49. *dūreṇa hyavaraṁ karma buddhiyogād dhanaṁjaya |*
buddhau śaraṇam anviccha kṛpaṇāḥ phalahetavaḥ ||

Mere action is far below the yoga of intelligence (buddhi yoga), O Conqueror of Wealth. Take refuge in the awakened intelligence (*buddhau śaraṇam*). Pathetic are those motivated by the fruit.

50. *buddhiyukto jahātīha ubhe sukṛtaduṣkṛte |*
tasmād yogāya yujyasva yogaḥ karmasu kauśalam ||

One whose buddhi is integrated, even here in the world, throws off both good and evil actions. Therefore, yoke yourself to yoga. Yoga is the art of skillful action.

51. *karmajaṁ buddhiyuktā hi phalaṁ tyaktvā manīṣiṇaḥ |*
janmabandhavinirmuktāḥ padaṁ gacchanty anāmayam ||

The wise who have let go of the fruits born of action are certainly of integrated intelligence. Released from the bonds of birth, they go to that abode free from misery.

52. *yadā te mohakalilaṁ buddhir vyatitariṣyati |*
tadā gantāsi nirvedaṁ śrotavyasya śrutasya ca ||

When your intelligence crosses beyond the quagmire of delusion then you will be indifferent to what is to be heard and to that which has been heard (the Veda).

53. *śrutivipratipannā te yadā sthāsyati niścalā |*
samādhāvacalā buddhis tadā yogama vāpsyasi ||

When your intelligence stands unwavering, fixed in deep meditation, unperplexed by the misinterpreting of Vedic texts, then you will attain yoga.

arjuna uvāca
54. *sthitaprajñasya kā bhāṣā samādhisthasya keśava |*
sthiṭadhīḥ kim prabhāṣeta kimāsīta vrajeta kim ||

Arjuna said:
What is the description of one who is of stable insight, who is steady in samādhi, O Keśava? How would one steady in thought speak? How would that one sit? How would that one travel?

śrībhagavān uvāca
55. *prajahāti yadā kāmān sarvān pārtha manogatān* |
ātmanyevātmanā tuṣṭaḥ sthitaprajñas tadocyate ||

The Beautiful Lord said:
When one abandons all desires coming from the mind, O Pārtha, when the self is content in the self (itself), then one is called stable in intelligence.

56. *duḥkheṣv anudvignamanāḥ sukheṣu vigataspṛhaḥ* |
vītarāgabhayakrodhaḥ sthitadhīr munir ucyate ||

One whose mind is not agitated in sorrow, who is free from clinging in the midst of joy, with passion, fear, and anger gone is called a sage, a *muni*, of steady mind.

57. *yaḥ sarvatrānabhisnehas tat-tat prāpya śubhāśubham* |
nābhinandati na dveṣṭi tasya prajñā pratiṣṭhitā ||

For one who is nongrasping on all sides, neither celebrating nor disliking while encountering this or that, pleasant or unpleasant, their insight is firmly established.

58. *yadā saṁharate cāyaṁ kūrmo 'ṅgānīva sarvaśaḥ* |
indriyāṇīndriyārthebhyas tasya prajñā pratiṣṭhitā ||

And when this one withdraws the senses from the objects of the senses completely like a tortoise withdraws its limbs, their insight is firmly established.

59. *viṣayā vinivartante nirāhārasya dehinaḥ* |
rasavarjaṁ raso 'pyasya paraṁ dṛṣṭvā nivartate ||

Sense objects turn away from the embodied one who does not feed on them, yet the flavor (the taste for them) remains, but having seen the supreme, even the taste turns away.

60. *yatato hyapi kaunteya puruṣasya vipaścitaḥ* |
indriyāṇi pramāthīni haranti prasabhaṁ manaḥ ||

The ever-disruptive senses forcefully carry away the mind of even the wise person striving for perfection.

61. *tāni sarvāṇi saṁyamya yukta āsīta matparaḥ* |
vaśe hi yasyendriyāṇi tasya prajñā pratiṣṭhitā ||

Controlling all these, one should sit, yoked in yoga, intent on Me. Surely in the one whose senses are tamed wisdom is firmly established.

62. *dhyāyato viṣayān puṁsaḥ saṅgasteṣūpajāyate* |
saṅgāt sañjāyate kāmaḥ kāmāt krodho 'bhijāyate ||

For one contemplating the objects of the senses, attachment to them is born; from attachment desire arises, from desire anger is born.

63. *krodhād bhavati sammohaḥ sammohāt smṛtivibhramaḥ* |
smṛtibhraṁśād buddhināśo buddhināśāt praṇaśyati ||

From anger delusion arises. From delusion memory and mindfulness wander away. From memory wandering there is destruction of the intelligence (buddhi). From destruction of the intelligence one is lost.

64. *rāgadveśaviyuktas tu viśayān indriyaiś caran* |
ātmavaśyair vidheyātmā prasādam adhigacchati ||

However, by disengaging with desire and repulsion a person with self-awareness and control, even though the senses are engaged with sense objects, attains clarity and tranquility.

65. *prasāde sarvaduḥkhānāṁ hānir asyo 'pajāyate* |
prasannacetaso hyāśu buddhiḥ paryavatiṣṭhate ||

In that tranquil clarity there is born for one a cessation of all suffering. For the clever mind the intelligence is quickly established.

66. *nāsti buddhir ayuktasya na cāyutasya bhāvanā* |
na cābhāvayataḥ śāntir aśāntasya kutaḥ sukham ||

For one not linked in yoga there is no singular intelligence and there is no deep meditation, and for one without meditation there is no peace. For one without peace, where is happiness?

67. *indriyāṇāṁ hi caratāṁ yanmano 'nuvidhīyate* |
tadasya harati prajñāṁ vāyur nāvam ivāmbhasi ||

When one's mind is continuously led around by the wandering senses, it carries away the discriminating wisdom like the wind carries away a ship on the water.

68. *tasmād yasya mahābāho nigṛhītāni sarvaśaḥ* |
indriyāṇīndriyārthebhyas tasya prajñā pratiṣṭhitā ||

Therefore, O Mighty Armed, one whose senses are not grasping at sense objects in any and all directions is firmly established in wisdom (*prajñā*).

69. *yā niśā sarvabhūtānāṁ tasyāṁ jāgarti saṁyamī* |
yasyāṁ jāgrati bhūtāni sā niśā paśyato muneḥ ||

That which is night for all beings is the time of awakening for the focused, the time of awakening for the beings is night for the sage who sees.

70. *āpūryamāṇam acalapratiṣṭhaṁ samudram āpaḥ praviśanti yadvat* |
tadvat kāmā yaṁ praviśanti sarve sa śāntim āpnoti na kāmakāmī ||

Just as the waters flow into the sea, which becomes full yet remains motionless, one into whom all desires enter and who remains unmoved, attains peace; not one who lusts after their own desires.

71. *vihāya kāmān yaḥ sarvān pumāṁś carati niḥspṛhaḥ* |
nirmamo nirahaṁkāraḥ sa śāntim adhigacchati ||

One who lets go of all desires and acts without longing, without being possessive, free of ego, goes to peace and clarity.

72. *eṣā brāhmī sthitiḥ pārtha naināṁ prāpya vimuhyati* |
sthitvā 'syām antakāle 'pi brahmanirvāṇam ṛcchati ||

This is the sacred balance, O Pārtha. Having attained this, one is not confused and is established in this, even at the end of time (death) and reaches the freedom of Brahman (Brahman-nirvāṇa).

Chapter 3

arjuna uvāca

1. *jyāyasī cet karmaṇas te matā buddhir janārdana* |
tat kiṁ karmaṇi ghore māṁ niyojayasi keśava ||

Arjuna said:
If it is your opinion that intelligence is better than action, O Janārdana, then why do you urge me to do this horrible action, O Keśava?

2. *vyāmiśreṇeva vākyena buddhiṁ mohayasīva me* |
tad ekaṁ vada niścitya yena śreyo 'ham āpnuyām ||

As if with contradictory, equivocal words you seem to bewilder my intelligence. Tell me the one thing for sure by which I can reach the highest goal.

śrībhagavān uvāca

3. *loke 'smin dvividhā niṣṭhā purā proktā mayānagha* |
jñānayogena sāṁkhyānāṁ karmayogena yoginām ||

The Beautiful Lord said:
In this world there is a twofold (dual) foundation of the path taught by Me from ancient times: the yoga of knowledge for the practitioners of contemplative Sāṁkhya, and the yoga of action for practitioners of yoga.

4. *na karmaṇāmanārambhān naiṣkarmyaṁ puruṣo 'śnute* |
na ca saṁnyasanād eva siddhiṁ samadhigacchati ||

It is not by abstaining from action that one (puruṣa) attains freedom from action, nor by renunciation (saṁnyāsa) alone does one reach perfection.

5. *na hi kaścit kṣaṇamapi jātu tiṣṭhatyakarmakṛt* |
kāryate hyavaśaḥ karma sarvaḥ prakṛtijairguṇaiḥ ||

Indeed, no one can exist, even for a moment, without performing action. Everyone is forced to do work, even against their will, by the guṇas born of prakṛti.

6. *karmendriyāṇi saṁyamya ya āste manasā smaran* |
indriyārthān vimūḍhātmā mithyācāraḥ sa ucyate ||

One who controls the organs of action while brooding over the objects of the senses with a deluded sense of self is said to be the hypocrite.

7. *yastvindriyāṇi manasā niyamyārbhate 'rjuna* |
karmendriyaiḥ karmayogam asaktaḥ sa viśiṣyate ||

But one who contains the senses with the mind, O Arjuna, and who, without attachment, uses the organs of action in the yoga of action, surpasses others and is the best.

8. *niyataṁ kuru karma tvaṁ karma jyāyo hyakarmaṇaḥ* |
śarīrayātrāpi ca te na prasidhyedakarmaṇaḥ ||

Do then the necessary action! Action is truly better than inaction. Even the maintaining of your body cannot be done without action.

9. *yajñārthāt karmaṇo 'nyatra loko 'yaṁ karmabandhanaḥ* |
tadarthaṁ karma kaunteya muktasaṅgaḥ samācara ||

This whole world is in bondage to action except for action done as and for sacrifice. O Son of Kuntī, perform action for the sake of sacrifice, free from attachments.

10. *sahayajñāḥ prajāḥ sṛṣṭvā purovāca prajāpatiḥ* |
anena prasaviṣyadhvam eṣa vo 'stviṣṭakāmadhuk ||

Having created sacrifice along with mankind, Prajāpati (the god Brahmā) said long ago, "By this (sacrifice) may you bring forth, and may this be the Cow of Plenty for your desires."

11. *devān bhāvayatānena te devā bhāvayantu vaḥ* |
parasparaṁ bhāvayantaḥ śreyaḥ paramavāpsyatha ||

By this may you nurture the gods and may the gods nurture you. By nurturing each other you will gain the highest happiness.

12. *iṣṭān bhogān hi vo devā dāsyante yajñabhāvitāḥ* |
tair dattān apradāyaibhyo yo bhuṅkte stena eva saḥ ||

Nourished by sacrifice the gods will certainly give you the desired pleasures. One who enjoys these gifts without any offering to them is merely a thief.

13. *yajñaśiṣṭāśinaḥ santo mucyante sarvakilbiṣaiḥ* |
bhuñjate te tvaghaṁ pāpā ye pacantyātmakāraṇāt ||

The good, eating the residual remains of sacrifice, are freed from all wrongs. But the wicked, who cook merely for themselves, eat their own misery.

14. *annād bhavanti bhūtāni parjanyād annasaṁbhavaḥ* |
yajñād bhavati parjanyo yajñaḥ karmasamudbhavaḥ ||

From food living beings come to be; from rain is the origin of food; from sacrifice comes the rain. It is action (karma) that gives birth to sacrifice.

15. *karma brahmodbhavaṁ viddhi brahmākṣarasamudbhavam* |
tasmāt sarvagataṁ brahma nityaṁ yajñe pratiṣṭhitam ||

Know action to be born of the Brahman (Vedic hymns), which is born from the imperishable. Therefore omnipresent, all-pervading Brahman is always established in sacrifice.

16. *evaṁ pravartitaṁ cakraṁ nānuvartayatīha yaḥ* |
aghāyurindriyārāmo moghaṁ pārtha sa jīvati ||

Thus the wheel is made to turn. One who, in this world, does not help to turn this wheel lives, O Son of Pṛthā, in vain; cruel and absorbed in sensuality.

17. *yas tvatāmaratireva syādātmatṛptaśca mānavaḥ* |
ātmanyeva ca saṁtuṣṭas tasya kāryaṁ na vidyate ||

For the person who takes delight in the self (ātman) alone, whose satisfaction is in the self (ātman), and who is totally contented in the self (ātman), for them there is no work that needs to be done.

18. *naiva tasya kṛtenārtho nākṛteneha kaścana* |
na cāsya sarvabhūteṣu kaścid arthavyapāśrayaḥ ||

They have no purpose to gain by action, nor anything at all by inaction. And no purpose or need at all from any and all beings.

19. *tasmād asaktaḥ satataṁ kāryaṁ karma samācara* |
asakto hyācaran karma param āpnoti pūruṣaḥ ||

Therefore, without attachment, always do the work that needs to be done. Truly, doing work without attachment, a person attains the highest.

20. *karmaṇaiva hi saṁsiddhim āsthitā janakādayaḥ* |
lokasaṁgrahamevāpi saṁpaśyan kartuṁ arhasi ||

It was by work alone that Janaka and others attained perfection. You should also act (do work) with the vision of holding together the world.

21. *yad yad ācarati śreṣṭhas tadtad evetaro janaḥ* |
sa yat pramāṇaṁ kurute lokastadanuvartate ||

Whatsoever the great person does, the rest of humanity does. Whatever standards that one sets the world follows.

22. *na me pārthāsti kartavyaṁ triṣu lokeṣu kiṁcana* |
nānavāptamavāptavyaṁ varta eva ca karmaṇi ||

For Me, O Pārtha, there is not anything at all to be done in the three worlds, nor is there anything to obtain or which has not been obtained. Yet, I engage in work.

23. *yadi hyahaṁ na varteyaṁ jātu karmaṇyatandritaḥ* |
mama vartmānuvartante manuṣyāḥ pārtha sarvaśaḥ ||

Indeed, if ever I did not engage in untiring work, mankind would follow my path incompletely, Son of Pṛthā.

24. *utsīdeyurime lokā na kuryāṁ karma cedaham* |
saṅkarasya ca kartā syām upahanyām imāḥ prajāḥ ||

If I did not do work, these worlds would fall to ruin. I would be the creator of confusion and I would destroy these beings.

25. *saktāḥ karmaṇyavidvāṁso yathā kurvanti bhārata* |
kuryād vidvāṁs tathā saktaś cikīrṣur lokasaṁgraham ||

Just as the ignorant do work with attachment, O Bhārata, the wise one should work thus with no attachment, with the aim of holding together the world.

26. *na buddhibhedaṁ janayed ajñānāṁ karmasaṅginām* |
joṣayet sarvakarmāṇi vidvān yuktaḥ samācaran ||

They (the wise) should not cause a splitting in the intelligence (buddhi) of the ignorant attached to action. The wise performing action as yoga should cause them to delight in all actions.

27. *prakṛteḥ kriyamāṇāni guṇaiḥ karmāṇi sarvaśaḥ* |
ahaṅkāravimūḍhātmā kartāham iti manyate ||

All actions everywhere are done by the guṇas of prakṛti. The being who is confused by egotism thinks, "I am the doer."

28. *tattvavittu mahābāho guṇakarmavibhāgayoḥ* |
guṇā guṇeṣu vartanta iti matvā na sajjate ||

But one who knows the true nature of things, the two roles of guṇa and karma, O Mighty Armed One, is not attached, having thought, "The guṇas are merely acting on the guṇas."

29. *prakṛter guṇasaṁmūḍhāḥ sajjante guṇakarmasu* |
tān akṛtsnavido mandān kṛtsnavin na vicālayet ||

Those who are deluded by the guṇas of prakṛti are attached to the actions of the guṇas. The one who knows the complete whole should not unsettle the minds of those who do not know the whole.

30. *mayi sarvāṇi karmāṇi saṁnyasyādhyātmacetasā* |
nirāśīr nirmamo bhūtvā yudhyasva vigatajvaraḥ ||

Offering and entrusting all actions to Me, conscious of the true ātman, having become free from desire and egotism, with your grief departed, fight!

31. *ye me matam idaṁ nityam anutiṣṭhanti mānavāḥ* |
śraddhāvanto 'nasūyanto mucyante te 'pi karmabhiḥ ||

Those who continuously practice this teaching of mine, full of trust and not spiteful/envious of others, are certainly released from the bonds of actions.

32. *ye tvetad abhyasūyanto nānutiṣṭhanti me matam* |
sarvajñānavimūḍhāṁs tān viddhi naṣṭānacetasaḥ ||

But those who sneer at and do not mindfully practice this teaching of mine, confusing all types of knowledge, know *them* to be lost and stupid.

33. *sadṛśaṁ ceṣṭate svasyāḥ prakṛter jñānavān api* |
prakṛtiṁ yānti bhūtāni nigrahaḥ kiṁ kariṣyati ||

One moves according to one's own nature (prakṛti), even those filled with wisdom. All beings follow their embodied nature. What will repression achieve?

34. *indriyasye ndriyasyārthe rāgadveṣau vyavasthitau* |
tayor na vaśamāgacchet tau hyasya paripanthinau ||

Attachment and repulsion are established in the very sensing of a sense object. One should not come under their power for they are one's two antagonists in every way.

35. *śreyān svadharmo viguṇaḥ paradharmāt svanuṣṭhitāt* |
svadharme nidhanaṁ śreyaḥ paradharmo bhayāvahaḥ ||

One's own dharma (duty) done imperfectly is better than another's dharma done perfectly. Death in doing one's true duty (svadharma) is better. Doing another's dharma invites great danger.

arjuna uvāca
36. *atha kena prayukto 'yaṁ pāpaṁ carati pūruṣaḥ* |
anicchannapi vārṣṇeya balād iva niyojitaḥ ||

Arjuna said:
By what then is a person impelled to commit evil, even against their will as if pushed by a force, O Vṛṣṇi's Clansman?

śrībhagavān uvāca
37. *kāma eṣa krodha eṣa rajoguṇasamudbhavaḥ* |
mahāśano mahāpāpmā viddhyenamiha vairiṇam ||

The Beautiful Lord said:
It is craving, it is wrathful anger born from the guṇa of passion (rajas), all consuming and greatly hurtful (evil). In this situation, know this to be the enemy.

38. *dhūmenāvriyate vahnir yathādarśo malena ca* |
yatholvenā vṛto garbhas tathā tenedam āvṛtam ||

As fire is covered by smoke, as a mirror by dust, and as an embryo is enveloped in a membrane, so is all this enveloped by that passion.

39. *āvṛtaṁ jñānam etena jñānino nityavairiṇā* |
kāmarūpeṇa kaunteya duṣpūrenānalena ca ||

It is wisdom (jñāna) that is covered by this form of lust and anger, by this insatiable fire, the constant enemy of the wise.

40. *indriyāṇi mano buddhir asyādhiṣṭhānam ucyate* |
etair vimohayatyeṣa jñānam āvṛtya dehinam ||

It is said that it dwells in the senses, the mind, and the intelligence. With these it deludes, veiling the wisdom of the embodied one.

41. *tasmāt tvaṁ indriyāṇyādau niyamya bharatarṣabha* |
pāpmānam prajahi hyenaṁ jñānavijñānanāśanam ||

Therefore from the beginning, control the senses, O Bull of the Bharatas, and slay this sinful destroyer of wisdom and discriminating knowledge.

42. *indriyāṇi parāṇyāhur indriyebhyaḥ paraṁ manaḥ* |
manasas tu parā buddhir yo buddheḥ paratas tu saḥ ||

They say that the senses are important. Higher than the senses is the mind (*manas*), greater than the mind (manas) is the intelligence (buddhi), but *this* is higher than the intelligence.

43. *evaṁ buddheḥ paraṁ buddhvā saṁstabhyātmānamātmanā* |
jahi śatruṁ mahābāho kāmarūpaṁ durāsadam ||

Therefore, having understood (buddhvā) that which is higher than the intelligence (buddhi), which holds the ātman with the ātman, slay the enemy in the form of desire who is so difficult to approach, O Mighty Armed.

Chapter 4

śrībhagavān uvāca

1. *imaṁ vivasvate yogaṁ proktavān aham avyayam* |
vivasvān manave prāha manur ikṣvākave 'bravīt ||

The Beautiful Lord said:
This imperishable yoga I taught to Vīvasvān. Vīvasvān transmitted it to Manu; Manu told it to Ikṣvāku.

2. *evaṁ paramparāprāptam imaṁ rājarṣayo viduḥ* |
sa kālene 'ha mahatā yogo naṣṭaḥ paraṁtapa ||

Received in this way passed from one to another, the royal seers knew it. After a long time here on earth yoga was lost, O Scorcher of the Foe.

3. *sa evāyaṁ mayā te 'dya yogaḥ proktaḥ purātanaḥ* |
bhakto 'si me sakhā ceti rahasyaṁ hyetaduttamam ||

This same ancient primeval yoga is proclaimed today by Me to you, since you are my devotee and my friend. This is truly the supreme secret.

arjuna uvāca

4. *aparaṁ bhavato janma paraṁ janma vivasvataḥ* |
katham etad vijānīyāṁ tvam ādau proktavāniti ||

Arjuna said:
Your birth was later and the birth of Vīvasvān was earlier. How should I understand this that you taught it in the beginning?

śrībhagavān uvāca

5. *bahūni me vyatītāni janmāni tava cārjuna* |
tānyahaṁ veda sarvāṇi na tvaṁ vettha paraṁtapa ||

The Beautiful Lord said:
Many of my births and yours too are gone. I know all of them, but you do not, O Scourge of the Opposition.

6. *ajo 'pi sann avyayātmā bhūtānām īśvaro 'pi san* |
prakṛtiṁ svām adhiṣṭhāya saṁbhavānyātmamāyayā ||

Though I am unborn and myself imperishable, though I am the beloved lord of all beings—established in my prakṛti, I come into embodied form through the creative power of my *māyā*.

7. *yadā yadā hi dharmasya glānir bhavati bhārata* |
abhyutthānamadharmasya tadātmānaṁ sṛjāmyaham ||

Whenever, wherever there is a waning of righteousness (dharma) and a rising up of unrighteousness (*adharma*), then I give forth myself.

8. *paritrāṇāya sādhūnāṁ vināśāya ca duṣkṛtām* |
dharmasaṁsthāpanārthāya saṁbhavāmi yuge yuge ||

To protect in all ways the good and to destroy the doers of evil, and for establishing dharma, I come into manifesting being, age after age.

9. *janma karma ca me divyam evaṁ yo vetti tattvataḥ* |
tyaktvā dehaṁ punarjanma naiti māmeti so 'rjuna ||

One who knows the actual nature of my divine birth and activities, when leaving the body is not born again but comes to Me, Arjuna.

10. *vītarāgabhayakrodhā manmayā māmupāśritāḥ* |
bahavo jñānatapasā pūtā madbhāvam āgatāḥ ||

With greed, fear, and anger gone, absorbed in Me, holding on to Me, many purified by the fire of wisdom have come to my state of being.

11. *ye yathā māṁ prapadyante tāṁs tathaiva bhajāmyaham* |
mama vartmānuvartante manuṣyāḥ pārtha sarvaśaḥ ||

In whatever way they resort to Me, I in that way adore them. People everywhere on all sides, follow my path O Son of Pṛthā.

12. *kāṅkṣantaḥ karmaṇāṁ siddhiṁ yajanta iha devatāḥ* |
kṣipraṁ hi mānuṣe loke siddhir bhavati karmajā ||

Desiring the perfections of ritual acts here on earth some offer sacrifices to the gods. Indeed, success born of ritual acts in this world of humans manifests quickly.

13. *cāturvarṇyaṁ māyā sṛṣṭaṁ guṇakarmavibhāgaśaḥ* |
tasya kartāramapi māṁ viddhyakartāram avyayam ||

The four caste types of persons were brought forth by Me according to the distributions of the guṇas. Even though I am the creator of them, know Me as the imperishable nondoer.

14. *na māṁ karmāni limpanti na me karmaphale spṛhā* |
iti māṁ yo 'bhijānāti karmabhir na sa badhyate ||

Actions do not defile Me. I have no yearning for any fruit of action. Therefore one who knows Me is not bound by actions.

15. *evaṁ jñātvā kṛtaṁ karma pūrvairapi mumukṣubhiḥ* |
kuru karmaiva tasmāt tvaṁ pūrvaiḥ purvataraṁ kṛtaṁ ||

Knowing this the ancient ones who sought liberation performed work. Therefore do your work as the ancient ones did in former times.

16. *kiṁ karma kim akarmeti kavayo 'pyatra mohitāḥ* |
tat te karma pravakṣyāmi yaj jṇātvā mokṣyase 'śubhāt ||

What is action? What is inaction? Even the great poets are bewildered by this. To you I will speak about action (karma), knowing which you will be free from viciousness.

17. *karmaṇo hyapi boddhavyaṁ boddhavyaṁ ca vikarmaṇaḥ* |
akarmaṇaśca boddhavyaṁ gahanā karmaṇo gatiḥ ||

Action is to be understood, wrong action is to be understood, and inaction is to be understood. Deeply profound is the way of action.

18. *karmaṇyakarma yaḥ paśyed akarmaṇi ca karma yaḥ* |
sa buddhimān manuṣyeṣu sa yuktaḥ kṛtsnakarmakṛt ||

One who sees inaction in action and who sees action in inaction is awakened among humans and does all actions linked in yoga.

19. *yasya sarve samārambhāḥ kāmasaṁkalpavarjitāḥ* |
jñānāgni dagdhakarmāṇaṁ tam āhuḥ paṇḍitaṁ budhaḥ ||

One who has shed desire and fanciful intentions from all their undertakings, whose actions have been consumed in the fire of knowledge, this one the awakened call a paṇḍit.

20. *tyaktvā karmaphalāsaṅgaṁ nityatṛpto nirāśrayaḥ* |
karmaṇy abhipravṛtto 'pi naiva kiñcit karoti saḥ ||

Having released any attachment to the fruits of action, always satisfied without any dependence, that one does not do anything at all even when immersed in action.

21. *nirāśiryatacittātmā tyaktasarvaparigrahaḥ* |
śārīraṁ kevalaṁ karma kurvannāpnoti kilviṣam ||

Free of aspiration, with thought and self-controlled, performing action with just the body alone, one obtains no evil.

22. *yadṛcchālābhasantuṣṭo dvandvātīto vimatsaraḥ* |
samaḥ siddhāvasiddhau ca kṛtvāpi na nibadhyate ||

Content with what comes by chance, beyond the dualities (happiness-suffering), with malice gone, the same in success and failure, even having acted, one is not bound.

23. *gatasaṅgasya muktasya jñānāvasthitacetasaḥ* |
yajñāyācarataḥ karma samagraṁ pravilīyate ||

The action (karma) of one whose attachments are gone, who is free, whose mind is established in wisdom (jñāna), and whose actions are done as sacrifice is completely, evenly dissolved.

24. *brahmārpaṇaṁ brahma havir brahmāgnau brahmaṇā hutam* |
brahmaiva tena gantavyaṁ brahmakarmasamādhinā ||

The act and the instrument of sacrifice is Brahman, the pouring of the oblation itself is Brahman, poured by Brahman into the fire, which is Brahman. Brahman is attained by one who contemplates action as Brahman.

25. *daivam evāpare yajñaṁ yoginaḥ paryupāste* |
brahmāgnāvapare yajñaṁ yajñeṇaivopajuhvati ||

Some yogīs perform sacrifice to the gods. Others offer sacrifice itself, by the sacrifice into the fire of Brahman.

26. *śrotrādīnīdriyāṇy anye saṁyamāgniṣu juhvati* |
śabdādīn viṣayān anya indriyāgniṣu juhvati ||

And others offer all the senses beginning with hearing into the fires of collected attention; and others pour all sense objects led by sound into the fires of the pure senses.

27. *sarvāṇīndriyakarmāṇi prāṇakarmāṇi cāpare* |
ātmasaṁyamayogāgnau juhvati jñānadīpite ||

Some offer all the movements of their senses and all the movements of their prāṇa into the fire of yoga, focused on the true ātman, ignited by wisdom.

28. *dravyayajñās tapoyajñā yogayajñās tathā 'pare* |
svādhyāyajñānayajñāśca yatayaḥ saṁśitavratāḥ ||

Others may also offer physical possessions, and some others austerities and yoga as sacrifice, and ascetics of sharpened vows offer knowledge, self-study, and chanting as sacrifice.

29. *apāne juhvati prāṇaṁ prāṇe 'pānaṁ tathā 'pare* |
prāṇāpānagatī ruddhvā prāṇāyāmaparāyaṇāḥ ||

Others, focused on prāṇāyāma, clearly defining the paths of inhalation and exhalation, offer the inhalation pattern (prāṇa) into the exhalation pattern (apāna) and the exhalation pattern (apāna) into the inhalation pattern (prāṇa).

30. *apare niyatāhārāḥ prāṇān prāṇeṣu juhvati* |
sarve 'pyete yajñavido yajñakṣapitakalmaṣāḥ ||

Others, controlling eating offer the different patterns of the prāṇas into those prāṇas. All of these know sacrifice and their impurities have been destroyed through sacrifice.

31. *yajñaśiṣṭāmṛtabhujo yānti brahma sanātnam* |
nāyaṁ loko 'styayajñasya kuto 'nyaḥ kurusattama ||

Enjoying the residual nectar of the sacrifice, they go to the primordial Brahman. This world is not for the nonsacrificing one. How then any other world, O best of the Kurus?

32. *evaṁ bahuvidhā yajñā vitatā brahmaṇo mukhe* |
karmajān viddhi tān sarvān evaṁ jñātvā vimokṣyase ||

Thus the many varieties of sacrifice spread out in the mouth of Brahman. Know all of them are born from action. Knowing this, you will be liberated.

33. *śreyān dravyamayād yajñāj jñānayajñaḥ parantapa* |
sarvaṁ karmākhilaṁ pārtha jñāne parisamāpyate ||

Better than the sacrifice of material possessions is the sacrifice of knowledge, O Scorcher of the Foe. All actions without any exception, Son of Pṛthā, fully culminate in knowledge.

34. *tad viddhi praṇipātena paripraśnena sevayā* |
upadekṣyanti te jñānaṁ jñāninas tattvadarśinaḥ ||

Learn this by humble reverence, by inquiring all around, and by rendering practical service. The wise, the seers of "thatness," will teach you wisdom.

35. *yaj jñātvā na punarmoham evaṁ yāsyasi pāṇḍava* |
yena bhūtānyaśeṣeṇa drakṣyasyātmanyatho mayi ||

Having known it, you will not fall into delusion again, Son of Pāṇḍu. And by which you will see all beings without exception in the ātman and then in me.

36. *api cedasi pāpebhyaḥ sarvebhyaḥ pāpakṛttamaḥ* |
sarvaṁ jñānaplavenaiva vṛjinaṁ santariṣyasi ||

Even if you are the most evil of all evildoers, you will completely cross over all deceit by the boat of wisdom.

37. *yathaidhāṁsi samiddho 'gnir bhasmasāt kurute 'rjuna |*
jñānāgniḥ sarvakarmāṇi bhasmasāt kurete tathā ||

Just as a kindled fire reduces firewood to ash, Arjuna, the fire of knowledge reduces all work to ash.

38. *na hi jñānena sadṛśaṁ pavitramiha vidyate |*
tat svayaṁ yogasaṁsiddhaḥ kālenātmani vindati ||

There is indeed no purifier here in the world equal to knowledge. One perfected by yoga in time, finds by means of themselves the self.

39. *śraddhāvāṅl labhate jñānaṁ tatparaḥ saṁyatendriyaḥ |*
jñānaṁlabdhvā parāṁ śāntim acireṇādhigacchati ||

Full of trust one attains wisdom. Holding that wisdom while seeing through the senses, one fully attains wisdom and goes quickly to the supreme peace.

40. *ajñaścāśraddadhānaśca saṁśayātmā vinaśyati |*
nāyaṁ loko 'sti na paro na sukhaṁ saṁśayātmanaḥ ||

One who is ignorant and not giving trusting faith, who is doubtful of the ātman, is destroyed. Neither in this world nor in the world beyond is there happiness for the doubting self.

41. *yogasaṁnyastakarmāṇaṁ jñānasaṁcchinnasaṁśayam |*
ātmavantaṁ na karmāṇi nibadhnanti dhanañjaya ||

O Conqueror of Wealth, actions do not bind one possessing the ātman, whose actions are placed down in yoga and whose doubt is cut through by wisdom.

42. *tasmādajñānasambhūtaṁ hṛtsthaṁ jñānasinātmanaḥ |*
chittvainaṁ saṁśayaṁ yogam ātiṣṭhottiṣṭha bhārata ||

Therefore, with the sword of knowledge having cut through this doubt in your heart (which comes from ignorance), do the yoga! Stand up, Descendant of Bhārata!

Chapter 5

arjuna uvāca

1. *saṁnyāsaṁ karmaṇāṁ kṛṣṇa punar yogaṁ ca śaṁsasi* |
   yacchreya etayor ekaṁ tan me brūhi suniścitam ||

Arjuna said:
You extol the renunciation of actions, O Kṛṣṇa, and again you extol yoga. Of these two, which is the better one? Explain this in a definitive way to me.

śrībhagavān uvāca

2. *saṁnyāsaḥ karmayogaś ca ca niḥśreyasakarāvubhau* |
   tayostu karmasaṁnyāsāt karmayogo viśiṣyate ||

The Beautiful Lord said:
Renunciation of work and work done in yoga (Karma yoga) both give the highest joy. Of the two, the yoga of action is better than the renunciation of action.

3. *jñeyaḥ sa nityasaṁnyāsī yo na dveṣṭi nakāṅkṣati* |
   nirdvandvo hi mahābāho sukhaṁ bandhāt pramucyate ||

One who neither hates nor covets is to be known as the perpetual saṁnyāsīn. Truly free of the pairs of opposites, O Mighty Armed Arjuna. They are easily released from bondage.

4. *sāṁkhyayogau pṛthāg bālāḥ pravadanti na paṇḍitāḥ* |
   ekam apyāsthitaḥ samyag ubhayor vindate phalam ||

The childish declare that Sāṁkhya and yoga are different, not the paṇḍits. Practicing either correctly, one finds the fruit of both.

5. *yat sāṁkhyaiḥ prāpyate sthānaṁ tadyogairapi gamyate* |
ekaṁ sāṁkhyañca yogañca yaḥ paśyati sa paśyati ||

The place attained by practitioners of Sāṁkhya is attained by practitioners of yoga. Sāṁkhya and yoga are one. One who sees this, really sees.

6. *saṁnyāsastu mahābāho duḥkhamāptumayogataḥ* |
yogayukto munirbrahma na cireṇādhigacchati ||

But saṁnyāsa (renunciation), O Mighty Armed Arjuna, is hard to gain without yoga. The sage (muni) focused in yoga reaches Brahman quickly.

7. *yogayukto viśuddhātmā vijitātmā jitendriyaḥ* |
sarvabhūtāmabhūtātmā kurvann api na lipyate ||

One focused in yoga who is purified in themselves, whose self has been won over with the senses controlled and whose True Self is the self of all beings, is not defiled by acting even when acting.

8. *naiva kiñcit karomīti yukto manyeta tattvavit* |
paśyan śṛṇvan spṛśañ jighrann aśnan gacchan svapañ śvasan ||

The knower of truth, linked in yoga, thinks, "I am not doing anything" even in seeing, hearing, touching, smelling, eating, walking, sleeping, breathing.

9. *pralapan visṛjan gṛhṇann unmiṣan nimiṣann api* |
indriyāṇīndriyārtheṣu vartanta iti dhārayan ||

When talking, excreting, grasping, opening the eyes, closing the eyes, they believe that only the senses are engaged with the objects of the senses.

10. *brahmaṇyādhāya karmāṇi saṅgaṁ tyaktvā karoti yaḥ* |
lipyate na sa pāpena padmapattram ivāmbhasā ||

One who places (their) actions into Brahman, releasing all attachments, is not defiled by wickedness or misdeeds any more than a lotus leaf by water.

11. *kāyena manasā buddhyā kevalairindriyairapi |*
yoginaḥ karma kurvanti saṅgaṁ tyaktvātmaśuddhaye ||

The yogīs do actions with merely the body, the mind, the intelligence, or even just the senses. (Having released attachment for the sake of self-purification.)

12. *yuktaḥ karmaphalaṁ tyaktvā śāntimāpnoti naiṣṭhikīm |*
ayuktaḥ kāmakāreṇa phale sakto nibadhyate ||

One who is linked in yoga, having released the fruits of actions, reaches complete peace. One who is not linked in yoga is attached to the fruits of action and is bound by desire.

13. *sarvakarmāṇi manasā saṁnyasyāste sukhaṁ vaśī |*
navadvāre pure dehī naiva kurvan na kārayan ||

Placing down all actions with the mind, the embodied one sits happily like a ruler in the city of nine gates, not acting and not causing action.

14. *na kartṛtvaṁ na karmāṇi lokasya sṛjati prabhuḥ |*
na karmaphalasaṁyogaṁ svabhāva stu pravartate ||

The primordial self, the Lord, does not make the means of action, the actions of creatures, nor the link between action and its fruit. Nature does all of these spontaneously.

15. *nādatte kasyacit pāpaṁ na caiva sukṛtaṁ vibhuḥ |*
ajñānenāvṛtaṁ jñānaṁ tena muhyanti jantavaḥ ||

The all-pervading does not accept the evil or the good actions of anyone. Wisdom is enveloped by ignorance, that by which living beings are deluded.

16. *jñānena tu tada jñānaṁ yeṣāṁ naśitam ātmanaḥ |*
teṣām ādityavaj jñānaṁ prakāśayati tat param ||

But for those whose ignorance of the self is destroyed by knowledge, their knowledge allows the supreme to shine like the sun.

17. *tadbuddhayas tadātmānas tanniṣṭhās tatparāyaṇāḥ |*
gacchantyapunarāvṛttiṁ jñānanirdhūtakalmaṣāḥ ||

Those whose intelligence is that knowledge, whose whole self is that, whose foundation is that, who hold that as the highest, they go to the end of rebirth, their faults washed away by knowledge.

18. *vidyāvinayasampanne brāhmaṇe gavi hastini* |
śuni caiva śvapāke ca paṇḍitāḥ samadarśinaḥ ||

The wise paṇḍits see equally a wise well-practiced Brahman, a cow, an elephant, a dog, or an outcast.

19. *ihaiva tairjitaḥ sargo yeṣāṁ sāmye sthitaṁ manaḥ* |
nirdoṣaṁ hi samaṁ brahma tasmād brahmaṇi te sthitāḥ ||

Even here on earth, rebirth is overcome by those whose mind is abiding in impartiality (equality). Brahman is flawless and equal to all, hence they are all abiding in Brahman.

20. *na prahṛṣyet priyaṁ prāpya nodvijet prāpya cāpriyam* |
sthirabuddhir asaṁmūḍho brahmavid brahmaṇi sthitaḥ ||

One should not rejoice when getting the desired nor shudder when the unwanted comes. The knower of Brahman with steady intelligence and undeluded is abiding in Brahman.

21. *bāhyasparśeṣvasaktātmā vindatyātmani yat sukham* |
sa brahmayogayuktātmā sukham akṣayam aśnute ||

One whose self (ātman) is not holding on to the touching of external contacts, who finds joy in the self (ātman), whose self (ātman) is united with Brahman in yoga attains indestructible joy.

22. *ye hi saṁsparśajā bhogā duḥkhayonaya eva te* |
ādyantavantaḥ kaunteya nā teṣu ramate budhaḥ ||

Pleasures born of merely the contact with sense objects are the wombs of suffering; they have a beginning and an end, Son of Kuntī. The awakened (*budhaḥ*) is not satisfied with them.

23. *śaknotīhaiva yaḥ soḍhuṁ prāk śarīravimokṣaṇāt* |
kāmakrodhodbhavaṁ vegaṁ sa yuktaḥ sa sukhī naraḥ ||

One who can, here on earth before giving up the body, be patient with the agitations of lust and anger, that one is steady in yoga and is a happy person.

24. *yo 'ntaḥsukho 'ntarārāmas tathāntarjyotir eva yaḥ* |
sa yogī brahmanirvāṇaṁ brahmabhūto 'dhigacchati ||

One whose happiness is within, whose delight is within, and therefore who has internal radiance, such a yogī attains Brahman-nirvāṇa, the absorption in Brahman.

25. *labhante brahmanirvāṇaṁ ṛṣayaḥ kṣīṇakalmaṣāḥ* |
chinnadvaidhā yatātmānaḥ sarvabhūtahite ratāḥ ||

The seers whose impurities are gone, whose dualities (doubts) have been severed, and who delight in the welfare of all beings attain Brahman-nirvāṇa.

26. *kāmakrodhaviyuktānāṁ yatīnāṁ yatacetasām* |
abhito brahmanirvāṇaṁ vartate viditātmanām ||

Brahman-nirvāṇa lies close to the knowers of the self, to the ascetics of subdued mind, unyoked from lust and anger.

27. *sparśān kṛtvā bahir bāhyāṁś cakṣuścai 'vantare bhruvoḥ* |
prāṇāpānau samau kṛtvā nāsābhyantaracāriṇau ||

Having excluded exterior contacts and placing the gaze between the eyebrows, making the prāṇa (inhalation) and the apāna (exhalation) move equally through the nostrils.

28. *yatendriyamanobuddhir munir mokṣaparāyaṇaḥ* |
vigatecchābhayakrodho yaḥ sadā mukta eva saḥ ||

The sage who holds liberation as the highest, whose senses, mind, and intelligence are controlled and from whom desire, fear, and anger are gone, is always free.

29. *bhoktāraṁ yajñatapasāṁ sarvalokamaheśvaram* |
suhṛdaṁ sarvabhūtānāṁ jñātvā māṁ śāntimṛcchati ||

Knowing Me as the enjoyer of sacrifices and austerities, as the great lord of all the worlds, and the beloved friend of all beings the sage attains peace.

Chapter 6

ṣrībhagavān uvāca
1. *anāśritaḥ karmaphalaṁ kāryaṁ karma karoti yaḥ* |
sa saṁnyāsī ca yogī ca na niragnir na cākriyaḥ ||

The Beautiful Lord said:
One who does the work that needs to be done, not needing the fruit of those actions, is a saṁnyāsī and a yogī. Not one who lights no (sacred) fire and does no (ritual) works.

2. *yaṁ saṁnyasamiti prāhur yogaṁ taṁ viddhi pāṇḍava* |
na hy asaṁnyastasaṁkalpo yogī bhavati kaścana ||

What they call saṁnyāsa, know that to be yoga, Son of Pāṇḍu. Certainly without the saṁnyāsa (placing down) of the imagined intention no one at all becomes a yogī.

3. *ārurukṣor muner yogaṁ karma kāraṇam ucyate* |
yogārūḍhasya tasyaiva śamaḥ kāraṇam ucyate ||

Work is said to be the method for the sage who wants to ascend to yoga. For one having ascended to yoga, calm clarity (*śamah*) is said to be the means.

4. *yadā hi nendriyārtheṣu na karmasvanuṣajjate* |
sarvasaṁkalpasaṁnyāsī yogārūḍhas tadocyate ||

When one is not clinging to the objects of the senses nor to actions and is renouncing (placing down) all purpose, then one is said to have ascended to yoga.

5. *uddhared ātmanātmānaṁ nātmānam avasādayet |*
ātmaiva hyātmano bandhur ātmaiva ripur ātmanaḥ ||

One should lift up the self by the self, not push down the self. Indeed the self alone is the friend of the self, and only the self is the enemy of the self.

6. *bandhur ātmātmanas tasya yenātmaivātmanā jitaḥ |*
anātmanas tu śatrutve vartetātmaiva śatruvat ||

By one who has mastered the self by the self, the self is a friend of the self. For one whose self is not mastered, the self stays hostile like an enemy.

7. *jitātmanaḥ praśāntasya paramātmā samāhitaḥ |*
śītoṣṇasukhaduḥkheṣu tathā mānāpamānayoḥ ||

For the peaceful one whose self is subdued, the higher self is integrated (steadfast) and composed in cold and heat, in happiness and suffering, and in honor and dishonor.

8. *jñānavijñānatṛptātmā kūṭastho vijitendriyaḥ |*
yukta ityucyate yogī samaloṣṭāśmakāñcanaḥ ||

The yogī whose self is satisfied by both knowledge as wisdom and contextual specific knowledge, who is unchanging with the senses tamed, for whom a clod of earth, a stone, and gold are the same is said to be integrated in yoga.

9. *suhṛnmitrāyudāsīna madhyasthadveṣyabandhuṣu |*
sādhuṣvapi ca pāpeṣu samabuddhir viśiṣyate ||

One not biased toward companion, friend, or enemy, standing in the middle between haters and supporters, equally mindful among the good and even the evil is preeminent among humans.

10. *yogī yuñjīta satatam ātmānaṁ rahasi sthitaḥ |*
ekākī yatacittātmā nirāśīr aparigrahaḥ ||

The yogī should continuously focus on the true ātman established privately and alone, with the mind and body concentrated, free of aspiration and without grasping anything in any direction.

11. *śucau deśe pratiṣṭhāpya sthiram āsanam ātmanaḥ |*
nātyucchritaṁ na 'tinīcaṁ cailājinakuśottaram ||

The yogī should place in a clean area a stable seat for themselves, neither too high nor too low, covered with kuśa grass, a deerskin, and a cloth.

12. *tatratikāgraṁ manaḥ kṛtvā yatacittendriyakriyaḥ |*
upaviśyāsane yuñjyād yogamātmaviśuddhaye ||

There, having sat on the āsana and having turned the mind toward a single object, minding thoughts and the activity of the senses, one should link to yoga for the purification of self.

13. *samaṁ kāyaśirogrīvaṁ dhārayann acalaṁ sthiraḥ |*
saṁprekṣya nāsikāgraṁ svaṁ diśaścānavalokayan ||

Holding erect the body, the head, and the neck, unmoving and steady, gazing at the end of one's own nose, and not looking all around in different directions.

14. *praśāntātmā vigatabhīr brahmacārivrate sthitaḥ |*
manaḥ saṁyamya maccitto yukta āsīta matparaḥ ||

With self made peaceful, with fear gone, observing a vow of celibacy, with the mind collected and thinking of Me, one should sit focused and devoted to Me.

15. *yuñjann evaṁ sadātmanaṁ yogī niyatamānasaḥ |*
śāntiṁ nirvāṇaparamāṁ matsaṁsthām adhigacchati ||

In this way the yogī, whose mind is integrated and always connecting with the true ātman, goes to clarity, the highest nirvāṇa, abiding with Me.

16. *nātyaśnatas tu yogo 'sti na caikāntam anaśnataḥ |*
na cātisvapnaśīlasya jāgrato naiva cārjuna ||

Yoga is not eating too much and it is certainly not fasting too much; not the practice of oversleeping and not staying awake too much, Arjuna.

17. *yuktāhāravihārasya yuktaceṣṭaysa karmasu |*
yuktasvapnāvabodhasya yogo bhavati duḥkhahā ||

For one who is moderate in food and play, mindfully linked to the performance of actions, balanced in sleeping and waking, yoga is the cessation of suffering.

18. *yadā viniyataṁ cittam ātmany evāvatiṣṭhate |*
niḥspṛhaḥ sarvakāmebhyo yukta ityucyate tadā ||

When the intelligence is precisely applied and one is abiding in the true ātman, free from all craving arising from desire, then one is said to be linked up (in yoga).

19. *yathā dīpo nivātastho neṅgate sopamā smṛtā |*
yogino yatacittasya yuñjato yogam ātmanaḥ ||

The comparison is remembered that as the flame of the lamp in a windless place does not flicker, such is the integrated mind of the yogī practicing the yoga of the ātman.

20. *yatroparamate cittaṁ niruddhaṁ yogasevaya |*
yatra caivātmanātmānaṁ paśyann ātmani tuṣyati ||

When the mind pauses, suspended by the attentive practice (service or *seva*) of yoga; when indeed the ātman is beheld by the ātman, one is completely satisfied by the ātman.

21. *sukham ātyantikaṁ yat tad buddhigrāhyam atīndriyam |*
vetti yatra na caivāyaṁ sthitaścalati tattvataḥ ||

Knowing this endless delight held by the intelligence (buddhi) and beyond the senses, this one knows and, so grounded, does not waiver from the truth.

22. *yaṁ labdhvā cāparaṁ lābhaṁ manyate nādhikaṁ tataḥ |*
yasmin sthito na duḥkhena guruṇāpi vicālyate ||

Gaining that, one thinks there is no greater gain. Established in this, one is not shaken even by heavy sorrow.

23. *taṁ vidyād duḥkhasaṁyoga viyogaṁ yogasaṁjñitam |*
sa niścayena yoktavyo yogo 'nirviṇṇacetasā ||

Let it be known that the unlinking of the union with suffering is known as yoga. This yoga is to be practiced with confident determination and an enthusiastic heart.

24. *saṅkalpaprabhavān kāmāṁs tyaktvā sarvān aśeṣataḥ* |
manasaivendriyagrāmaṁ viniyamya samantataḥ ||

Letting go, without any exceptions, of all desires born of selfish intention (saṅkalpa), and with the mind precisely monitoring the aggregate of all the senses on all sides.

25. *śanaiḥśanairuparamed buddhyā dhṛtigṛhītaya* |
ātmasaṁsthaṁ manaḥ kṛtvā na kiñcid api cintayet ||

Slowly, slowly, step-by-step one should become quiet by means of the intelligence being firmly grounded. Having established the mind in the ātman, one should not think of anything.

26. *yato yato niścarati manaś cañcalam asthiram* |
tatastato niyamyaitad ātmany eva vaśaṁ nayet ||

When and wherever the ungrounded wavering mind wanders, from there one should lead it back to the domain of the ātman.

27. *praśāntamanasaṁ hyenaṁ yoginaṁ sukham uttamam* |
upaiti śāntarajasaṁ brahmabhūtam akalmaṣam ||

Indeed, such a one, the yogī, with the mind at peace, goes to the highest happiness, with passions pacified, without any ill intent, united with Brahman.

28. *yuñjann evaṁ sadātmānaṁ yogī vigatakalmaṣaḥ* |
sukhena brahmasaṁsparśam atyantaṁ sukham aśnute ||

Always linking into the self, freed from evil, the yogī reaches boundless happiness, easily touching Brahman.

29. *sarvabhūtastham ātmānaṁ sarvabhūtāni cātmani* |
īkṣate yogayuktātmā sarvatra samadarśanaḥ ||

Seeing the ātman abiding in all beings and all beings in the ātman, the self linked in yoga sees the same everywhere.

30. *yo māṁ paśyati sarvatra sarvaṁ ca mayi paśyati |*
tasyāhaṁ na praṇaśyāmi sa ca me na praṇaśyati ||

One who sees Me everywhere, who sees all in Me; I am not lost to that one and that one is not lost to Me.

31. *sarvabhūtasthitaṁ yo māṁ bhajat yekatvam āsthitaḥ |*
sarvathā vartamāno 'pi sa yogī mayi vartate ||

Established in oneness adoring Me abiding in all beings, in whatever way turning or acting, the yogī dwells in Me.

32. *ātmaupamyena sarvatra samaṁ paśyati yo 'rjuna |*
sukhaṁ vā yadi vā duḥkhaṁ sa yogī paramo mataḥ ||

One who, with empathy and compassion within themselves, sees all things equally, whether it is happiness or suffering, is considered to be the highest yogī.

arjuna uvāca
33. *yo 'yaṁ yogas tvayā proktaḥ sāmyena madhusūdana |*
etasyāhaṁ na paśyāmi cañcalatvāt sthitiṁ sthirām ||

Arjuna said:
This yoga of equal mind taught by you, O Slayer of Madhu, I see no lasting foundation for it because the mind is so unstable.

34. *cañcalaṁ hi manaḥ kṛṣṇa pramāthi balavad dṛḍham |*
tasyāhaṁ nigrahaṁ manye vāyor iva suduṣkaram ||

The mind is certainly always wavering, O Kṛṣṇa, troubling, strong, and stubborn. I think it is as difficult to control as the wind (*vāyu*).

śrībhagavān uvāca
35. *asaṁśayaṁ mahābāho mano durnigrahaṁ calam |*
abhyāsena tu kaunteya vairāgyeṇa ca gṛhyate ||

The Beautiful Lord said:
There is no doubt, O Mighty Armed, the mind is hard to contain and is always wavering—but, O Son of Kuntī, by continuous practice (abhyāsa) and releasing (vairāgyam) it can be held.

36. *asaṁyatātmanā yogo duṣprāpa iti me matiḥ* |
vaśyātmanā tu yatatā śakyo 'vāptum upāyataḥ ||

I think yoga is difficult to grasp when there is no continued focus on the ātman, but by resolute attention to the ātman, yoga is attainable by skillful means.

arjuna uvāca
37. *ayatiḥ śraddhayopeto yogāc calitamānasaḥ* |
aprāpya yogasaṁsiddhiṁ kāṁ gatiṁ kṛṣṇa gacchati ||

Arjuna said:
One who is uncontrolled, but who has faith (śraddhā), whose mind has wandered away from yoga, who does not attain perfection in yoga, which path do they take, O Kṛṣṇa?

38. *kaccin nobhayavibhraṣṭaś chinnābhram iva naśyati* |
apratiṣṭho mahābāho vimūḍho brahmaṇaḥ pathi ||

Is it not true that they have fallen from both paths, lost like a disintegrating cloud, without any ground and bewildered in the path of Brahman?

39. *etan me saṁśayaṁ kṛṣṇa chettum arhasy aśeṣataḥ* |
tvadanyaḥ saṁśayasyāsya chettā na hy upapadyate ||

This is my doubt, O Kṛṣṇa. You are able to dispel it without any remainder. Besides you, no other dispeller of doubt exists.

śrībhagavān uvāca
40. *pārtha naiveha nāmutra vināśastasya vidyate* |
na hi kalyāṇakṛt kaścid durgatiṁ tāta gacchati ||

The Beautiful Lord said:
O Pārtha neither here on earth nor in heaven above is there destruction for them. No one who does virtuous good, my friend, is on the path of grief.

41. *prāpya puṇyakṛtāṁ lokān uṣitvā śāśvatīḥ samāḥ* |
śucīnāṁ śrīmatāṁ gehe yogabhraṣṭo 'bhijāyate ||

Having reached the worlds of the virtuous and dwelling there for endless years, the one who fell from yoga is born in the house of the joyous and the illustrious.

42. *athavā yoginām eva kule bhavati dhīmatām* |
etad dhi durlabhataraṁ loke janma yad īdṛśam ||

Or one appears in the family of wise yogīs. Such a birth in the world is more difficult to obtain.

43. *tatra taṁ buddhisaṁyogaṁ labhate paurvadehikam* |
yatate ca tato bhūyaḥ saṁsiddhau kurunandana ||

There the interlinking of the yoga of intelligence derived from the former incarnation awakens and one strives on once again toward perfection, O Joy of the Kurus.

44. *pūrvābhyāsena tenaiva hriyate hy avaśo 'pi saḥ* |
jijñāsur api yogasya śabdabrahmātivartate ||

Through previous practice, pulled irresistibly on through the heart, even against intentions (the will). Even the mere inquirer into yoga goes beyond Vedic ritual.

45. *prayatnād yatamānas tu yogī saṁśuddhakilbiṣaḥ* |
anekajanmasaṁsiddhas tato yāti parāṁ gatim ||

From continuous exertion and guiding the mind, the yogī is totally cleansed of impurities and through many lifetimes is successful, and then attains the highest goal.

46. *tapasvibhyo 'dhiko yogī jñānibhyo 'pi mato 'dhikaḥ* |
karmibhyaś cādhiko yogī tasmād yogī bhavārjuna ||

The yogī goes beyond the ascetics, is thought to be beyond the learned, the wise, and is beyond the doer of sacrificial ritual. Therefore be a yogī, Arjuna!

47. *yoginām api sarveṣāṁ madgatenāntarātmanā* |
śraddhāvān bhajate yo māṁ sa me yuktatamo mataḥ ||

Of all these yogīs, one who has gone to Me with their innermost self, who adores Me with complete trust, is considered by Me to be the most linked to Me.

Chapter 7

śrībhagavān uvāca

1. *mayyāsaktamanāḥ pārtha yogaṁ yuñjan madāśrayaḥ* |
asaṁśayaṁ samagraṁ māṁ yathā jñāsyasi tac chṛṇu ||

The Beautiful Lord said:
Son of Pṛthā, with the mind absorbed in Me, practicing yoga, taking refuge in Me, you will, without a doubt, know Me fully. Now hear how.

2. *jñānaṁ te 'haṁ savijñānam idaṁ vakṣyāmyaśeṣataḥ* |
yaj jñātvā neha bhūyo 'nyaj jñātavyamavaśiṣyate ||

I will explain to you this knowledge (jñāna) and this discriminating knowledge (*vijñāna*) completely, without any residue; by understanding these, nothing beyond remains to be known here.

3. *manuṣyāṇaṁ sahasreṣu kaścid yatati siddhaye* |
yatatām api siddhānāṁ kaścin māṁ vetti tattvataḥ ||

Among thousands of people maybe one reaches for perfection; of those so endeavoring and even of those perfected, scarcely one knows Me in truth.

4. *bhūmir āpo 'nalo vāyuḥ khaṁ mano buddhir eva ca* |
ahaṁkāra itīyaṁ me bhinnā prakṛtir aṣṭadhā ||

Earth, water, fire, air, space, mind, intelligence, and the ego function, this is the eightfold division of my prakṛti (creative energy).

5. *apareyam itas tvanyāṁ prakṛtiṁ viddhi me parām |*
jīvabhūtāṁ mahābāho yayedaṁ dhāryate jagat ||

This is my lower prakṛti. But know my other prakṛti, the higher, the individual beings, O Mighty Armed, by which this world is held.

6. *etadyonīni bhūtāni sarvāṇīty upadhāraya |*
ahaṁ kṛtsnasya jagataḥ prabhavaḥ pralayastathā ||

Understand that this forms the wombs for all beings. I am the birth and also the dissolution of the entire world.

7. *mattaḥ parataraṁ nānyat kiñcid asti dhanañjaya |*
mayi sarvam idaṁ protaṁ sūtre maṇigaṇā iva ||

There is nothing at all higher than Me, O Winner of Wealth. All of this is strung upon Me as jewels are strung on a thread.

8. *raso 'ham apsu kaunteya prabhāsmi śaśisūryayoḥ |*
praṇavaḥ sarvavedeṣu śabdaḥ khe pauruṣaṁ nṛṣu ||

I am the taste of water, Son of Kuntī, I am the light of the moon and the sun. I am the syllable (Oṁ) in all the Vedas, the sacred sound of space and the virility in men.

9. *puṇyo gandhaḥ pṛthivyāṁ ca tejaścāsmi vibhāvasau |*
jīvanaṁ sarvabhūteṣu tapaścāsmi tapasviṣu ||

I am the sacred fragrance of the earth, the brilliant splendor of the sun, the individual life in all beings, and the austerity of ascetics.

10. *bījaṁ māṁ sarvabhūtānāṁ viddhi pārtha sanātanam |*
buddhir buddhimatām asmi tejas tejasvinām aham ||

Know Me to be the original, primeval seed of all beings, Son of Pṛthā. I am the intelligence of the intelligent and the radiance of the radiant.

11. *balaṁ balavatāṁ cāham kāmarāgavivarjitam |*
dharmāviruddho bhūteṣu kāmo 'smi bharatarṣabha ||

I am the power of the powerful, freed from lust and passion. In beings I am erotic love consistent with dharma (which does not oppose the dharma).

12. *ye caiva sāttvikā bhāvā rājasās tāmasāś ca ye |*
matta eveti tān viddhi na tvahaṁ tesu te mayi ||

And whatever those states of being, sattvic (harmonious), rajasic (passionate), tamasic (fixed), know them to be from Me. But I am not affected by them, they are in Me.

13. *tribhir guṇamayair bhāvair ebhiḥ sarvam idaṁ jagat |*
mohitaṁ nābhijānāti mām ebhyaḥ param avyayam ||

This whole world is deluded by these states of being (*bhāvas*) composed of the three guṇas. It does not recognize Me; I am higher than these and imperishable.

14. *daivī hy eṣā guṇamayi mama māyā duratyayā |*
mām eva ye prapadyante māyām etāṁ taranti te ||

Divine indeed is my guṇa-composed māyā and very hard to go beyond. Only those who take refuge in Me cross over this divine illusion.

15. *na māṁ duṣkṛtino mūḍhāḥ prapadyante narādhamāḥ |*
māyayāpahṛtajñānā āsuraṁ bhāvam āśritāḥ ||

Rascals, fools, the worst of humans, those whose knowledge has been taken away by illusion and who resort to the nature of demons do not take refuge in me.

16. *caturvidhā bhajante māṁ janāḥ sukṛtino 'rjuna |*
ārto jijñāsur arthārthī jñānī ca bharatarṣabha ||

Of benevolent people four types adore Me, Arjuna: the distressed, the inquisitive seeker of knowledge, the seeker of wealth, and the wise, O Bull of the Bharatas.

17. *teṣāṁ jñānī nityayukta ekabhaktir viśiṣyate |*
priyo hi jñānino 'tyartham ahaṁ sa ca mama priyaḥ ||

Of all those, the one always linked in yoga, and loving but the one alone, this one alone is the best. I am extraordinarily fond of the wise one (jñānī) and that one is fond of Me.

18. *udārāḥ sarva evaite jñānī tvātmaiva me matam |*
āsthitaḥ sa hi yuktātmā mām evānuttamāṁ gatim ||

All of these are indeed exalted, but the wise one (jñānī) is thought to be my very self. Steadfastly linked to the self, this one abides in Me as the supreme way.

19. *bahūnāṁ janmanām ante jñānavān māṁ prapadyate |*
vāsudevaḥ sarvam iti sa mahātmā sudurlabhaḥ ||

At the end of many births the wise one takes full refuge in Me, knowing "Vāsudeva (Kṛṣṇa) is all." Such a great being is hard to find.

20. *kāmais taistair hṛtajñānāḥ prapadyante 'nyadevatāḥ |*
taṁ taṁ niyamam āsthāya prakṛtyā niyatāḥ svayā ||

Those whose knowledge has been stolen by these and those desires, resort to other gods and practice this and that religious ritual, controlled by their own nature (prakṛti).

21. *yo yo yāṁ yāṁ tanuṁ bhaktaḥ śraddhayārcitum icchati |*
tasya tasyācalāṁ śraddhāṁ tām eva vidadhāmy aham ||

Whoever and whomever and whatever and whatever form a devotee desires to honor with faith, I bestow unwavering faith on whomever the devotee is.

22. *sa tayā śraddhyā yuktas tasyā 'rādhanam īhate |*
labhate ca tataḥ kāmān mayaiva vihitān hi tān ||

Yoked with that trusting faith, the devotee desires to satisfy such a one and from it obtains their desires, which are in fact given by Me alone.

23. *antavattu phalaṁ teṣāṁ tad bhavaty alpamedhasām |*
devān devayajo yānti madbhaktā yānti mām api ||

But temporary is this fruit for them of little understanding. The worshippers of the gods go to the gods, but loving Me they surely come to Me.

24. *avyaktaṁ vyaktim āpannaṁ manyante mām abuddhayaḥ |*
paraṁ bhāvam ajānanto mamāvyayam anuttamam ||

Those of no understanding think of Me, unmanifested as falling into manifestation, not knowing my supreme nature imperishable and incomparable.

25. *nāhaṁ prakāśaḥ sarvasya yogamāyāsamāvṛtaḥ* |
mūḍho 'yaṁ nābhijānāti loko mām ajam avyayam ||

I am not visible to all beings wrapped and enveloped by the illusory magic of yoga. This confused world does not recognize Me; unborn, unchangeable.

26. *vedāhaṁ samatītāni vartamānāni cārjuna* |
bhaviṣyāṇi ca bhūtāni māṁ tu veda na kaścana ||

I know those departed, who have passed, and the living, Arjuna, and those yet to come, but not anyone knows Me.

27. *icchādveṣasamutthena dvandvamohena bhārata* |
sarvabhūtāni saṁmohaṁ sarge yānti paraṁtapa ||

By the arising of desire and hate, by the dualities of misperception, O Bhārata, all beings fall into delusion when born, Conqueror of Foe.

28. *yeṣāṁ tv antagataṁ pāpaṁ janānāṁ puṇyakarmaṇām*|
te dvandvamohanirmuktā bhajante māṁ dṛḍharvatāḥ ||

But people whose actions are virtuous, in whom evil has come to an end, free from the dualities of misperception, they adore Me with steady vows.

29. *jarāmaraṇamokṣāya mām āśritya yatanti ye* |
te brahma tad viduḥ kṛtsnam adhyātmaṁ karma cākhilam ||

Those who strive for freedom from old age and death, taking refuge in Me, know entirely Brahman (the primordial self) and action (karma) without any gap.

30. *sādhibhūtādhidaivaṁ māṁ sādhiyajñaṁ ca ye viduḥ* |
prayāṇakāle 'pi ca māṁ te vidur yuktacetasaḥ ||

They who know Me as all of the manifest world and all of the divine functions, as well as the process of sacrifice. With their minds stable in yoga, they know Me at the time of departure.

Chapter 8

arjuna uvāca

1. *kiṁ tadbrahma kim adhyātmaṁ kiṁ karma puruṣottama* |
adhibhūtaṁ ca kiṁ proktam adhidaivaṁ kim ucyate ||

Arjuna said:
What is this Brahman? What is the original self and what is action, O Best of Persons? And what is said to be the primordial domain of the elements, and who is the original divinity?

2. *adhiyajñaḥ kaṭhaṁ ko 'tra dehe 'smin madhusūdana* |
praypāṇakāle ca kaṭhaṁ jñeyo 'si niyatātmabhiḥ ||

How and what is the nature of sacrifice here in this body, O Slayer of Madhu? And how are you to be known at the time of death by the self-controlled?

śrībhagavān uvāca

3. *akṣaraṁ brahma paramaṁ svabhāvo 'dhyātmam ucyate* |
bhūtabhāvodbhavakaro visargaḥ karmasaṁjñitaḥ ||

The Beautiful Lord said:
Brahman is the imperishable, the supreme. The essential nature (*svabhāva*) is the primordial self, which causes the production of all beings. Karma (action) is understood as the creative power.

4. *adhibhūtaṁ kṣaro bhāvaḥ puruṣaś cādhidaivatam* |
adhiyajño 'ham evātra dehe dehabhṛtāṁ vara ||

The primordial domain of elements (adhibhūta) is the perishable existence. The puruṣa (the witness) is the basis of the divine creations. And I myself am all the sacrifices here in the body, O Best of the Embodied.

5. *antakāle ca mām eva smaran muktvā kalevaram* |
yaḥ prayāti sa madbhāvaṁ yāti nāstyatra saṁśayaḥ ||

And at the end of time, remembering Me, having released the body, the one who goes forth comes to my state of being. Here, there is no doubt.

6. *yaṁ yaṁ vāpi smaran bhāvaṁ tyajaty ante kalevaram* |
taṁ tam evaiti kaunteya sadā tadbhāvabhāvitaḥ ||

Moreover, whatever state of being is contemplated or remembered at the releasing of the body at the end, to *that* one goes, O Son of Kuntī, always becoming that state of being.

7. *tasmāt sarveṣu kāleṣu mām anusmara yudhya ca* |
mayy arpitamanobuddhir māmevaiṣyasyasaṁśayaḥ ||

Therefore, at all times, meditate on Me and fight. With mind and intelligence set on Me, you will come to Me without any doubt.

8. *abhyāsayogayuktena cetasā nānyagāminā* |
paramaṁ puruṣaṁ divyaṁ yāti pārthānucintayan ||

O Son of Pṛthā, by engaging in the practice of yoga with the attention not wandering off to another thing, continuously meditating, one comes to the highest, divine consciousness.

9. *kaviṁ purāṇam anuśāsitāram aṇor aṇīyāṁsam anusmared yaḥ* |
sarvasya dhātāram acintyarūpam ādityavarṇaṁ tamasaḥ parastāt ||

One should mindfully meditate on the poet, the ancient, the ruler, more subtle than an atom, the support of all, of unthinkable form, the color of the sun, beyond darkness.

10. *prayāṇakāle manasā 'calena bhaktyā yukto yogabalena caiva* |
bhruvor madhye prāṇam āveśya samyak sa taṁ paraṁ puruṣam upaiti divyam ||

At the time of departure with an unwavering mind, enmeshed in love and with the strength of yoga, having made the prāṇa go correctly to the middle of the eyebrows, this one approaches this supreme, divine consciousness (puruṣa).

11. *yad akṣaraṁ vedavido vadanti viśanti yad yatayo vītarāgāḥ* |
yad icchanto brahmacaryaṁ caranti tat te padaṁ saṁgraheṇa pravakṣye ||

I will explain to you briefly the path the knower of the Vedas call the imperishable, into which ascetics free of passion enter, desiring which, they follow the path of celibacy.

12. *sarvadvārāṇi saṁyamya mano hṛdi nirudhya ca* |
mūrdhnyādhāyātmanaḥ prāṇam āsthito yogadhāraṇām ||

Attending to all of the gates (of the body) and suspending the mind in the heart, having placed one's own prāṇa in the head, established in yogīc concentration.

13. *aum ity ekākṣaraṁ brahma vyāharam mām anusmaran* |
yaḥ prāyāti tyajan dehaṁ sa yāti paramāṁ gatim ||

Saying "Oṁ," the one syllable Brahman, meditating continuously on Me, the one who comes forth while releasing the body goes to the highest path.

14. *anayacetāḥ satataṁ yo māṁ smarati nityaśaḥ* |
tasyāhaṁ sulabhaḥ pārtha nityayuktasya yoginaḥ ||

One who constantly remembers (is mindful of) Me, whose attention does not go to elsewhere, for that one, the yogī ever linked, I am easy to attain, Son of Pṛthā.

15. *mām upetya punarjanma duḥkhālayam aśāśvatam* |
nāpnuvanti mahātmānaḥ saṁsiddhiṁ paramāṁ gatāḥ ||

Having come close to Me, these great beings do not incur another birth in the impermanent abode of suffering, for they have gone to the greatest perfection.

16. *ābrahmabhuvanāllokāḥ punarāvartino 'rjuna* |
mām upetya tu kaunteya punarjanma na vidyate ||

Up to the realm of Brahmā, all the worlds are places of rebirth, Arjuna. But in coming to Me, Son of Kuntī, there is no rebirth to be found.

17. *sahasrayugaparyantam aharyad brahmaṇo viduḥ* |
rātriṁ yugasahasrāntāṁ te 'horātravido janāḥ ||

Those who know that the day of Brahmā lasts for a thousand *yugas* and the night of Brahmā ends after a thousand yugas are the "knowers of the day and night."

18. *avyaktād vyaktayaḥ sarvāḥ prabhavantyaharāgame* |
rātryāgame pralīyante tatraivāvyaktasaṁjñake ||

At the dawn of the day all things manifest from the unmanifest; at the coming of the night they dissolve back there into that known as the unmanifest.

19. *bhūtagrāmaḥ sa evāyaṁ bhūtvā bhūtvā pralīyate* |
rātryāgame 'vaśaḥ pārtha prabhavatyaharāgame ||

This multitude of existences, having risen up again and again, helplessly dissolves at the coming of night, O Pārtha, and then again arises into being at the coming of the day.

20. *paras tasmāt tu bhāvo 'nyo 'vyakto 'vyaktāt sanātanaḥ* |
yaḥ sa sarveṣu bhūteṣu naśyatsu na vinaśyati ||

But there is higher than this unmanifest, a primeval unmanifest, which does not perish when all manifestations perish.

21. *avyakto 'kṣara ityuktas tamāhuḥ paramāṁ gatim* |
yaṁ prāpya na nivartante taddhāma paramaṁ mama ||

This unmanifest they declare as the supreme goal, arriving there they do not return. This is my supreme abode.

22. *puruṣaḥ sa paraḥ pārtha bhaktyā labhyastvananyayā* |
yasyāntaḥsthāni bhūtāni yena sarvam idaṁ tatam ||

This is the highest being (puruṣa), Son of Pṛthā, attained by love and nothing else, in whom all beings stand, by whom all this is pervaded.

23. *yatra kāle tvanāvṛttim āvṛttiṁ caiva yoginaḥ* |
prayātā yānti taṁ kālaṁ vakṣyāmi bharatarṣabha ||

I will tell, O Best of Bhāratas, of this time where in yogīs departing return and the time where they do not return.

24. *agnirjyotirahaḥ śuklaḥ ṣaṇmāsā uttarāyaṇam* |
tatra prayātā gacchanti brahma brahmavido janāḥ ||

Fire, light, day, the bright lunar fortnight, and the six months of the northern path of the sun are when Brahman-knowing people go to Brahman.

25. *dhūmo rātristathā kṛṣṇaḥ ṣaṇmāsā dakṣiṇāyanam* |
tatra cāndramasaṁ jyotir yogī prāpya nivartate ||

Smoke, night, the dark lunar fortnight (kṛṣṇaḥ) and the six months of the southern path of the sun are when the yogī returns gaining the lunar light.

26. *śuklakṛṣṇe gatīhyete jagataḥ śāśvate mate* |
ekayā yātyanāvṛttim anyayāvartate punaḥ ||

These two paths, the light and the dark, are thought to be perpetual in the world. By the first, one goes to not return, by the other, one returns again.

27. *naite sṛtī pārtha jānan yogī muhyati kaścana* |
tasmāt sarveṣu kāleṣu yogayukto bhavārjuna ||

Knowing these two paths, Son of Pṛthā, the yogī is not deluded in any way. Therefore, Arjuna, at all times be firm in yoga.

28. *vedeṣu yajñeṣu tapaḥsu caiva dāneṣu yat puṇyāphalaṁ pradiṣṭam* |
atyeti tat sarvamidaṁ viditvā yogī paraṁ sthānamupaiti cādyam ||

Having known all this the yogī goes beyond the virtuous fruits prescribed by the Vedas, in sacrifices, in austerities, and in gift giving, and arrives at the primordial supreme abode.

Chapter 9

śrībhagavān uvāca

1. *idaṁ tu te guhyatamaṁ pravakṣyāmyanasūyave* |
jñānaṁ vijñānasahitaṁ yajjñātvā mokṣyase 'śubhāt ||

The Beautiful Lord said:
To you, who are without envy and spite, I will explain this ultimate secret of both wisdom (jñāna) and contextual knowledge (vijñāna) together. Knowing which you will be free from evil.

2. *rājavidyā rājaguhyaṁ pavitramidam uttamam* |
pratyakṣāvagamaṁ dharmyaṁ susukhaṁ kartuṁ avyayam ||

This is the royal knowledge, the royal secret, and the ultimate purifier. Its comprehension is of what is right before our eyes, the true dharma (law), pleasant to practice and imperishable.

3. *aśraddahānāḥ puruṣā dharmasyāsya paraṁtapa* |
aprāpya māṁ nivartante mṛtyusaṁsāravartmani ||

People who hold no trust in this dharma, O Scorcher of Foe, do not reach Me and return again to the path of mortality and saṃsāra.

4. *mayā tatam idaṁ sarvaṁ jagadavyaktamūrtinā* |
matsthāni sarvabhūtāni na cāhaṁ teṣvavasthitaḥ ||

This whole world is pervaded by Me in my unmanifested form. All beings dwell within Me and I am not resting in them.

5. *na ca matsthāni bhūtāni paśya me yogamaiśvaram* |
bhūtabhṛn na ca bhūtastho mamātmā bhūtabhāvanaḥ ||

And yet all beings do not dwell in Me. Just see my majestic, mysterious connection. I myself am manifesting all beings, supporting all beings, and not dwelling in all beings.

6. *yathākāśasthito nityaṁ vāyuḥ sarvatrago mahān* |
tathā sarvāṇi bhūtāni matsthānītyupadhāraya ||

As the great wind blowing everywhere, always abides in open space, so all beings abide in Me. Contemplate this!

7. *sarvabhūtāni kaunteya prakṛtiṁ yānti māmikām* |
kalpakṣaye punastāni kalpādau visṛjāmyaham ||

O Son of Kuntī, at the end of a *kalpa* (cosmic cycle) all beings pass into my prakṛti. At the beginning of a kalpa I pour them forth.

8. *prakṛtim svāmavaṣṭabhya visṛjāmi punaḥ punaḥ* |
bhūtagrāmam imaṁ kṛtsnam avaśaṁ prakṛtervaśāt ||

Having animated my own prakṛti, I send forth again and again this whole multitude of beings who are helpless under prakṛti's power.

9. *na ca māṁ tāni karmāṇi nibadhnanti dhanañjaya* |
udāsīnavad āsīnam asaktaṁ teṣu karmasu ||

And these actions do not bind Me, Dhanañjaya (one who is victorious over wealth), like one sitting aside impartially, unattached to these actions.

10. *mayādhyakṣeṇa prakṛtiḥ sūyate sacarācaram* |
hetunānena kaunteya jagad viparivartate ||

With me as the eyewitness prakṛti generates everything animate and inanimate. From this process, O Son of Kuntī, the whole universe revolves.

11. *avajānanti māṁ mūḍhā mānuṣīṁ tanumāśritam* |
paraṁ bhāvamajānanto mama bhūtanaheśvaram ||

Fools despise Me clad in human form, ignorant of my higher nature as the great lord of all beings.

12. *moghāśā moghakarmāṇo moghajñānā vicetasaḥ* |
rākṣasīm āsurīṁ caiva prakṛtiṁ mohinīṁ śritāḥ ||

Clinging to deluded nature, fiendish and demonic, their hopes are futile, their actions fruitless, their knowledge vain, and their judgment gone.

13. *mahātmānas tu māṁ pārtha daivīṁ prakṛtimāśritāḥ* |
bhajantyananyamanaso jñātvā bhūtādim avyayam ||

But great beings, O Pārtha, dwelling in divine prakṛti, single-mindedly adore Me, knowing Me as the imperishable beginning of all beings.

14. *satataṁ kīrtayanto māṁ yatantaśca dṛḍhavratāḥ* |
namasyantaśca māṁ bhaktyā nityayuktā upāsate ||

Always celebrating, singing of Me, striving fully with steady vows, greeting Me with love, continuously engaged, they honor Me.

15. *jñānayajñena cāpyanye yajanto māmupāsate* |
ekatvena pṛthāktvena bahudhā viśvatomukham ||

And others, sacrificing with the sacrifice of knowledge, worship Me as the one and as the many and as the great variety facing all directions.

16. *ahaṁ kraturahaṁ yajñaḥ svadhā 'hamahamauṣadhaṁ* |
mantro 'ham aham evājyam ahamagniraham hutam ||

I am the ceremonial action, I am the sacrifice, I am the offering, I am the medicinal herb, I am the mantra, I am the clarified butter, I am the fire, I am the pouring.

17. *pitā 'ham asya jagato mātā dhātā pitāmahaḥ* |
vedyaṁ pavitram auṅkāra ṛk sāma yajureva ca ||

I am the father of this world, the mother, the grandfather, the object of knowledge, the purifier, the syllable Oṁ, and indeed the Ṛg, Sāma, and Yajur Vedas.

18. *gatirbhartā prabhuḥ sākṣī nivāsaḥ śaraṇaṁ suhṛt* |
prabhavaḥ pralayaḥ sthānaṁ nidhānaṁ bījam avyayam ||

I am the goal, the supporter, the lord, the witness, the home, the refuge, the friend, the origin, the dissolution, the ground, the repository of essence, and the imperishable seed.

19. *tapāmyahamahaṁ varṣaṁ nigṛhṇāmyutsṛjāmi ca* |
amṛtañcaiva mṛtyuśca sadasaccāham arjuna ||

I give off heat. I hold back and send forth the rain, as well as I am immortality and death. I am reality and illusion, Arjuna.

20. *traividyā māṁ somapāḥ pūtapāpā yajñairiṣṭvā svargatiṁ prārthayante* |
te puṇyamāsādya surendralokamnaśnanti divyān divi devabhogān ||

The knowers of the three Vedas, drinking the *soma* juice, cleansed of evil, worship Me with sacrifices seeking the path to heaven. They, the pious, go to the world of Indra. There in the divine heaven they enjoy the pleasures of the gods.

21. *te taṁ bhuktvā svargalokaṁ viśālaṁ kṣīṇe punye martyalokaṁ viśanti* |
evaṁ trayīdharmam anuprapannā gatāgataṁ kāmakāmā labhante ||

Having enjoyed this extensive world of heaven, with their virtue and merit used up, they reenter the world of mortality. Thus, having gone along with the dharma of the three Vedas, desiring objects of enjoyment, they obtain that which comes and goes.

22. *ananyāścintayanto māṁ ye janāḥ paryupāste* |
teṣāṁ nityābhiyuktānāṁ yogakṣemaṁ vahāmyaham ||

Those who adore Me everywhere, their thoughts going to Me and not to another; for them constantly linked in yoga, I carry their maintenance and needs.

23. *ye 'pyanyadevatā bhaktā yajhante 'sraddhayā 'nvitāḥ* |
te 'pi māmeva kaunteya yajantyavidhipūrvakam ||

Even for those who adore other gods, worshipping with great trust but not using traditional rules, they also are worshipping Me, O Son of Kuntī.

24. *ahaṁ hi sarvayajñānāṁ bhoktā ca prabhureva ca* |
nātu mām abhijānanti tattvenātaś cyavanti te ||

I am indeed the enjoyer and lord of all sacrifices. But those not recognizing Me in truth (as "thatness"), they fall.

25. *yānti devavratā devān pitṛn yānti pitṛvratāḥ* |
bhūtāni yānti bhūtejyā yānti madyājino 'pi māṁ ||

Devotees of the gods go to the gods. Devotees of the ancestors go to the ancestors. Those who sacrifice to the spirits go to the spirits. Those who sacrifice to Me come to Me.

26. *patraṁ puṣpaṁ phalaṁ toyaṁ yo me bhaktyā prayacchati* |
tadahaṁ bhaktyupahṛtam aśnāmi prayatātmanaḥ ||

For one who offers to Me with love a leaf, a flower, a fruit, or water, I accept that offering of love, which is from one whose heart is pure.

27. *yat karoṣi yadaśnāsi yajjuhoṣi dadāsi yat* |
yat tapasyasi kaunteya tat kuruṣva madarpaṇam ||

Whatever you do, whatever you eat, whatever you offer in sacrifice, whatever you give, and whatever you perform as austerity, do that, Son of Kuntī, as an offering to Me.

28. *śubhāśubhaphalair evaṁ mokṣyase karmabandhanaiḥ* |
saṁnyāsayogayuktātmā vimukto māmupaiṣyate ||

In this way you will be free from the bonds of action, from its good and evil fruits. With your True Self linked into the yoga of renunciation you will be free and will come to Me.

29. *samo 'haṁ sarvabhūteṣu na me dveṣyo 'sti na priyaḥ* |
ye bhajanti tu māṁ bhaktyā mayi te teṣu cāpyaham ||

I am the same in all beings. There is no one hated or favored by Me. But those who love Me with devotion, they are in Me and I am also in them.

30. *api cet sudurācāro bhajate māmananyabhāk* |
sādhureva sa mantavyaḥ samyag vyavasito hi saḥ ||

If one of vile action adores Me with undivided devotion, they are to be considered as virtuous, for they are correctly resolved.

31. *kṣipraṁ bhavati dharmātmā śaśvacchāntiṁ nigacchati* |
kaunteya pratijānīhi na me bhaktaḥ praṇaśyati ||

They quickly become one whose self is noble and they go to eternal peace. Son of Kuntī, understand that no devotee of mine is ever lost.

32. *māṁ hi pārtha vyapāśritya ye 'pi syuḥ pāpayonayaḥ* |
striyo vaiśyāstathā śūdrās te'pi yānti parāṁ gatim ||

All those who take refuge in Me, O Pārtha, even if they come from demonic wombs and also women, *Vaiśyas*, and *Śūdras* attain the highest goal.

33. *kiṁ punarbrāhmaṇāḥ puṇyā bhaktā rājarṣayas tathā* |
anityamasukhaṁ lokam imaṁ prāpya bhajasva mām ||

What again for the pure true Brāhmans and the devoted royal sages? Having entered this impermanent, unhappy world, devote yourself to Me.

34. *manmanā bhava madbhakto madyājī māṁ namaskuru* |
māmevaiṣyasi yuktvaivam ātmānaṁ matparāyaṇaḥ ||

Establish your mind in Me. To Me be devoted. Give to Me. Make salutations. You will come to Me steady in yoga with Me as the supreme aim into yourself.

Chapter 10

śrībhagavān uvāca

1. *bhūya eva mahābāho śṛṇu me paramaṁ vacaḥ* |
yat te 'haṁ prīyamāṇāya vakṣyāmi hitakāmyayā ||

The Beautiful Lord said:
Hear from Me once again, O Mighty Armed Arjuna, the highest word that I will declare, with a desire for your welfare, to you who are sincerely delighted.

2. *na me viduḥ suragaṇāḥ prabhavaṁ na maharṣayaḥ* |
ahamādirhi devānāṁ maharṣīṇāṁ ca sarvaśaḥ ||

Neither the hosts of gods nor the great seers know my source. Indeed I am the origin of the gods and the great seers in every way.

3. *yo māmajamanādiṁ ca vetti lokamaheśvaram* |
asaṁmūḍhaḥ sa martyeṣu sarvapāpaiḥ pramucyate ||

One who knows Me who is birthless and beginningless, knows the great lord of all worlds. Among mortals that one is undeluded and is released from all evils.

4. *buddhirjñānamasaṁmohaḥ kṣamā satyaṁ damaḥ śamaḥ* |
sukhaṁ duḥkhaṁ bhavo 'bhavo bhāyaṁ cābhayam eva ca ||

Intelligence, knowledge, freedom from delusion, patience, truthfulness, self-control, calm equanimity, happiness and suffering, existence and nonexistence, fear and fearlessness.

5. *ahiṁsā samatā tuṣṭis tapo dānaṁ yaśo 'yaśaḥ* |
bhavanti bhāvā bhūtānāṁ matta eva pṛthagvidhāḥ ||

Nonviolence, impartiality, contentment, austerity, generosity, fame, and ill repute—these many varieties of conditions of all beings arise from Me alone.

6. *maharṣayaḥ sapta pūrve catvāro manavastathā* |
madbhāvā mānasā jātā yeṣāṁ loka imāḥ prajāḥ ||

The primordial seven great seers, also the four Manus (ancestors of all humans) from whom sprang all of the creatures of these worlds, originated from my nature, born from my mind.

7. *etāṁ vibhūtiṁ yogaṁ ca mama yo vetti tattvataḥ* |
so 'vikampena yogena yujyate nātra saṁśayaḥ ||

There is no doubt that one who knows the truth (thatness) of this splendorous connection and power of mine, is united by unwavering yoga.

8. *ahaṁ sarvasya prabhavo mattaḥ sarvaṁ pravartate* |
iti matvā bhajante māṁ budhaḥ bhavasamanvitāḥ ||

I am the manifesting of all. From Me everything unfolds. Comprehending this the awakened ones (budhaḥ) adore Me completely absorbed into deep states of being.

9. *maccittā madgataprāṇā bodhayantaḥ parasparam* |
kathayantaśca māṁ nityaṁ tuṣyanti ca ramanti ca ||

With all their thoughts in Me, with the prāṇas (vital breaths and all sensations) flowing to Me, awakening each other, always conversing about Me, they are content and delighted.

10. *teṣāṁ satatayuktānāṁ bhajatāṁ prītipūrvakam* |
dadāmi buddhiyogaṁ taṁ yena māmupayānti te ||

To those who are continuously devoted and filled with joyous love, I give this yoga of intelligence by which they come to Me.

11. *teṣām evānukampārtham ahamajñānajaṁ tamaḥ* |
nāśayāmyātmabhāvastho jñānadīpena bhāsvatā ||

Out of compassion for them I, dwelling in their hearts, destroy with the shining lamp of wisdom, the darkness born of ignorance.

arjuna uvāca
12. *paraṁ brahma paraṁ dhāma pavitraṁ paramaṁ bhavān* |
puruṣaṁ śāśvatam divyam ādidevamajaṁ vibhum ||

Arjuna said:
Thou art the highest Brahman, the ultimate abode, the supreme purifier, the constant divine pure awareness, the primordial god, birthless and omnipresent.

13. *āhustvāmṛṣayaḥ sarve devarṣir nāradas tathā* |
asito devalo vyāsaḥ svayaṁ caiva bravīṣi me ||

All of the *ṛṣiṣ* (seers) say this of you, and also the divine seer, Nārada, as well as Asita, Devala, Vyāsa, and even you, yourself tell me.

14. *sarvametadṛtaṁ manye yanmāṁ vadasi keśava* |
na hi te bhagavan vyaktiṁ vidurdevā na dānavāḥ ||

I believe all of this that you are telling me is true, O Keśava. Indeed, neither the gods nor the demons understand your manifestation.

15. *svayamevātmanātmānaṁ vettha tvaṁ puruṣottama* |
bhūtabhāvana bhūteśa devadeva jagatpate ||

You alone know yourself through yourself, O Highest Being, the source of welfare for all beings, the lord of all beings, god of gods, shelter of the world.

16. *vaktum arhasyaśeṣeṇa divyā hyātmavibhūtayaḥ* |
yābhirvibhūtibhirlokān imāṁs tvaṁ vyāpya tiṣṭhasi ||

Please describe in all detail the divine self-manifestations by which you penetrate and also dwell within these worlds.

17. *kaṭhaṁ vidyām ahaṁ yogiṁs tvāṁ sadā paricintayan* |
keṣu keṣu ca bhāveṣu cintyo 'si bhagavan mayā ||

O Yogī, how may I know you constantly meditating in all ways all around? In what various aspects are you to be thought of by me, O Opulent One?

18. *vistareṇātmano yogaṁ vibhūtiṁ ca janārdana |*
bhūyaḥ kathaya tṛptirhi śṛṇvato nāsti me 'mṛtam ||

Explain further to me in fine detail, O Janārdana, Kṛṣṇa, the power of manifestation of the self. I am indeed never satiated with listening to this nectar.

śrībhagavān uvāca
19. *hanta te kathayiṣyāmi divyā hyātmavibhūtayaḥ |*
prādhānyataḥ kuruśreṣṭha nāstyanto vistarasya me ||

The Beautiful Lord said:
Look! I will tell you only of the most prominent manifesting forms, Best of the Kurus, for there is no end to my magnitude.

20. *ahamātmā guḍākeśa sarvabhūtāśayasthitaḥ |*
ahamādiśca madhyañca bhūtānām anta eva ca ||

O Guḍākeśa, I am the ātman (True Self) standing in the heart of all beings. I am the beginning, the middle, and also the end of beings.

21. *ādityānāmahaṁ viṣṇur jyotiṣāṁ raviraṁśumān |*
marīcirmarutāmasmi nakṣātrāṇām ahaṁ śaśī ||

Of the Ādityas (Vedic gods) I am Viṣṇu; of lights I am the shining sun. I am Marīci of the Maruts; in the mansions of the stars, I am the moon.

22. *vedānāṁ sāmavedo 'smi devānāmasmi vāsavaḥ |*
indriyāṇām manaścāsmi bhūtānāmasmi cetanā ||

Of the Vedas I am the Sāma Veda; of gods I am Indra; of the senses I am the mind; and in all beings I am consciousness.

23. *rudrāṇāṁ śaṁkaraścāsmi vitteśo yakṣarakṣasām |*
vasūnāṁ pāvakaścāsmi meruḥ śikhariṇām aham ||

Of the Rudras I am Śaṁkara (Maker of Peace); of Yakṣas and Rakṣas I am Kubera (the lord of wealth); of the Vasus I am Agni (fire); and of mountain peaks I am Meru.

24. *purodhasāṁ ca mukhyaṁ māṁ viddhi pārtha bṛhaspatim* |
senānīnāmahaṁ skandaḥ sarasāmasmi sāgaraḥ ||

Of chief priests know Me to be the head, Bṛhaspati, O Son of Pṛthā. Of the commanders of armies I am Skanda (god of war). Of reservoirs of water I am the ocean.

25. *maharṣīṇāṁ bhṛgurahaṁ girāmasmyekamakṣaram* |
yajñānāṁ japayajño 'smi sthāvarāṇāṁ himālayaḥ ||

Of the great seers I am Bhṛgu. Of utterances I am the single syllable (Oṁ). Of sacrifices I am *japayajña* (whispered mantra), and of immovable things, the Himālaya.

26. *aśvatthaḥ sarvavṛkṣāṇāṁ devarṣīṇāñca nāradaḥ* |
gandharvāṇāṁ citrarathaḥ siddhānāṁ kapilo muniḥ ||

Of all trees I am the *aśvattha* (sacred fig) and of the divine seers, Nārada; of the Gandharvas (celestial musicians) I am Citraratha; and of the perfected I am Kapila, the sage.

27. *uccaiḥśravasam aśvāṇāṁ viddhi māmamṛtodbhavam* |
airāvataṁ gajendrāṇāṁ narāṇāñca narādhipam ||

Of horses know Me to be Uccaihśravas, born of nectar; of princely elephants, Āirāvata; and of humans, the monarch.

28. *āyudhānāmahaṁ vajraṁ dhenūnāmasmi kāmadhuk* |
prajanaścāsmi kandarpaḥ sarpāṇāmasmi vāsukiḥ ||

Of weapons I am the lightning bolt; of cows I am the Kāmadhuk (the wish fulfiller). Of progenitors I am Kandarpa (the god of love); of serpents I am Vāsuki.

29. *anantaś cāsmi nāgānāṁ varuṇo yādasāmaham* |
pitṛnāmaryamā cāsmi yamaḥ saṁyamatāmaham ||

Of the divine serpents (Nāgas) I am Ananta (infinity). Of sea creatures I am Varuṇa; and of all the ancestors I am Aryaman. Of enforcers I am Yama (death).

30. *prahlādaścāsmi daityānāṁ kālaḥ kalayatāmaham |*
mṛgāṇāñca mṛgendro 'haṁ vainateyaś ca pakṣiṇām ||

And of the Daityas (the enemies of the gods) I am Prahlāda. Of judges I am time; of beasts I am the lion; and of birds I am the son of Vinatā (Garuda).

31. *pavanaḥ pavatāmasmi rāmaḥ śastrabhṛtāmahaṁ |*
jhaṣāṇāṁ makaraścāsmi srotasāmasmi jāhnavī ||

Of purifiers I am the wind; of wielders of weapons I am Rāma. Of fish I am the shark; of rivers I am Jāhnavī (the Ganges).

32. *sargāṇām ādirantaś ca madhyañcaivāham arjuna |*
adhyātmavidyā vidyānāṁ vādaḥ pravadatāmaham ||

Of creations I am the beginning and the end, and also the middle, Arjuna. Of sciences I am the science of the primordial self. Of those who debate I am the dialectic.

33. *akṣarāṇakāro 'smi dvandvaḥ sāmāsikasya ca |*
ahamevākṣayaḥ kālo dhātā 'haṁ viśvatomukhaḥ ||

Of letters I am the letter *a*, and of the types of compounds I am the copulative dual. Indeed I am endless time; I am the giver, facing all directions.

34. *mṛtyuḥ sarvaharaścāham udbhavaśca bhaviṣyatām |*
kīrtiḥ śrīr vāk ca nārīṇāṁ smṛtirmedhā dhṛtiḥ kṣamā ||

I am all destroying death and the source of all things yet to be. Of feminine things I am good name, prosperity, language, memory, intelligence, stability, and patience.

35. *bṛhatsāma tathā sāmnāṁ gāyatrī chandasāmahaṁ |*
māsānāṁ mārgaśīrṣo 'ham ṛtūnāṁ kusumākaraḥ ||

Of Sāma Veda chants I am the Bṛhatsāma. Of meters I am the Gāyatrī. Of months I am Mārga-śīrṣa, the "Deer Head"; of seasons, the flowery spring.

36. *dyūtaṁ chalayatāmasmi tejastejasvināmaham |*
jayo 'smi vyavasāyo 'smi sattvaṁ sattvavatāmaham ||

I am the gambling of the con artist. I am the splendor of the splendid. I am victory, and I am firm resolve. I am the goodness of the good.

37. *vṛṣṇīnāṁ vāsudevo 'smi pāṇḍavānāṁ dhanañjayaḥ* |
munīnāmapyahaṁ vyāṣaḥ kavīnāmuśanā kaviḥ ||

Of the Vṛṣṇi family I am Vāsudeva (Kṛṣṇa), of the sons of Pāṇḍu I am Dhanañjaya (Arjuna). Also of sages I am Vyāsa; of poets, the poet Uśanā.

38. *daṇdo damayatāmasmi nītirasmi jigīṣatām* |
maunaṁ caivāsmi guhyānāṁ jñānaṁ jñānavatāmaham ||

I am the rod of chastisers. I am diplomacy for those wanting victory, and I am the silence of secrets. I am the wisdom of the wise.

39. *yaccāpi sarvabhūtānāṁ bījaṁ tadahamarjuna* |
na tadasti vinā yat syān mayā bhūtaṁ carācaram ||

And I am that which is the seed of all beings, Arjuna. There is nothing, moving or unmoving, that is without Me.

40. *nānto 'sti mama divyānāṁ vibhūtīnāṁ parantapa* |
eṣa tūddeśataḥ prokto vibhūtervistaro mayā ||

There is no end to my divine manifestations, O Scorcher of the Foe, Arjuna. All of these have been presented by Me as an illustration of limitless manifestation.

41. *yad yad vibhūtimat sattvaṁ śṛīmadūrjitameva vā* |
tattad evāvagaccha tvaṁ mama tejo 'ṁśasaṁbhavam ||

Whatever glorious existence there is, beautiful or even majestic, you should understand in every case it manifests from a fraction of my radiance.

42. *athavā bahunaitena kiṁ jñātena tavārjuna* |
viṣṭabhyāhamidam kṛtsnam ekāṁśena sthito jagat ||

But what to you is all of this detailed knowledge, Arjuna? I constantly support the entire world in any single fraction (of myself).

Chapter 11

arjuna uvāca

1. *madanugrahāya paramaṁ guhyam adhyātmasaṁjñitam* |
yat tvayoktaṁ vacastena moho 'yaṁ vigato mama ||

Arjuna said:
Out of kindness for me the words about the greatest secret known as the Primordial Being were spoken by you. By this the delusion of mine is gone.

2. *bhavāpyayau hi bhūtānāṁ śrutau vistaraśo mayā* |
tvattaḥ kamalapatrākṣa māhātmyamapi cāvyayam ||

The appearance and dissolution of all beings has been heard by me from you in elaborate detail, O Lotus Petal Eyed, and also of your imperishable greatness of being.

3. *evametad yathāttha tvam ātmānaṁ parameśvara* |
draṣṭumicchāmi te rūpam aiśvaraṁ puruṣottama ||

As you have described yourself, so it is, O Ultimate Lord. I want to see your majestic divine form, O Ultimate Pure Being.

4. *manyase yadi tacchakyaṁ mayā draṣṭumiti prabho* |
yogeśvara tato me tvaṁ darśayātmānam avyayam ||

O Lord, if you think it can be experienced, then show to me your imperishable True Self, O Lord of Yoga.

śrībhagavān uvāca

5. *paśya me pārtha rūpāṇi śataśo 'tha sahasraśaḥ* |
nānāvidhāni divyāni nānāvarṇākṛtīni ca ||

The Beautiful Lord answered:
Just look, O Pārtha, at my forms, a hundredfold; by the hundreds, by the thousands, all varieties of types divine, all kinds of colors and shapes.

6. *paśyādityān vasūn rudrān aśvinau marutas tathā* |
bahūnyadṛṣṭapūrvāṇi paśyāścaryāṇi bhārata ||

Behold the Ādityas, the Vasus, the Rudras, the two Aśvins, and the Maruts as well. Behold many wonders never before seen, Bhārata (Arjuna).

7. *ihaikstham jagat kṛtsnaṁ paśyādya sacarācaram* |
mama dehe guḍākeśa yaccānyad draṣṭumicchasi ||

See here standing as one the whole universe with all things moving and unmoving, here together, here in my body, O Guḍākeśa. And whatever else you want to see.

8. *na tu māṁ śakyase draṣṭum anenaiva svaccakṣuṣā* |
divyaṁ dadāmi te cakṣuḥ paśya me yogam aiśvaram ||

But you cannot behold Me with your own eye. I give you the divine eye. Behold my glorious yoga.

sañjaya uvāca

9. *evamuktvā tato rājan mahāyogeśvaro hariḥ* |
darśayāmāsa pārthāya paramaṁ rūpam aiśvaram ||

Sañjaya said:
O King, having spoken this, Hari—the great master of yoga—showed the Son of Pṛthā the supreme glorious form.

10. *anekavaktranayanam anekādbhutadarśanam* |
anekadivyābharaṇaṁ divyānekodyatāyudham ||

Not of one, but many mouths and eyes, many wondrous visions, many divine ornaments, many raised divine weapons.

11. *divyamālyāmbaradharaṁ divyagandhānulepanam |*
sarvāścaryamayaṁ devam anantaṁ viśvatomukham ||

Wearing divine garlands and apparel with divine fragrances and ointments and composed of all wonders, the Lord infinite with faces turned everywhere.

12. *divi sūryasahasrasya bhaved yugapadutthitā |*
yadi bhāḥ sadṛśī sā syād bhāsastasya mahātmanaḥ ||

If a thousand suns rose at once in the sky, such a brilliance might be the splendor of this great being.

13. *tatraikasthaṁ jagat kṛtsnaṁ pravibhaktamanekadhā |*
apaśyaddevadevasya śarīre pāṇḍavastadā ||

There the Pāṇḍava saw in the body of the god of gods the whole world with its countless divisions as one.

14. *tataḥ sa vismayāviṣṭo hṛṣṭaromā dhanañjayaḥ |*
praṇamya śirasā devaṁ kṛtāñjalirabhāṣata ||

Then the Conqueror of Wealth, stunned with awe, all his hair standing on end, bowed his head to the lord with hands folded together.

arjuna uvāca
15. *paśyāmi devāṁstava deva dehe sarvāṁs tathā bhūtaviśeṣasaṅghān |*
brahmāṇamīśaṁ kamalāsanastham ṛṣīṁśca sarvānuragāṁśca divyān ||

Arjuna said:
I see in your body all of the gods and all of the distinct variegated families of beings, the beloved god Brahmā sitting in a lotus flower, and all the true seers and all the divine water serpents.

16. *anekabāhūdaravaktranetraṁ paśyāmi tvāṁ sarvato 'nantarūpam |*
nāntaṁ na madhyaṁ na punastavādiṁ paśyāmi viśveśvara viśvarūpa ||

O Lord, Beloved of the Universe, O Form of the Universe, I do not see your end, your middle, or your beginning. I see you with endless form on all sides, with endless arms, bellies, faces, and eyes.

17. *kirīṭnaṁ gadinaṁ cakriṇañca tejorāśim sarvato dīptimantam* |
paśyāmi tvāṁ durnirīkṣyaṁ samantād dīptānalārkadyutim aprameyam ||

Wearing a crown, holding a club, spinning a discus, a massive radiance shining in all directions, I see you who are difficult to see completely and who are the immeasurable radiance of fire and the sun.

18. *tvamakṣaraṁ paramaṁ veditavyaṁ tvamasya viśvasya paraṁ nidhānam* |
tvaṁavyayaḥ śāśvatadharmagoptā sanātanastvaṁ puruṣo mato me ||

You are the indestructible supreme to be realized. You are the true, highest resting place and refuge of all this. You are the imperishable keeper of the dharma, the eternal law. I think you are the primordial consciousness, the conscious spirit.

19. *anādimadhyāntam anantavīryam anantabāhuṁ śaśisūryanetram* |
paśyāmi tvāṁ dīptahutāśavaktraṁ svatejasā viśvamidaṁ tapantam ||

I see you without beginning, middle, or end, unlimited, infinitely powerful with endless arms, with the moon and the sun as eyes, with your oblation consuming mouth as blazing fire, whose brilliance burns up this world.

20. *dyāvāpṛthivyoridamantaraṁ hi vyāptaṁ tvayaikena diśaśca sarvāḥ* |
dṛṣṭvā 'dbhutaṁ rūpamugraṁ tavedaṁ lokatrayaṁ pravyathitaṁ mahātma ||

Between heaven and earth in all directions, this is filled by you alone. O Great One, seeing this awesome and horrible form of yours, the three worlds tremble.

21. *amī hi tvāṁ surasaṅghā viśanti kecidbhītāḥ prāñjalayo gṛṇanti* |
svastītyuktvā maharṣisiddhasaṅghāḥ stuvanti tvāṁ stutibhiḥ puṣkalābhiḥ ||

Over there communities of gods are entering into you; some terrified, they sing praises with reverent gestures. The hosts of great seers and perfected beings, while calling out "*svastī,*" praise you with abundant, splendorous songs.

22. *rudrādityā vasavo ye ca sādhyā viśve 'śvinau marutaścoṣmapāśca* |
gandharvayakṣāsurasiddhasaṅghā vīkṣante tvāṁ vismitāścaiva sarve ||

The Rudras, the Ādityas, the Vasus, the Sādhyas, the Viśvas, the two Aśvins, the Maruts, and the stream-drinking Ūṣmapās, the communities of the Gandharvas, Yakṣas, Āsuras, and Siddhas all look at you in wonder.

23. *rūpaṁ mahat te bahuvaktranetraṁ mahābāho bahubāhūrupādam* |
bahūdaraṁ bahudaṁṣṭrākarālaṁ dṛṣṭvā lokāḥ pravyathitāstathāham ||

Having seen your great form, O Mighty Armed, all the worlds and I too tremble with its many mouths and eyes, its numberless arms, thighs, and feet, and your form, which has many bellies and mouths gaping with many horrible tusks.

24. *nabhaḥspṛśaṁ dīptamanekavarṇaṁ vyāttānanaṁ dīptaviśālanetram* |
dṛṣṭvā hi tvāṁ pravyathitāntarātmā dhṛtiṁ na vindāmi śamaṁ ca viṣṇo ||

Having seen you touching the sky, blazing with many colors, with gaping, open mouths and gigantic fiery eyes—I am shivering deep through in my very being. I cannot find stability or peace, O Viṣṇu!

25. *daṁṣṭrākarālāni ca te mukhāni dṛṣṭvaiva kālānalasannibhāni* |
diśo na jane na labhe ca śarma prasīda deveśa jagannivāsa ||

Having seen your many mouths filled with tusks, like the fires of time, I have no sense of direction, and I cannot find shelter or comfort. Be merciful, Lord of Gods, Shelter of the Universe!

26. *amī ca tvāṁ dhṛtarāṣṭrasya putrāḥ sarve sahaivāvanipālasaṅghaiḥ* |
bhīṣmo droṇaḥ sūtaputras tathā 'sau sahāsmadīyair api yodhamukhyaiḥ ||

And over there all of the sons of Dhṛtarāṣṭra enter into you. Indeed all of the throngs of kings and rulers too. And there, on our side, Bhīṣma, Droṇa, and Karṇa, the Son of the Charioteer, together with even our own chief warriors.

27. *vaktrāṇi te tvaramāṇā viśanti daṁṣṭrākarālāni bhayānakāni* |
kecidvilagnā daśanāntareṣu saṁdṛśyante cūrṇitair uttamāṅgaiḥ ||

They enter quickly into your many mouths, which are filled with dreadful tusks. Some are seen stuck between the teeth with their heads crushed!

28. *yathā nadīnāṁ bahavo 'mbuvegāḥ samudramevābhimukhā dravanti* |
tathā tavāmī naralokavīrā viśanti vaktrāṇyabhivijvalanti ||

As many torrents of water, rivers, and streams flow to the ocean, so too these heroes of the human world flow into your flaming mouths.

29. *yathā pradīptaṁ jvalanaṁ pataṅgā viśanti nāśāya samṛddhavegāḥ* |
tathaiva nāśāya viśanti lokās tavāpi vaktrāṇi samṛddhavegāḥ ||

Just as moths into a bright light with such speed fly to their destruction, so these worlds quickly enter your mouths to their destruction.

30. *lelihyase grasamānaḥsamantāl lokān samagrān vadanairjvaladbhiḥ* |
tejobhirāpūrya jagat samagraṁ bhāsastavogrāḥ pratapanti viṣṇo ||

You lick and swallow from all directions all of the worlds with flaming mouths. O Viṣṇu, your fierce and terrible brilliance fills and consumes the whole universe with splendor.

31. *ākhyāhi me ko bhavānugrarūpo namo 'stu te devavara prasīda* |
vijñātum icchāmi bhavantamādyaṁ na hi prajānāmi tava pravṛttim ||

Tell me who you are, O Terrible Form. Salutation to you, Finest of Gods. Be kind, merciful. I want to understand you, O Original Being.

śrībhagavān uvāca
32. *kālo 'smi lokakṣayakṛt pravṛddho lokān samāhartumiha pravṛttaḥ* |
ṛte 'pi tvāṁ na bhaviṣyanti sarve ye 'vasthitāḥ pratyanīkeṣu yodhāḥ ||

The Beautiful Lord said:
I am time, the powerful, ripe, mature destruction of the universe, arising here to thoroughly eliminate the worlds. Even without you the warriors arranged in opposing formations shall all cease to be.

33. *tasmāt tvaṁ uttiṣṭha yaśo labhasva jitvā śatrūn bhuṅkṣva rājyaṁ samṛddham |*
māyāivaite nihatāḥ pūrvameva nimittamātraṁ bhava svayasācin ||

Therefore you should stand up and gain glory and honor. Having conquered foes, enjoy a thriving kingdom; they have already been destroyed by me. Be merely the instrument, O Ambidextrous Archer.

34. *droṇañca bhīṣmañca jayadrathañca karnaṁ tathā 'nyānapi yodhavīrān |*
mayā hatāṁstvaṁ jahi mā vyathiṣṭhā yudhyasva jetāsi raṇe sapatnān ||

Droṇa, Bhīṣma, Jayadratha, Karṇa, and the other courageous warriors are already slain by me. Don't be afraid. Slay. Fight. You will defeat the rivals in battle.

sañjaya uvāca
35. *etacchrutvā vacanaṁ keśavasya kṛtāñjalirvepamānaḥ kirīṭī |*
namaskṛtvā bhūya evāha kṛṣṇaṁ sagadgadaṁ bhītabhītaḥ prāṇamya ||

Sañjaya said:
Having heard these words of Keśava (Handsome Hair), the trembling Diademed One made salutations with hands folded in front of his heart. Bowing yet again extremely frightened, he spoke to Kṛṣṇa in a stammering voice.

arjuna uvāca
36. *sthāne hṛṣikeśa tava prakīrtyā jagat prahṛṣyatyanurajyate ca |*
rakṣāṁsi bhītāni diśo dravanti sarve namasyanti ca siddhasaṁghāḥ ||

Arjuna said:
The world rightly rejoices and is delighted by your manifestations. The demons are terrified and run in all directions. The throngs of perfected beings send salutations.

37. *kasmācca te na nameran mahātman garīyase brahmaṇo 'pyādikartre |*
ananta deveśa jagannivāsa tvamakṣaraṁ sadasat tat paraṁ yat ||

And why would they not make homage to you, O Great Being, greater, weightier than Brahmā, the original creator, O Infinite God of Gods, shelter of the universe, you are the imperishable, the real and the unreal and beyond that.

38. *tvamādidevaḥ puruṣaḥ purāṇas tvamasya viśvasya paraṁ nidhānam* |
vettāsi vedyañca parañca dhāma tvayā tataṁ viśvamanantarūpa ||

You are the primordial god, the original person. You are the ultimate refuge of the world. You are the knower and the known, and the ultimate goal and purpose. This world is pervaded by you, O Infinite Form.

39. *vāyuryamo 'gnir varuṇaḥ śaśāṅkaḥ prajāpatistvaṁ prapitāmahaśca* |
namo namaste 'stu sahasrakṛtvaḥ punaśca bhūyo 'pi namo namaste ||

You are Vāyu, Yama, Agni, Varuṇa, Śaśānka, and Prajāpati, lord of all creatures; and you are the primal great-grandfather. Salutations to you a thousand times. Salutations again and then again.

40. *namaḥ purastād atha pṛṣṭhataste namo 'stu te sarvata eva sarva* |
anantavīryāmitavikramastvaṁ sarvaṁ samāpnoṣi tato 'si sarvaḥ ||

Adoration and reverence to you from the front and from behind. Salutations to you, who are all things, from all sides. You are infinite courage and immeasurable power. You envelope and penetrate all things, so you are all; everything.

41. *sakheti matvā prasabhaṁ yaduktaṁ he kṛṣṇa he yādava he sakheti* |
ajānatā mahimānaṁ tavedaṁ mayā pramādāt praṇayena vāpi ||

Thinking as a friend and impetuously saying to you, "Hey Kṛṣṇa, hey Yādava, hey Sakha (my pal)," not knowing your great majesty, through intoxication or even through affection.

42. *yaccāvahāsārthamasatkṛto 'si vihāraśayyāsanabhojaneṣu* |
eko 'thavāpyacyuta tatsamakṣaṁ tat kṣāmaye tvām aham aprameyam ||

And as if for the purpose of joking you were treated without respect while playing or when you were in bed, or seated, or while eating, when alone, O Unshakable One, or even right before the eyes of the others. I ask for your pardon, O Immeasurable One!

43. *pitā 'si lokasya carācarasya tvamasya pūjyaśca gururgarīyān |*
na tvatsamo 'styabhyadhikaḥ kuto 'nyo lokatraye
'pyapratimaprabhāva ||

You are the father of the world, of the moving and the unmoving, to be worshipped and adored by it as the most venerable guru. There is nothing comparable to you in all the three worlds. How could there be another surpassing you, O Incomparable Being?

44. *tasmāt praṇamya praṇidhāya kāyaṁ prasādaye tvāmahamīśamīḍyam |*
piteva putrasya sakheva sakhyuḥ priyaḥ priyāyārhasi deva soḍhum ||

Therefore, making obeisances and prostrating the body, I beg for your indulgence, O Lord to Be Honored. Like a father to a son, a friend to a friend, a lover to a beloved, please be merciful, O Deva.

45. *adṛṣṭapūrvaṁ hṛṣito 'smi dṛṣṭvā bhayena ca pravyathitaṁ mano me |*
tadeva me darśaya deva rūpaṁ prasīda deveśa jagannivāsa ||

I am delighted seeing that which has never before been seen and my mind is trembling with fear. Show me your normal form, O Lord. Be merciful, Beloved of Gods and Shelter of the Worlds.

46. *kirīṭinaṁ gadinaṁ cakrahastam icchāmi tvāṁ draṣṭum ahaṁ tathaiva |*
tenaiva rūpeṇa caturbhujena sahasrabāho bhava viśvamūrte ||

I want to see you wearing your crown, holding your club, and spinning your discus. Become the form with four arms, O Thousand Armed, O Form of All the Worlds.

śrībhagavān uvāca
47. *mayā prasannena tavārjunedaṁ rūpaṁ paraṁ darśitamātmayogāt |*
tejomayaṁ viśvamanantamādyaṁ yanme tvadanyena na
dṛṣṭapūrvam ||

The Beautiful Lord said:
By my grace to you, Arjuna, the supreme form manifested from the yoga of the True Self, luminous, all things, infinite and primordial, never before seen by any, other than you.

48. *na vedayajñādhyayanairna dānair na ca kriyābhir na tapobhirugraiḥ* |
evaṁrūpaḥ śakya ahaṁ nṛloke draṣṭum tvadanyena kurupravīra ||

Not by Vedic sacrifice or chanting, not by giving charity, not by ceremonial acts or by terrible austerities can I be seen with such a form in this human world by anyone else but you, O Hero of the Kurus.

49. *mā te vyathā mā ca vimūḍhabhāvo dṛṣṭvā rūpaṁ ghoramīdṛṅmamedam* |
vyapetabhīḥ prītamanāḥ punastvaṁ tadeva me rūpamidaṁ prapaśya ||

Don't be afraid. Don't be bewitched, seeing this frightening form of mine. Free of fear and cheerful at heart, behold this form of me.

sañjaya uvāca
50. *ityarjunaṁ vāsudevastathoktvā svakaṁ rūpaṁ darśayāmāsa bhūyaḥ* |
āśvāsayāmāsa ca bhītamenaṁ bhūtvā punaḥ saumyavapurmahātmā ||

Sañjaya said:
Having spoken this to Arjuna, Vāsudeva showed his own form again. The Mahātmā, the great being, becoming again gentle, sweet in form, he calmed the terrified Arjuna.

arjuna uvāca
51. *dṛṣṭvedaṁ mānuṣaṁ rūpaṁ tava saumyaṁ janārdana* |
idānīm asmi saṁvṛttaḥ sacetāḥ prakṛtiṁ gataḥ ||

Arjuna said:
Seeing this sweet human form of yours, O Janārdana, I am composed in mind and have returned to my natural state.

śrībhagavān uvāca
52. *sudurdarśamidaṁ rūpaṁ dṛṣṭavānasi yanmama* |
devā apyasya rūpasya nityaṁ darśanakāṅkṣiṇaḥ ||

The Beautiful Lord said:
This form that you have seen Me in is difficult to see. Even the gods are always eager to behold this form.

53. *nāhaṁ vedairna tapasā na dānena na cejyayā |*
śakyaevaṁvidho draṣṭuṁ dṛṣṭavānasi māṁ yathā ||

I cannot be seen as you are seeing Me by the Veda, nor by austerity, nor by giving gifts and not by ritual sacrifice.

54. *bhaktyā tvananyayā śakya ahamevaṁvidho 'rjuna |*
jñātuṁ draṣṭuṁ ca tattvena praveṣṭuṁ ca paraṁtapa ||

By undistracted devotion alone I can be known and seen in this way. And be truly attained, O Paraṁtapa.

55. *matkarmakṛn matparamo madbhaktaḥ saṅgavarjitaḥ |*
nirvairaḥ sarvabhūteṣu yaḥ sa māmeti pāṇḍava ||

One who performs all action for Me, considers Me the goal and loves Me, gives up all attachments and without enmity to any and all beings comes to Me, Son of Pāṇḍu.

Chapter 12

arjuna uvāca

1. *evaṁ satatayuktā ye bhaktās tvāṁ paryupāsate* |
ye cāpyakṣamavyaktaṁ teṣāṁ ke yogavittamāḥ ||

Arjuna said:
Of those continuously engaged, who worship you with love everywhere, and of those who worship the imperishable unmanifest; which of these has the better knowledge of yoga?

śrībhagavān uvāca

2. *mayyāveśya mano ye māṁ nityayuktā upāsate* |
śraddhayā parayopetās te me yuktatamā matāḥ ||

The Beautiful Lord said:
The ones who fix the mind on Me and worship Me continuously yoked, possessed of the highest faith, they are considered the most devoted to Me.

3. *ye tvakṣaram anirdeśyam avyaktaṁ paryupāste* |
sarvatragamacintyañca kūṭastham acalaṁ dhruvam ||

But those who worship the undestroyable, the undefinable, the unmanifest, the all-pervading and unthinkable, the unchanging, the unwavering, the continuous.

4. *saṁniyamyendriyagrāmaṁ sarvatra samabuddhayaḥ* |
te prāpnuvanti māmeva sarvabhūtahite ratāḥ ||

Containing the multitude of the senses, with even-minded intelligence in all directions, rejoicing in the welfare of all beings, indeed they also reach Me.

5. *kleśo 'dhikatarasteṣām avyaktāsaktacetasām* |
avyaktā hi gatirduḥkhaṁ dehavadbhiravāpyate ||

The pain is greater for those whose minds cling to the unmanifest. The goal of the unmanifest is reached with difficulty by embodied beings.

6. *ye tu sarvāṇi karmāṇi mayi saṁnyasya matparāḥ* |
ananyenaiva yogena māṁ dhyāyanta upāsate ||

But those who place down all their actions before Me, holding Me as the highest with undistracted yoga, meditating on Me, honor Me.

7. *teṣāmahaṁ samuddhartā mṛtyusaṃsārasāgarāt* |
bhavāmi na cirāt pārtha mayyāveśitacetasām ||

Those whose thoughts have entered into Me, I soon deliver them from the ocean of the cycles of death, O Pārtha.

8. *mayyeva mana ādhatsva mayi buddhiṁ niveśaya* |
nivasiṣyasi mayyeva ata ūrdhvaṁ na saṁśayaḥ ||

Place the mind in Me alone. Make the intelligence (buddhi) enter Me. Without any doubt, from there onward you will live in Me.

9. *atha cittaṁ samādhātuṁ na śaknoṣi mayi sthiram* |
abhyāsayogena tato māmicchāptuṁ dhanañjaya ||

Now if you are not able to absorb the mind steadily in Me, then seek to reach Me by the practice of yoga, O Dhanañjaya.

10. *abhyāse 'pyasamartho 'si matkarmaparamo bhava* |
madartham api karmāṇi kurvan siddhimavāpsyasi ||

If you are unable to practice, be one whose highest intention is my work (service). Performing work (service) for my sake, you will reach perfection.

11. *athaitadapyaśakto 'si kartuṁ madyogamāśritaḥ* |
sarvakarmaphalatyāgaṁ tataḥ kuru yatātmavān ||

If you are not able to do even this, then act, letting go of the fruits of all actions, depending on my wondrous nature, with the self-controlled.

12. *śreyo hi jñānamabhyāsāj jñānād dhyānaṁ viśiṣyate* |
dhyānāt karmaphalatyāgas tyāgācchāntiranantaram ||

Knowledge is better than practice. Better than knowledge is meditation. Better than meditation is letting go (tyāga) of the fruit of action; from letting go (tyāga) there is immediate peace.

13. *adveṣṭā sarvabhūtānāṁ maitraḥ karuṇa eva ca* |
nirmamo nirahaṁkāraḥ samaduḥkhasukhaḥ kṣamī ||

One who has no hatred for any and all beings, who is friendly and compassionate, free from possessiveness and egotism, equal to pain and pleasure, who is patient.

14. *santuṣṭaḥ satataṁ yogī yatātmā dṛḍhaniścayaḥ* |
mayyarpitamanobuddhir yo madbhaktaḥ sa me priyaḥ ||

Always, a completely content yogī, who is self-controlled, unwavering in resolve, with the mind and the intelligence merged with Me, one who is devoted to Me, is beloved to Me.

15. *yasmān nodvijate loko lokānnodvijate ca yaḥ* |
harṣāmarṣabhayodvegair mukto yaḥ sa ca me priyaḥ ||

From whom the world does not pull back and who does not pull back from the world, who is free of pleasures, impatience, fear, and misery, is also dear to Me.

16. *anapekṣaḥ śucirdakṣa udāsīno gatavyathaḥ* |
sarvārambhaparityāgī yo madbhaktaḥ sa me priyaḥ ||

One who is impartial, pure, dexterous, unprejudiced, untroubled, who has let go of all undertakings and who is devoted to Me, is beloved to Me.

17. *yo na hṛṣyati na dveṣṭi na śocati na kāṅkṣati* |
śubhāśubhaparityāgī bhaktimān yaḥ sa me priyaḥ ||

One who neither rejoices nor hates, who neither grieves nor lusts, who has let go of good and evil, who is filled with love, is dear to Me.

18. *samaḥ śatrau ca mitre ca tathā mānāpamānayoḥ* |
śitoṣṇasukhaduḥkheṣu samaḥ saṅga vivarjitaḥ ||

One who is the same to enemy and to friend and also to their own honor and disgrace, who is alike to cold and heat, happiness and distress, and who is free of attachment.

19. *tulyanindāstutir maunī santuṣṭo yena kenacit* |
aniketaḥ sthiramatir bhaktimān me priyo naraḥ ||

Who is equal to blame and praise, who observes silence, content with anything, who is without a house, with steady judgment, filled with love, this person is dear to Me.

20. *ye tu dharmyāmṛtamidaṁ yathoktaṁ paryupāsate* |
śraddadhānā matparamā bhaktāste 'tīva me priyāḥ ||

Those who follow everywhere this nectar of wisdom just expounded, with trusting faith, having Me as their ultimate aim, such devotees are extremely dear to Me.

Chapter 13

arjuna uvāca
prakṛtiṁ puruṣaṁ caiva kṣetraṁ kṣetrajñam eva ca |
etad veditum icchāmi jñānaṁ jñeyaṁ ca keśava ||

Arjuna said:
Prakṛti and puruṣa, the field and the knower of the field, knowledge and the object of knowledge (the known), these I would like to know, O Keśava.

śrībhagavān uvāca
1. *idaṁ śarīraṁ kaunteya kṣetram ity abhidhīyate* |
etad yo vetti taṁ prāhuḥ kṣetrajña iti tadvidaḥ ||

The Beautiful Lord said:
This body, Son of Kuntī, is said to be the field. That which knows it is declared by the wise to be the knower of the field.

2. *kṣetrajñañ cāpi māṁ viddhi sarvakṣetreṣu bhārata* |
kṣetrakṣetrajñayor jñānaṁ yat taj jñānaṁ mataṁ mama ||

Know Me as the knower of the field in all fields, O Bhārata. Knowledge of the field and the field knower are considered by Me to be true knowledge.

3. *tat kṣetraṁ yac ca yādṛk ca yadvikāri yataśca yat* |
sa ca yo yatprabhāvaś ca tat samāsena me śṛṇu ||

Hear from Me in brief what this field is, of what function, of what various modifications and from where they come, and who the one (knower of the field) is and what its powers are.

4. *ṛṣibhir bahudhā gītaṁ chandobhir vividhaiḥ pṛthak* |
brahmasūtrapadaiś cai va hetumadbhir viniścitaiḥ ||

This has been sung by the great seers distinctly and in many different ways in various sacred hymns and also presented with good, clear reasoning in the *sūtras* of Brahman.

5. *mahābhūtāny ahaṅkāro buddhir avyaktam eva ca* |
indriyāṇi daśai 'kaṁ ca pañca cendriyagocarāḥ ||

The five elements, the I-maker (ego-maker), the intelligence, and the unmanifest, the ten senses, the mind, and the five objects of the senses.

6. *icchā dveṣaḥ sukhaṁ duḥkhaṁ saṁghātaś cetanā dhṛtiḥ* |
etat kṣetraṁ samāsena savikāram udāhṛtam ||

Desire, hatred, happiness and distress, the whole organism, intelligence and courage, this is the field with its capacity for change briefly explained.

7. *amānitvam adambhitvam ahiṁsā kṣāntir ārjavam* |
ācāryopāsanaṁ śaucaṁ sthairyam ātmavinigrahaḥ ||

Lack of pride, absence of deceit, nonviolence, patience, virtue, attending to (sitting beside) a teacher, cleanliness, grounded stability, and self-control.

8. *indriyārtheṣu vairāgyam anahaṅkāra eva ca* |
janmamṛtyujarāvyādhi duḥkhadoṣānudarśanam ||

Letting go of sense objects, absence of egotism and a continuous seeing of the problems of birth, death, old age, disease, and suffering.

9. *asaktir anabhiṣvaṅgaḥ putradāragṛhādiṣu* |
nityaṁ ca samacittatvam iṣṭāniṣṭopapattiṣu ||

Nonattachment, not clinging to children, spouse, house, and so on, and a continuous, even mindfulness of the desired and the undesired.

10. *mayi cā 'nanyayogena bhaktir avyabhicāriṇi* |
viviktadeśasevitvam aratirjanasaṁsadi ||

An unwavering love for Me (using) a single-focused yoga, resorting to secluded places, a distaste for crowds of people.

11. *adhyātmajñānanityatvaṁ tattvajñānārthadarśanam* |
etaj jñānam iti proktam ajñānaṁ yad ato 'nyathā ||

Continual knowing of the primordial ātman, seeing the purpose of knowing the actual truth (*tattva*) is said to be this knowledge. Anything otherwise is ignorance.

12. *jñeyaṁ yat tat pravakṣyāmi yaj jñātvā 'mṛtam aśnute* |
anādimat paraṁ brahma na sat tan nā 'sad ucyate ||

I will explain that which is to be known, knowing which one reaches immortality. It is the beginningless, supreme Brahman, said to be neither permanent nor impermanent (neither sat nor asat).

13. *sarvataḥpāṇipādaṁ tat sarvatokṣiśiromukham* |
sarvataḥśrutimal loke sarvam āvṛtya tiṣṭhati ||

With hands and feet everywhere, eyes, heads, and faces all around, with ears listening everywhere, it stands enveloping all in the world.

14. *sarvendriyaguṇābhāsaṁ sarvendriyavivarjitam* |
asaktaṁ sarvabhṛc cai va nirguṇaṁ guṇabhoktṛ ca ||

It has the qualities of all the senses and yet is free from the senses, unattached and still supporting everything, without and free of the guṇas and yet enjoying the guṇas.

15. *bhair antaśca bhūtānām acaraṁ caram eva ca* |
sūkṣmatvāt tad avijñeyaṁ dūrasthaṁ cā 'ntike ca tat ||

Outside of and inside of all beings, not moving and also moving, too subtle to be known, it is far away and yet near.

16. *avibhaktaṁ ca bhūteṣu vibhaktam iva ca sthitam* |
bhūtabhartṛ ca taj jñeyaṁ grasiṣṇu prabhaviṣṇu ca ||

Undivided and established in all beings as if divided, it is to be known as the support of all beings; both their devourer and creator.

17. *jyotiṣām api taj jyotis tamasaḥ param ucyate* |
jñānaṁ jñeyaṁ jñānagamyaṁ hṛdi sarvasya dhiṣṭhitam ||

It is the light of lights, is said to be beyond darkness, knowledge, the known and that gained by knowledge, seated in the heart of all.

18. *iti kṣetraṁ tathā jñānaṁ jñeyaṁ co 'ktaṁ samāsataḥ* |
madbhakta etad vijñāya madbhāvāyo 'papadyate ||

And so the field, knowledge, and the object of knowledge have been concisely described. One who loves Me, understanding this, enters my state of being.

19. *prakṛtiṁ puruṣaṁ cai 'va viddhy anādī ubhāv api* |
vikārāṁś ca guṇāṁś caiva viddhi prakṛtisaṁbhavān ||

Know that prakṛti and puruṣa are both without beginning. And know that all modifications and the guṇas too arise from prakṛti.

20. *kārya karaṇa kartṛtve hetuḥ prakṛtir ucyate* |
puruṣaḥ sukhaduḥkhānāṁ bhoktṛtve hetur ucyate ||

Prakṛti is said to be the reason for the action, the instrument and means of action, and the doer of action; puruṣa is said to be the reason for the experiencing of happiness and suffering.

21. *puruṣaḥ prakṛtistho hi bhuṅkte prakṛtijān guṇān* |
kāraṇaṁ guṇasaṅgo 'sya sadasadyonijanmasu ||

The puruṣa situated in prakṛti enjoys the guṇas born of prakṛti. Attachment to the guṇas is the cause of its births in good and bad wombs.

22. *upadraṣṭā 'numantā ca bhartā bhoktā maheśvaraḥ* |
paramātmeti cāpyukto dehe 'smin puruṣaḥ paraḥ ||

In this body the highest puruṣa is called the supreme self (paramātman), the great beloved lord, the witness and the approver, the supporter, and the enjoyer.

23. *ya evaṁ vetti puruṣaṁ prakṛtiṁ ca guṇaiḥ saha* |
sarvathā vartamāno 'pi na sa bhūyo 'bhijāyate ||

One who knows in this way puruṣa and prakṛti along with the guṇas in whatever phase of unfolding, is not born again.

24. *dhyānenātmani paśyanti kecid ātmānam ātmanā* |
anye sāṁkhyena yogena karmayogena cā 'pare ||

By meditation some see the self within the self by the self; others by Sāṁkhya yoga and yet others by Karma yoga.

25. *anye tv evam ajānantaḥ śrutvā 'nyebhya upāsate* |
te 'pi cātitaranty eva mṛtyuṁ śrutiparāyaṇāḥ ||

However, some, not knowing these, worship by listening to others. And they also cross beyond death devoted to listening.

26. *yāvat sañjāyate kiñcit sattvaṁ sthāvarajaṅgamam* |
kṣetrakṣetrajñasaṁyogāt tad viddhi bharatarṣabha ||

Any being whatever that is born, moving or unmoving, comes from the union of the field and the knower of the field. Know that, Bull of the Bharatas!

27. *samaṁ sarveṣu bhūteṣu tiṣṭhantaṁ parameśvaram* |
vinaśyatsv avinaśyantaṁ yaḥ paśyati sa paśyati ||

One who sees the supreme beloved situated the same in all beings, not perishing when they perish, actually sees.

28. *samaṁ paśyan hi sarvatra samavasthitam īśvaram* |
na hinasty ātmanā 'tmānaṁ tato yāti parāṁ gatim ||

Seeing the lord equally and evenly existing everywhere, one does not hurt the self by the self and then attains the highest goal.

29. *prakṛtyai 'va ca karmāṇi kriyamāṇāni sarvaśaḥ* |
yaḥ paśyati tathā 'tmānam akartāraṁ sa paśyati ||

One who sees that all actions are performed entirely by prakṛti, and that the self (or they themselves) is not the performer, truly sees.

30. *yadā bhūtapṛthagbhāvam ekastham anupaśyati* |
tata eva ca vistāraṁ brahma saṁpadyate tadā ||

When one continuously, mindfully sees the multiplicity of the states of being abiding in the one and from there alone expanding out, they then attain Brahman.

31. *anāditvān nirguṇatvāt paramātmā 'yam avyayaḥ* |
śarīrastho 'pi kaunteya na karoti na lipyate ||

By having no beginning and by having no guṇas (transforming qualities), this paramātman, the supreme self, even though abiding in the body, neither acts nor is stained, Son of Kuntī.

32. *yathā sarvagataṁ saukṣmyād ākāśaṁ no 'palipyate* |
sarvatrā 'vasthito dehe tathātmā no 'palipyate ||

Just as all-pervading space is not stained because of its subtlety, so the ātman, abiding in all bodies everywhere, is never tainted.

33. *yathā prakāśayaty ekaḥ kṛtsnaṁ lokam imaṁ raviḥ* |
kṣetraṁ kṣetrī tathā kṛtsnaṁ prakāśayati bhārata ||

Just as this whole world is illuminated by one sun, so the lord of the field illuminates the whole field, O Bhārata.

34. *kṣetrakṣetrajñayor evam antaraṁ jñānacakṣuṣā* |
bhūtaprakṛtimokṣaṁ ca ye vidur yānti te param ||

Those who know with the eye of wisdom the difference between the field and the knower of the field and also the liberation of beings from creative energy, prakṛti, come to the highest.

Chapter 14

śrībhagavān uvāca

1. *paraṁ bhūyaḥ pravakṣyāmi jñānānaṁ jñānamuttamam* |
yaj jñātvā munayaḥ sarve parāṁ siddhimito gatāḥ ||

The Beautiful Lord said:
I will explain the ultimate even further, the highest knowledge of all forms of knowledge, knowing which all of the wise ones have gone from here to the highest perfection.

2. *idaṁ jñānamupāśritya mama sādharmyam āgatāḥ* |
sarge 'pi nopajāyante pralaye na vyathanti ca ||

Resting upon this knowledge they become the same nature as Me. They are not even born at the creation nor are they disturbed at the dissolution.

3. *mama yonirmahadbrahma tasmin garbhaṁ dadhāmy aham* |
sambhavaḥ sarvabhūtānāṁ tato bhavati bhārata ||

For Me Brahman is the *yoni* (womb); I give the seed. From that is the birth of all beings, O Bhārata.

4. *sarvayoniṣu kaunteya mūrtayaḥ saṁbhavanti yāḥ* |
tāsāṁ brahma mahadyonir ahaṁ bījapradaḥ pitā ||

O Son of Kuntī, of any forms coming to be in any and all wombs, Brahman is the great yoni and I am the seed-giving father.

5. *sattvaṁ rajastama iti guṇāḥ prakṛtisambhavāḥ* |
nibadhnanti mahābāho dehe dehinamavyayam ||

Thus, sattva, rajas, and tamas are the guṇas born of prakṛti. O Mighty Armed, they bind the imperishable dweller of the body in the body.

6. *tatra sattvaṁ nirmalatvāt prakāśakamanāmayam* |
sukhasaṅgena badhnāti jñānasaṅgena cānagha ||

Of these, sattva being free of faults, gives brilliance and good health. O Pure One, it binds you by attachment to happiness and by attachment to knowledge.

7. *rajo rāgātmakaṁ viddhi tṛṣṇāsaṅgasamudbhavam* |
tannibadhnāti kaunteya karmasaṅgena dehinam ||

Know that rajas has the nature of passion rising up from desire and attachment. O Son of Kuntī, it ties up the embodied one with attachment to action.

8. *tamastvajñānajaṁ viddhi mohanaṁ sarvadehinām* |
pramādālasyanidrābhis tannibadhnāti bhārata ||

But know that tamas is born of ignorance deluding all embodied beings. It binds them down, O Bhārata, with delusion, laziness, and sleepiness.

9. *sattvaṁ sukhe sañjayati rajaḥ karmaṇi bhārata* |
jñānamāvṛtya tu tamaḥ pramāde sañjayatyuta ||

Sattva makes attachment to happiness, rajas to action, O Bhārata, but tamas, obscuring knowledge, causes attachment to delusion.

10. *rajas tamaścābhibhūya sattvaṁ bhavati bhārata* |
rajaḥ sattvaṁ tamaścaiva tamaḥ sattvaṁ rajas tathā ||

Sattva arises prevailing over rajas and tamas, O Bhārata. Rajas then comes over sattva and tamas; likewise tamas over sattva and rajas.

11. *sarvadvāreṣu dehe 'smin prakāśa upajāyate*|
jñānaṁ yadā tadā vidyād vivṛddhaṁ sattvamityuta ||

When the radiance of knowledge is born in all of the gates of this body, then may it be known that sattva is indeed dominant.

12. *lobhaḥ pravṛttirārambhaḥ karmaṇāmaśamaḥ spṛhā |*
rajasyetāni jāyante vivṛddhe bharatarṣabha ||

When rajas is dominant, Bull of the Bharatas, these are born: greed, exertion, the commencing of actions, restlessness, and lust.

13. *aprakāśo 'pravṛttiśca pramādo moha eva ca |*
tamasyetāni jāyante vivṛddhe kurunandana ||

Lack of brilliance, inertness, negligence, and delusion are born when tamas is dominant, Joy of the Kurus.

14. *yadā sattve pravṛddhe tu pralayaṁ yāti dehabhṛt |*
tadottamavidāṁ lokān amalān pratipadyate ||

When within the dominance of sattva the embodied one goes to dissolution, then it enters the stainless worlds of the knowers of the ultimate.

15. *rajasi pralayaṁ gatvā karmasaṅgiṣu jāyate |*
tathā pralīnastamasi mūḍhayoniṣu jāyate ||

Going to dissolution in rajas, one is born among those attached to action; and dying in tamas one is born from the wombs of the deluded.

16. *karmaṇaḥ sukṛtasyāhuḥ sāttvikaṁ nirmalaṁ phalam |*
rajasas tu phalaṁ duḥkham ajñānaṁ tamasaḥ phalam ||

They say the fruit of action done well is sattvic and pure. But the fruit of rajasic action is suffering and of tamasic is ignorance.

17. *sattvāt sañjāyate jñānaṁ rajaso lobha eva ca |*
pramādamohau tamaso bhavato 'jñānameva ca ||

From sattva knowledge is born; from rajas, greed; and from tamas, distraction, delusion, and also ignorance.

18. *ūrdhvaṁ gacchanti sattvasthā madhye tiṣṭhanti rājasāḥ |*
jaghanyaguṇavṛttisthā adho gacchanti tāmasāḥ ||

Those established in sattva go upward; the rajasic remain in the middle; the tamasic, stuck in the lowest guṇa, go downward.

19. *nānyaṁ guṇebhyaḥ kartāraṁ yadā draṣṭā 'nupaśyati |*
guṇebhyaśca paraṁ vetti madbhāvaṁ so 'dhigacchati ||

When the seer sees mindfully, no doer besides the guṇas, and knows that which is beyond the guṇas, they attain my being.

20. *guṇānetānatītya trīn dehī dehasamudbhavān |*
janmamṛtyujarāduḥkhair vimukto 'mṛtam aśnute ||

When someone with a body goes beyond these three guṇas, which rise up together from and through the body, they attain the nectar of immortality and are freed from birth, death, old age, and suffering.

arjuna uvāca
21. *kairliṅgaistrīn guṇānetān atīto bhavati prabho |*
kimācāraḥ kathaṁ caitāṁs trīn guṇān ativartate ||

Arjuna said:
What are the characteristics in one going beyond these three guṇas, O Noble One? How is their conduct and how do they transcend these three guṇas?

śrībhagavān uvāca
22. *prakāśañca pravṛttiñca mohameva ca pāṇḍava |*
na dveṣṭi sampravṛttāni na nivṛttāni kāṅkṣatī ||

The Beautiful Lord said:
They neither hate nor wish for the occurrence or the absence of the illumination of sattva, the activity of rajas, or the delusion of tamas, Son of Pāṇḍu.

23. *udāsīnavad āsīno guṇairyo na vicālyate |*
guṇā vartanta ityeva yo 'vatiṣṭhati neṅgate ||

One who is seated as if disinterested, who is not shaken or disturbed by the guṇas knowing that only the guṇas are turning, stands firm and does not react.

24. *samaduḥkhasukhaḥ svasthaḥ samaloṣṭāśmakāñcanaḥ |*
tulyapriyāpriyo dhīras tulyanindātmasaṁstutiḥ ||

Equal in distress and happiness, self-satisfied, for whom a clod of earth, a stone, and gold are the same, who is steady and equal with the loved and the unloved and for whom blame and praise are equal.

25. *mānāpamānayostulyas tulyo mitrāripakṣayoḥ* |
sarvārambhaparityāgī guṇātītaḥ sa ucyate ||

One is said to have transcended the guṇas who is the same in honor and dishonor and is equal to the sides of both friends and foes, and who lets go of starting all actions.

26. *māṁ ca yo 'vyabhicāreṇa bhaktiyogena sevate* |
sa guṇān samatītyaitān brahmabhūyāya kalpate ||

One who serves Me with the yoga of unwavering devotion going beyond these three guṇas is ready for merging in Brahman.

27. *brahmaṇo hi pratiṣṭhā 'ham amṛtasyāvyayasya ca* |
śāśvatasya ca dharmasya sukhasyaikāntikasya ca ||

I am the abode of Brahman, of the nectar of the imperishable, and of the everlasting dharma and of unconditional, absolute happiness.

Chapter 15

śrībhagavān uvāca

1. *ūrdhvamūlamadhaḥ śākham aśvatthaṁ prāhur avayayam |*
chandāṁsi yasya parṇāni yas taṁ veda sa vedavit ||

The Beautiful Lord said:
They talk of the imperishable aśvattha tree (saṃsāra) with roots above and branches below, of which the leaves are the sacred hymns. One who knows this is the knower of the true Veda.

2. *adhaścordhvaṁ prasṛtāstasya śākhā guṇapravṛddhā viṣayapravālāḥ |*
adhaśca mūlānyanusantatāni karmānubandhīni manuṣyaloke ||

Its branches spread endlessly below and above with sense objects as it sprouts, nourished by the guṇas. And below (karmic) roots stretch forth endlessly promoting actions in the world of humans.

3. *na rūpamasyeha tathopalabhyate nānto na cādirna ca sampratiṣṭhā |*
aśvatthamenam suvirūḍhamūlam asaṅgaśastreṇa dṛḍhena chittvā ||

It is complete for it is not perceptible here in this world; not its end, not its beginning, nor its continuing interpenetrating existence. Having cut the aśvattha tree with its fully developed root with the powerful sword of nonattachment.

4. *tataḥ padaṁ tat parimārgitavyaṁ yasmin gatā na nivartanti bhūyaḥ* |
tameva cādyaṁ puruṣaṁ prapadye yataḥ pravṛttiḥ prasṛtā purāṇī ||

Then having gone to that state, which is sought after by paths all around, they do not turn back. "I take refuge in the original being, from whom moving, spiraling activity has streamed forever."

5. *nirmānamohā jitasaṅgadoṣā adhyātmanityā vinivṛttakāmāḥ* |
dvandvair vimuktāḥ sukhaduḥkhasaṁjñair gacchantyamūḍhāḥ padam avyayaṁ tat ||

Without pride and delusion those who have defeated the mistake of attachment, who are always in the primal being, with the endless forms of desire turned away, free from the dualities known as happiness and distress, the undeluded go to this imperishable state.

6. *na tadbhāsayate sūryo na śaśāṇko na pāvakaḥ* |
yad gatvā na nivartante taddhāma paramaṁ mama ||

In this state the sun does not illuminate, nor the moon, nor fire. Having gone they do not return. This is my supreme abode.

7. *mamaivāṁśo jīvaloke jīvabhūtaḥ sanātanaḥ* |
manaḥṣaṣṭhānīndriyāṇi prakṛtisthāni karṣati ||

Only a part of Me becomes the continuous individual in the world of the living and pulls to itself the five senses and the mind (the sixth sense), that all rest in prakṛti.

8. *śarīraṁ yadavāpnoti yaccāpyutkrāmatīśvaraḥ* |
gṛhītvaitāni saṁyāti vāyurgandhānivāśayāt ||

When Īśvara takes up a body and then gives it up, he takes these along as the breeze carries perfumes from their source.

9. *śrotraṁ cakṣuḥ sparśanañca rasanaṁ ghrāṇameva ca* |
adhiṣṭhāya manaścāyaṁ viṣayān upasevate ||

Presiding over them, Īśvara enjoys the objects of the senses—hearing, seeing, touching, tasting, and smelling, as well as the mind.

10. *utkrāmantaṁ sthitaṁ vāpi bhuñjānaṁ vā guṇānvitam* |
vimūḍhā nānupaśyanti paśyanti jñānacakṣuṣaḥ ||

The deluded do not see clearly Īśvara, departing, staying still, or indulging in contact with the guṇas. Those whose eyes are wisdom itself actually see.

11. *yatanto yoginaścainaṁ paśyanty ātmany avasthitam* |
yatanto 'pyakṛtātmāno nainaṁ paśyanty acetaseaḥ ||

Yogīs, while practicing, see this one existing in the ātman. But the mindlessness of the unworked, unpracticed, unprepared selves, though striving and practicing, do not see this one.

12. *yadādityagataṁ tejo jagad bhāsayate 'khilam* |
yaccandramasi yaccāgnau tat tejo viddhi māmakam ||

That brilliance of the sun, which lights this world without interruption, is in the moon and in fire—know that brilliance to be Me (mine).

13. *gām āviśya ca bhūtāni dhārayāmyahamojasā* |
puṣṇāmi cauṣadhīḥ sarvāḥ somo bhūtvā rasātmakaḥ ||

And being the ground, I support all beings with internal *ojas* (power). I make all of the plants and herbs blossom and flower, having become the juicy aesthetic and flavor of the soma.

14. *ahaṁ vaiśvānaro bhūtvā prāṇināṁ dehamāśritaḥ* |
prāṇāpāna samāyuktaḥ pacāmyannaṁ caturvidham ||

I become digestive fire in all humans. I inhabit the body of all who breathe, linking together the full inhaling pattern and the full exhaling pattern. I digest the four kinds of food.

15. *sarvasya cāhaṁ hṛdi sanniviṣṭo mattaḥ smṛtirjñānamapohanañca* |
vedaiśca sarvairahameva vedyo vedāntakṛd vedavid eva cāham ||

I am seated in the hearts of all. From Me are memory, knowledge, and reasoning ability. By all of the Vedas I am known. I am the knower of the Vedas and the creator of the Vedanta (the end or conclusion of the Veda).

16. *dvāvimau puruṣau loke kṣaraścākṣara eva ca |*
kṣaraḥ sarvāṇi bhūtāni kūṭastho 'kṣara ucyate ||

There are two conscious knowers in the world: the perishable and the imperishable. All beings are perishable; the unchanging is called the imperishable.

17. *uttamaḥ puruṣastvanyaḥ paramātmetyudāhṛtaḥ |*
yo lokatrayam āviśya bibhartyavyaya īśvaraḥ ||

But the highest puruṣa (knower) is another, called the paramātman who enveloping the three worlds supports them as Īśvara.

18. *yasmāt kṣaramatīto 'ham akṣarādapi cottamaḥ |*
ato 'smi loke vede ca prathitaḥ puruṣottamaḥ ||

Since I transcend the perishable and am beyond the imperishable I am in this world and in the Vedas extolled as the highest being.

19. *yo māmevam asaṁmūḍho jānāti puruṣottamam |*
sa sarvavid bhajati māṁ sarvabhāvena bhārata ||

An undeluded one who knows Me as the highest being understands everything and loves Me with all of their being, O Bhārata.

20. *iti guhyatamaṁ śāstram idamuktaṁ mayā 'nagha |*
etad buddhvā buddhimān syāt kṛtakṛtyaśca bhārata ||

This teaching of the ultimate secret has been laid out by Me, O Blameless One. Understanding this, one will become fully awake, with all duties and actions completed, O Bhārata.

Chapter 16

śrībhagavān uvāca

1. *abhayaṁ sattvasaṁśuddhir jñānayoga vyavasthitiḥ* ||
dānaṁ damaśca yajñaśca svādhyāyastapa ārjavam || *[[*

The Beautiful Lord said:
Fearlessness, purity of heart, perseverance in knowledge and yoga, generosity, self-control, and sacrifice, as well as self-study, austerity, and sincerity.

2. *ahimsā satyamakrodhas tyāgaḥ śāntirapaiśunam* |
dayā bhūteṣvaloluptvaṁ mārdavaṁ hrīracāpalam ||

Nonviolence, truthfulness, freedom from anger, renunciation, peacefulness, not fault finding, kindness to all beings, freedom from desire, gentleness, modesty, steadiness.

3. *tejaḥ kṣamā dhṛtiḥ śaucam adroho nātimānitā* |
bhavanti saṁpadaṁ daivīm abhijātasya bhārata ||

Vigor, patience, stability, purity, lack of hatred, lack of excessive pride; these are the gifts of those born of divine qualities, O Bhārata.

4. *dambho darpo 'bhimānaśca krodhaḥ pāruṣyam eva ca* |
ajñānam cābhijātasya pārtha saṁpadam āsurīm ||

Ostentation, arrogance, and conceit and also anger, cruel language, and ignorance are the endowments of one born with demonic qualities, Son of Pṛthā.

5. *daivī saṁpadivimokṣāya nibandhāyāsurī matā* |
mā śucaḥ saṁpadaṁ daivīm abhijāto 'si pāṇḍava ||

It is thought that the divine characteristics lead to liberation, while demonic ones lead to bondage. Don't worry, Son of Pāṇḍu, you were born with divine character.

6. *dvau bhūtasargau loke 'smin daiva āsura eva ca* |
daivo vistaraśaḥ prokta āsuraṁ pārtha me śṛṇu ||

There are two types of created beings in this world: the divine and the demonic. The divine has been explained in detail, Son of Pṛthā. Hear from Me of the demonic.

7. *pravṛttiñca nivṛttiñca janā na vidurāsurāḥ* |
na śaucaṁ nāpi cācāro na satyaṁ teṣu vidyate ||

The demonic (the Āsuras) do not understand appropriate action and appropriate inaction. There is no purity, certainly no good behavior, and no honesty found in them.

8. *asatyam apratiṣṭhaṁ te jagadāhuranīśvaram* |
aparasparasambhūtaṁ kim anyat kāmahaitukam ||

They maintain that the universe is without any truth, without any moral ground, has no lord, and has not been brought into being by evolutionary process. By what then? Merely by passionate desire.

9. *etāṁ dṛṣṭimavaṣṭabhya naṣṭāmāno 'lpabuddhayaḥ* |
prabhavanty ugrakarmāṇaḥ kṣayāyā jagato 'hitāḥ ||

Clinging to this point of view these persons, having lost themselves with small intelligence and of cruel, evil actions, manifest as enemies of the world for its destruction.

10. *kāmamāśritya duṣpūraṁ dambhamānamadānvitāḥ* |
mohād gṛhītvā 'sadgrāhān pravartante 'śucivratāḥ ||

Clinging to unfulfillable desires, full of fraudulent hypocrisy, arrogance, and the intoxication of lust, accepting untrue ideas, they act with unclean vows and rules.

11. *cintām aparimeyāñca pralayāntāmupāśritāḥ* |
kāmopabhogaparamā etāvad iti niścitāḥ ||

Clutching on to countless mental anxieties, which end only in death, having no doubt that enjoyment of desires is the highest goal.

12. *āśāpāśaśatairbaddhāḥ kāmakrodhaparāyaṇāḥ* |
īhante kāmabhogārtham anyāyenārthasañcayān ||

Bound by a hundred nooses made of aspirations, blindly devoted to desire and anger, they seek hoards of wealth, by unethical means, to enjoy their desires.

13. *idamadya mayā labham idaṁ prāpsye manoratham* |
idamastīdam api me bhaviṣyati punardhanam ||

"Today this was obtained by me, this desire (chariot of mind) I will attain. And this and also *this* property are mine."

14. *asau mayā hataḥ śatrur haniṣye cāparānapi* |
īśvaro 'ham ahaṁ bhogī siddho 'haṁ balavān sukhī ||

"That enemy has been killed by me and I will kill others too; I am the lord, I am the enjoyer, I am accomplished, powerful, and happy!"

15. *āḍhyo 'bhijanavānasmi ko 'nyo 'sti sadṛśo mayā* |
yakṣye dāsyāmi modiṣya ityajñānavimohitāḥ ||

"I am opulently rich and well born. What other is there like me? I shall make sacrifice, I shall give charity, I shall celebrate." In this way they are bewildered by ignorance.

16. *anekacittavibhrāntā mohajālasamāvṛtāḥ* |
prasaktāḥ kāmabhogeṣu patanti narake 'śucau ||

Carried away by so many thoughts, completely entangled in the net of delusion, addicted to the gratification of desire, they fall into a foul hell.

17. *ātmasambhāvitāḥ stabdhā dhanamānamadānvitāḥ* |
yajante nāmayajñaiste dambhenāvidhipūrvakam ||

Obsessed with themselves, obstinate, filled with pride and arrogance of wealth, they make sacrifices that are such only in name, with fraudulent hypocrisy and with no regard for traditional rules.

18. *ahaṅkāraṁ balaṁ darpaṁ kāmaṁ krodhañca saṁśritāḥ* |
māmātmaparadeheṣu pradviṣanto 'bhyasūyakāḥ ||

Clinging to ego, force, and arrogance, as well as lust and anger, these indignantly envious ones hate Me, dwelling in their own and in other's bodies.

19. *tānahaṁdviṣataḥ krūrān saṁsāreṣu narādhamān* |
kṣipāmyajasramaśubhān asurīṣveva yoniṣu ||

I constantly throw them, the haters, the cruel, vile, and vicious humans, into the wombs of the demonic in the cycle of saṃsāra.

20. *āsurīṁ yonim āpannā mūḍhā janmanijanmani* |
mām aprāpyaiva kaunteya tato yāntyadhamāṁ gatim ||

Flowing down to the wombs of demons, birth after birth, the deluded do not attain Me, Son of Kuntī. From there they follow the worst path.

21. *trividhaṁ narakasyedaṁ dvāraṁ nāśanamātmanaḥ* |
kāmaḥ krodhas tathā lobhas tasmādetat trayaṁ tyajet ||

The gate of this hell, so destructive of the self. It is threefold: lust, anger, and greed. Therefore, one should give up these three.

22. *etairvimuktaḥ kaunteya tamodvārais tribhirnaraḥ* |
ācaratyātmanaḥ śreyas tato yāti parāṁ gatim ||

A person who is freed from these three gates of darkness, O Son of Kuntī, does what is best for the Self (ātman) and thereupon goes to the highest path.

23. *yaḥ śāstravidhim utsṛjya vartate kāmakārataḥ* |
na sa siddhimavāpnoti na sukhaṁ na parāṁ gatim ||

But one who ignores the wisdom of the scriptures and does as desires urge, does not attain perfection, happiness, or the highest path.

24. *tasmācchāstraṁ pramāṇaṁ te kāryākāryavyavasthitau* |
jñātvā śāstravidhānoktaṁ karma kartumihārhasi ||

Therefore, let the scriptures be your guide for what is and what is not to be done. You should do your work here in this world, knowing the recommended scriptural teaching.

Chapter 17

arjuna uvāca

1. *ye śāstravidhimutsṛjya yajante śraddhayānvitāḥ* |
teṣāṁ niṣṭhā tu kā kṛṣṇa sattvamāho rajastamaḥ ||

Arjuna said:
What is the position (situation) of those who, throwing aside the injunctions of the scriptures, yet filled with śraddhā, offer sacrifices, O Kṛṣṇa? Is it sattvic, rajasic, or tamasic?

śrībhagavān uvāca

2. *trividhā bhavati śraddhā dehināṁ sā svabhāvajā* |
sāttvikī rājasī caiva tāmasī ceti tāṁ śṛṇu ||

The Beautiful Lord said:
The śraddhā of those embodied is of three types, born of their intrinsic nature: sattva, rajas, and tamas. Now hear about them.

3. *sattvānurūpā sarvasya śraddhā bhavati bhārata* |
śraddhāmayo 'yaṁ puruṣo yo yacchraddhaḥ sa eva saḥ ||

Śraddhā closely follows the form of one's nature. Humans are composed of their trust in their metaphysical assumptions. What one's śraddhā is, *that* one is.

4. *yajante sāttvikā devān yakṣarakṣāṁsi rājasāḥ* |
pretān bhūtagaṇāṁścānye yajante tāmasā janāḥ ||

Sattvic people worship the gods; rajasic, the spirits and the demons (Yakṣas and Rakṣas) of the departed. Others, tamasic people, worship the spirits and the hordes of ghosts.

5. *aśāstravihitaṁ ghoraṁ tapyante ye tapo janāḥ* |
dambhāhaṅkārasaṁyuktāḥ kāmarāgabalānvitāḥ ||

People who perform terrible austerities not ordained by the scriptures, joined with hypocrisy and egotism, accompanied by lust, passion, and force.

6. *karśayantaḥ śarīrasthaṁ bhūtagrāmamacetasaḥ* |
māṁ caivāntaḥśarīrasthaṁ tān viddhyāsuraniścayān ||

Unthinking, torturing the multitude of elements within the body and also Me dwelling within the body, know them to be of demonic intention.

7. *āhārastvapi sarvasya trividho bhavati priyaḥ* |
yajñastapastathā dānaṁ teṣāṁ bhedamimaṁ ṣṛṇu ||

But also the food preferred by all is of those three kinds, as are the sacrifices, austerities, and gifts. Listen to the distinctions between them.

8. *āyuḥsattvabalārogya sukhaprītivivardhanāḥ* |
rasyāḥ snigdhāḥ sthirā hṛdyā āhārāḥ sāttvikapriyāḥ ||

Foods dear to the sattvic (people) nourish life, harmony, strength, freedom from disease, happiness, and satisfaction (good cheer) and are flavorful, smooth, firm, and pleasant.

9. *kaṭvamlalavaṇātyuṣṇa tīkṣṇarūkṣavidāhinaḥ* |
āhārā rājasasyeṣṭā duḥkhaśokāmayapradāḥ ||

Foods desired by the rajasic cause pain, grief, and sickness and are bitter, sour, too salty, too hot, harsh, astringent, and burning.

10. *yātayāmaṁ gatarasaṁ pūti paryuṣitañca yat* |
ucchiṣṭam api cāmedhyaṁ bhojanaṁ tāmasapriyam ||

Spoiled, tasteless, putrid, leftover, which is rejected and impure, is the food dear to the tamasic.

11. *aphalākāṅkṣibhiryajño vidhidṛṣṭo ya ijyate* |
yaṣṭavyameveti manaḥ samādhāya sa sāttvikaḥ ||

Sacrifice that is done with an eye to scriptural direction, by those with no longing for the fruit, concentrating the mind on only what is to be offered, that is sattvic.

12. *abhisandhāya tu phalaṁ dambhārtham api caiva yat* |
ijyate bharataśreṣṭha taṁ yajñaṁ viddhi rājasam ||

But having in mind the fruit or for the sake of show, know, O Best of Bharatas, that sacrifice is rajasic.

13. *vidhihīnamasṛṣṭānnaṁ mantrahīnamadakṣiṇam* |
śraddhāvirahitaṁ yajñaṁ tāmasaṁ paricakṣate ||

Sacrifice empty of śraddhā, without scriptural direction, where no food is offered, no mantra chanted, and no compensation given to the priest, is seen as tamasic.

14. *devadvijaguruprājña pūjanaṁ śaucamārjavam* |
brahmacaryamahiṁsā ca śārīraṁ tapa ucyate ||

Attending reverence to the gods, the twice-born, the teachers and the wise; cleanliness, virtue, continence, and nonviolence are said to be the austerity of the body.

15. *anudvegakaraṁ vākyaṁ satyaṁ priyahitañca yat* |
svādhyāyabhyasanaṁ caiva vāṅmayaṁ tapa ucyate ||

Words that do not cause distress, that are honest, pleasant, and beneficial, as well as the recitation of sacred hymns, are the austerity of speech.

16. *manaḥprasādaḥ saumyatvaṁ maunam ātmavinigrahaḥ* |
bhāvasaṁśuddhirityetat tapo mānasam ucyate ||

Calm, clarity of the mind, gentleness, silence, detailed attention to the self, cleanliness of the deeper mind, this is called the austerity of mind.

17. *śraddhayā parayā taptaṁ tapastat trividhaṁ naraiḥ* |
aphalākāṅkṣibhiryuktaiḥ sāttvikaṁ paricakṣate ||

This threefold austerity practiced with the deepest śraddhā by people who are not longing for fruits and are steady in yoga is seen as sattvic.

18. *satkāramānapūjārthaṁ tapo dambhena caiva yat* |
kriyate tadiha proktaṁ rājasaṁ calam adhruvam ||

Austerity practiced for the goal of gaining good favor, honor, and reverence, practiced with hypocrisy, here in this world, is rajasic, wavering, and ungrounded.

19. *mūḍhagrāheṇātmano yat pīḍayā kriyate tapaḥ* |
parasyotsādanārthaṁ vā tat tāmasam udāhṛtam ||

Tapas done with deluded ideas of oneself that are competitive, tortured, and done for the sake of destroying another is said to tamasic.

20. *dātavyamiti yaddānaṁ dīyate 'nupakāriṇe* |
deśe kāle ca pātre ca taddānaṁ sāttvikaṁ smṛtam ||

The gift made at the correct time and place, thinking only, "It is to be given," to a worthy person who has not done a prior favor, is understood to be sattvic.

21. *yat tu pratyupakārārthaṁ phalamuddiśya vā punaḥ* |
dīyate ca parikliṣṭaṁ taddānaṁ rājasaṁ smṛtam ||

But the gift that is given reluctantly with the purpose of gaining a favor or again with regard to a fruit is considered to be rajasic.

22. *adeśakāle yaddānam apātrebhyaśca dīyate* |
asatkṛtam avajñātaṁ tat tāmasam udāhṛtam ||

That gift given at the wrong time or wrong place or to an unworthy person without respect and without wisdom is declared to be tamasic.

23. *auṁ tat sat iti nirdeśo brahmaṇas trividhaḥ smṛtaḥ* |
brāhmaṇāstena vedāśca yajñāśca vihitāḥ purā ||

"Oṁ tat sat" has been seen to be the threefold designation of Brahman. With this the Brāhmans, Vedas, and sacrifices were consecrated in ancient times.

24. *tasmād aum ityudāhṛtya yajñadānatapaḥkriyāḥ* |
pravartante vidhānoktāḥ satataṁ brahmavādinām ||

Therefore, with the chanting of Oṁ, acts of sacrifice, the giving of gifts, and the performing of austerities prescribed in the scriptures are always begun by the teachers of Brahman.

25. *tadityanabhisandhāya phalaṁ yajñatapaḥkriyāḥ* |
dānakriyāśca vividhāḥ kriyante mokṣakāṅkṣibhiḥ ||

With tat and without any interest in a fruit, acts of sacrifice and austerity, and all sorts of acts of giving, are done by those longing for freedom (*mokṣa*).

26. *sadbhāve sādhubhāve ca sadityetat prayujyate* |
praśaste karmaṇi tathā sacchabdaḥ pārtha yujyate ||

Sat is used with the meaning "reality" and also "goodness." Thus, for an admirable action the word *sat* is also used, Son of Pṛthā.

27. *yajñe tapasi dāni ca sthitiḥ saditi cocyate* |
karma caiva tadarthīyaṁ sadityevābhidhīyate ||

Steadiness in sacrifice, austerity, and giving is also called sat, and any work serving that purpose is proclaimed as sat.

28. *aśraddhayā hutaṁ dattaṁ tapastaptaṁ kṛtañca yat* |
asad ityucyate pārtha na ca tat pretya no iha ||

Any oblation offered, austerity performed, or ritual done without śraddhā is called asat, O Pārtha; it is nothing to us here in the world or hereafter.

Chapter 18

arjuna uvāca

1. *saṁnyāsaya mahābāho tattvam icchāmi veditum |*
tyāgasya ca hṛṣīkeśa pṛthak keśiniṣūdana ||

Arjuna said:
Mighty Armed, I want to know the distinguishing truth of saṁnyāsa and that of tyāga, O Hṛṣīkeśa, O Slayer of Kesin.

śrībhagavān uvāca

2. *kāmyānāṁ karmaṇāṁ nyāsaṁ saṁnyāsaṁ kavayo viduḥ |*
sarvakarmaphalatyāgaṁ prāhus tyāgaṁ vicakṣaṇāḥ ||

The Beautiful Lord said:
The poets know the placing down of actions that come from desire as saṁnyāsa. The clear-sighted declare releasing of the fruit of all actions to be tyāga.

3. *tyājyaṁ doṣavadityeke karma prāhurmanīṣiṇaḥ |*
yajñadānatapaḥkarma na tyājyaiti cāpare ||

Some learned men say, "Action should be given up as evil." Other wise men say, "The actions of sacrifice, giving, and practice should not be given up."

4. *niścayaṁ śṛṇu me tatra tyāge bharatasattama |*
tyāgo hi puruṣavyāghra trividhaḥ samprakīrtitaḥ ||

Hear my conclusion on tyāga, Best of the Bharatas. Tyāga is indeed designated to be of three types.

5. *yajñadānatapaḥkarma na tyājyaṁ kāryameva tat* |
yajño dānaṁ tapaścaiva pāvanāni manīṣiṇām ||

The actions of sacrifice, giving, and practice are not to be abandoned but should be done. Sacrifice, giving, and practice are purifiers of those who are already wise.

6. *etānyapi tu karmāṇi saṅgaṁ tyaktvā phalāni ca* |
kartavyānīti me pārtha niścitaṁ matam uttamam ||

These actions, however, are to be done completely, releasing attachment to the fruits. This is definitely my highest opinion, Son of Pṛthā.

7. *niyatasya tu saṁnyāsaḥ karmaṇo nopapadyate* |
mohāt tasya parityāgas tāmasaḥ parikīrtitaḥ ||

But renunciation of necessary action is not appropriate. Giving it up because of delusion is said to be tamasic.

8. *duḥkhamityeva yat karma kāyakleśabhayāt tyajet* |
sa kṛtvā rājasaṁ tyāgaṁ naiva tyāgaphalaṁ labhet ||

One who gives up an action merely because it is difficult or from fear of suffering of the body is doing rajasic renunciation. They do not get the fruit of that renunciation.

9. *kāryamityeva yat karma niyataṁ kriyate 'rjuna* |
saṅgaṁ tyaktvā phalaṁ caiva sa tyāgaḥ sāttviko mataḥ ||

This tyāga renunciation is thought to be sattvic, O Arjuna, when action is done because it ought to be done, giving up attachment to the fruit.

10. *na dveṣṭyakuśalaṁ karma kuśale nānuṣajjate* |
tyāgī sattvasamāviṣṭo medhāvī chinnasaṁśayaḥ ||

The renouncer, the wise one, whose doubt has been cut away and who is filled with luminous harmony, has no repulsion to disagreeable actions and no clinging to agreeable actions.

11. *na hi dehabhṛtā śakyaṁ tyaktuṁ karmāṇyaśeṣataḥ* |
yastu karmaphalatyāgī sa tyāgītyabhidhīyate ||

Indeed those inhabiting bodies are not able to give up actions without some residue. The one who lets go of the fruit of the action is then said to be the real renouncer.

12. *aniṣṭamiṣṭaṁ miśrañca trividhaṁ karmanaḥ phalam* |
bhavatyatyāgināṁ pretya na tu saṁnyāsināṁ kvacit ||

For those who have not let go, the fruits of their actions are of three types: unwanted, desired, and mixed. But for true saṁnyāsīns (renouncers) there is none at all.

13. *pañcai 'tāni mahābāho kāraṇāni nibodha me* |
sāṁkhye kṛtānte proktāni siddhaye sarvakarmaṇām ||

O Mighty Armed, learn from Me the five factors as taught in the original Sāṁkhya for the perfection of all actions.

14. *adhisthānaṁ tathā kartā karaṇañca pṛthagavidhaṁ* |
vividhāśca pṛthak ceṣṭā daivañcaivātra pañcamam ||

The seat of action and then the agent, the different types of instruments and efforts of perception and work, and then divine providence (the gods) as the fifth.

15. *śarīravāṅmanobhiryat karma prārabhate naraḥ* |
nyāyyaṁ vā viparītaṁ vā pañcaite tasya hetavaḥ ||

Any action a person commences with the body, the speech, or the mind, whether it is good or bad, has these five factors.

16. *tatraivaṁ sati kartāram ātmānaṁ kevalaṁ tu yaḥ* |
paśyatyakṛtabuddhitvān na sa paśyati durmatiḥ ||

This being the situation, the fool of unrefined intelligence sees their self as the sole agent. They do not really see.

17. *yasya nāhaṅkṛto bhāvo buddhiryasya na lipyate* |
hatvāpi sa imāṁllokān na hanti na nibadhyate ||

One who is not in an egotistical state, whose intelligence is not corrupted even slaying all these worlds, is not slaying them and is not bound by actions.

18. *jñānaṁ jñeyaṁ parijñātā trividhā karmacodanā* |
karaṇaṁ karma karte 'ti trividhaḥ karmasaṁgrahaḥ ||

Knowledge, the object of the knowledge, and the knower are the three components stimulating action. The instrument, the action, and the doer (the agent) are the three components composing any action.

19. *jñānaṁ karma ca kartā ca tridhaiva guṇabhedataḥ* |
procyate guṇasaṁkhyāne yathāvacchṛṇu tānyapi ||

It is taught in the guṇa theory of Sāṁkhya that knowledge, action, and the agent are of three kinds determined by the guṇas. Hear about these too.

20. *sarvabhūteśu yenaikaṁ bhāvamavyayamīkṣate* |
avibhaktaṁ vibhakteśu taj jñānaṁ viddhi sāttvikam ||

Know that knowledge to be sattvic by which one sees the imperishable being in all beings; undivided in the divided.

21. *pṛthaktvena tu yaj jñānaṁ nānābhāvān pṛthagvidhān* |
vetti sarveṣu bhūtesu taj jñānaṁ viddhi rājasam ||

But know knowledge that, as rajasic, sees in all beings separate kinds of distinct beings of various types.

22. *yat tu kṛtsnavad ekasmin kārye saktam ahetukam* |
atattvārthavadalpañca tat tāmasam udāhṛtam ||

But that (knowledge) that is clinging to only one single effect as if it were the whole without interest in cause, without clear purpose, is proclaimed to be tamasic.

23. *niyataṁ saṅgarahitam arāgadveṣataḥ kṛtam* |
aphalaprepsu nā karma yat tat sāttvikamucyate ||

An action that needs to be done and that is free of attachment, done without desire or hatred, without wishing to get the fruit is said to be sattvic.

24. *yat tu kāmepsunā karma sahaṅkarenā vā punaḥ* |
kriyate bahulāyāsaṁ tad rājasam udāhṛtam ||

But action done wishing to obtain desires with self-centered egotism or, again, with excessive exertion is declared to be rajasic.

25. *anubandhaṁ kṣayaṁ hiṁsām anapekṣya ca pauruṣam* |
mohādārabhyate karma yat tat tāmasamucyate ||

Action undertaken from delusion disregarding ongoing consequences, destruction, or inquiry to others' and even one's own ability is said to be tamasic.

26. *muktasaṅgo 'nahaṁvādi dhṛtyutsāhasamanvitaḥ* |
siddhyasiddhyor nirvikāraḥ kartā sāttvika ucyate ||

The one who is released from clinging, without talking about themselves, accompanied with courage and clear resolution, not affected by success or failure is said to be sattvic.

27. *rāgī karmaphalaprepsur lubdho hiṁsātmako 'śuciḥ* |
harṣaśokānvitaḥ kartā rājasaḥ parikīrtitaḥ ||

The one who is impulsively passionate, hoping to get the fruit of action, greedy, violent by nature, impure, and swayed by happiness and misery is universally declared to be rajasic.

28. *ayuktaḥ prākṛtaḥ stabdhaḥ śaṭho naikṛtiko 'lasaḥ* |
viṣādī dīrghasūtrī ca kartā tāmasa ucyate ||

The one who is unyoked, ostentatious, stubborn, deceitful, lazy, disparate, and procrastinating is called tamasic.

29. *buddherbhedaṁ dhṛteścaiva guṇatastrividhaṁ śṛṇu* |
procyamānam aśeṣeṇa pṛthaktvena dhanañjaya ||

Hear the threefold distinction according to the guṇas of both intelligence and steadfastness presented completely and separately, O Arjuna, Conqueror of Wealth.

30. *pravṛttiñca nivṛttiñca kāryākārye bhayābhaye* |
bandhaṁ mokṣañca yā vetti buddhiḥ sā pārtha sāttvikī ||

O Son of Pṛthā, intelligence that perceives action in inaction, what is to be done and what is not to be done, what is to be feared and what is not to be feared, and what is bondage and what is liberation is sattvic.

31. *yayā dharmamadharmañca kāryaṁ cā 'kāryam eva ca* |
ayathāvat prajānāti buddhiḥ sā pārtha rājasī ||

O Son of Pṛthā, intelligence is rajasic by which right and wrong and that which should be done and that which should not be done are distinguished incorrectly.

32. *adharmaṁ dharmamiti yā manyate tamasāvṛtā* |
sarvārthān viparītāṁś ca buddhiḥ sā pārtha tāmasī ||

Intelligence enveloped in darkness, imagining wrong to be right (adharma to be dharma), and all aims and purposes turned backward is tamasic, Son of Pṛthā.

33. *dhṛtyā yayā dhārayate manaḥprāṇendriyakriyāḥ* |
yogenāvyabhicāriṇyā dhṛtiḥ sā pārtha sāttvikī ||

The firmness that holds movements steady is sattvic, when the prāṇa, the mind, and the activities of the senses are stabilized through unswerving, focused yoga, Son of Pṛthā.

34. *yayā tu dharmakāmārthān dhṛtyā dhārayate 'rjuna* |
prasaṅgena phalākāṅkṣī dhṛtiḥ sā pārtha rājasī ||

Firmness by which one strongly holds on to duty, selfish pleasure, and wealth with attachment and the desire for fruits is rajasic, Pārtha.

35. *yayā svapnaṁ bhayaṁ śokaṁ viṣādaṁ madam eva ca* |
navimuñcati durmedhā dhṛtiḥ sā pārtha tamasī ||

Firmness by which the dull-witted do not let go of dreamy sleep, fear, sorrow, melancholy, and arrogance is tamasic, Pārtha.

36. *sukhaṁ tvidānīṁ trividhaṁ śṛṇu me bharatarṣabha* |
abhyāsād ramate yatra duḥkhāntañca nigacchati ||

But now hear from Me, O Bull of the Bharatas, the three kinds of happiness that one comes to enjoy by lengthy practice and by which suffering comes to an end.

37. *yat tadagre viṣamiva pariṇāme 'mṛtopamam |*
tat sukhaṁ sāttvikaṁ proktam ātmabuddhiprasādajam ||

That which is like poison at the beginning but transforms into nectar is declared to be sattvic and is born from the clear intelligence of oneself.

38. *viṣayendriyasaṁyogād yat tadagre 'mṛtopamam |*
pariṇāme viṣam iva tat sukhaṁ rājasam smṛtam ||

That happiness coming from connecting to sense objects, which is like nectar at the beginning and then transforms into poison, is recognized as rajasic.

39. *yadagre cānubandhe ca sukhaṁ mohanam ātmanaḥ |*
nidrālasyapramādotthaṁ tat tāmasam udāhṛtam ||

That happiness which is confusing of the actual self both in the beginning and later in its results, which arises from sleep, sloth, and confusion, is said to be tamasic.

40. *na tad asti pṛthivyām vā divi deveṣu vā punaḥ |*
sattvaṁ prakṛtijair muktaṁ yadebhiḥ syāt tribhirguṇaiḥ ||

There is no being on earth or even in heaven among the gods who exists free from these three guṇas born of prakṛti.

41. *brāhmaṇakṣatriyaviśāṁ śūdrāṇāñca parantapa |*
karmāṇi pravibhaktāni svabhāvaprabhavair guṇaiḥ ||

O Conqueror of the Foe, the actions (works) of Brāhmans, Kṣatriyas, Vaiśyas, and Śūdras are arranged by the guṇas arising from their intrinsic nature.

42. *śamo damastapaḥ śaucaṁ kṣāntirārjavam eva ca |*
jñānaṁ vijñānamāstikyaṁ brahmakarma svabhāvajam ||

Serenity, self-control, austerity, and cleanliness, as well as wisdom, knowledge, and trust are the work of the Brāhman born of intrinsic nature.

43. *śauryaṁ tejo dhṛtirdākṣyaṁ yuddhe cāpyapalāyanam |*
dānamīśvarabhāvaśca kṣātraṁ karma svabhāvajam ||

Heroism, dignity, courage, dexterity, not fleeing in war, generosity, and a noble spirit are the work of the Kṣatriya born of their intrinsic nature.

44. *kṛṣigaurakṣyavāṇijyaṁ vaiśyakarma svabhāvajam |*
paricaryātmakaṁ karma śūdrasyāpi *svabhāvajam ||*

Agriculture, cow herding, and commerce are the work of the Vaiśya born of intrinsic nature. Service all around is the work of the Śūdra born of their intrinsic nature.

45. *sve sve karmaṇyabhirataḥ saṁsiddhiṁ labhate naraḥ |*
svakarmaniratah siddhiṁ yathā vindati tacchṛṇu ||

A human attains complete perfection, the perfection of being satisfied with one's true duty, by devotion to those actions in line with their true nature. Now hear how one attains the state of being deeply satisfied with one's own true duty.

46. *yataḥ pravṛttirbhūtānāṁ yena sarvamidaṁ tatam |*
svakarmaṇā tam abhyarcya siddhiṁ vindati mānavaḥ ||

By adoring with their own true work, the one from whom all beings manifest, by whom all of this is pervaded, humans find fulfillment.

47. *śreyān svadharmo viguṇaḥ paradharmāt svanuṣṭhitāt |*
svabhāvaniyataṁ karma kurvan nāpnoti kilbiṣam ||

It is better to do one's own dharma imperfectly than to do the dharma of another well. Doing the duty given by one's true nature and circumstances, one obtains no evil.

48. *sahajaṁ karma kaunteya sadoṣamapi na tyajet |*
sarvārambhā hi doṣeṇa dhūmenāgnirivāvṛtāḥ ||

O Son of Kuntī, one should not renounce their work arising from birth and actual circumstances even though it might have some fault. Indeed all undertakings have some faults, just as fire is enveloped by smoke.

49. *asaktabuddhiḥ sarvatra jitātmā vigataspṛhaḥ* |
naiṣkarmyasiddhiṁ paramāṁ saṁnyāsenādhigacchati ||

One whose intelligence is not grasping anywhere, who is victorious in the self (in themselves) and whose craving has gone, attains the great perfection of freedom from action by the placing down of true saṁnyāsa.

50. *siddhiṁ prāpto yathā brahma tathāpnoti nibodha me* |
samāsenaiva kaunteya niṣṭhā jñānasya yā parā ||

Learn from Me, O Son of Kuntī, how having gotten such perfection, one then attains Brahman, which is the highest wisdom.

51. *buddhyā viśuddhayā yukto dhṛtyātmānaṁ niyamya ca* |
śabdādīn viṣayāṁs tyaktvā rāgadveṣau vyudasya ca ||

Hooked up with the purest function of the intelligence, firmly focused on the ātman, leaving be all separated sense objects (beginning with sound), and throwing aside attraction and repulsion.

52. *viviktasevī laghvāśī yatavākkāyamānasaḥ* |
dhyānayogaparo nityaṁ vairāgyaṁ samupāśritaḥ ||

Dwelling apart from others, eating lightly, moderating speech, body, and mind, continuously devoted to meditation and yoga, being upheld by nonattachment.

53. *ahaṅkāraṁ balaṁ darpaṁ kāmaṁ krodhaṁ parigraham* |
vimucya nirmamaḥ śānto brahmabhūyāya kalpate ||

Giving up egotism, forcefulness, pride, lust, anger, and possessiveness—unselfish and peaceful, one becomes the very being of Brahman.

54. *brahmabhūtaḥ prasannātmā na śocati na kāṅkṣati* |
samaḥ sarveṣu bhūteṣu madbhaktiṁ labhate paraṁ ||

Being of Brahman and tranquil in self, one grieves not and desires not; equal to all beings, one attains supreme love for Me.

55. *bhaktyā māmabhijānāti yāvān yaścāsmi tattvataḥ* |
tato māṁ tattvato jñātvā viśate tadanantaram ||

By devotion one comes to know my extent and who I am in reality. Having then known Me in truth, one thereupon enters Me.

56. *sarvakarmāṇyapi sadā kurvāṇo madvyapāśrayaḥ* |
matprasādād avāpnoti śāśvataṁ padam avyayam ||

Doing all actions continuously while taking refuge in Me, by my kindness they reach the timeless, imperishable state.

57. *cetasā sarvakarmāṇi mayi saṁnyasya matparaḥ* |
buddhiyogam upāśritya maccittaḥ satataṁ bhava ||

In all thoughts, offering all actions to Me, regarding Me as the supreme, taking refuge in buddhi yoga, continuously think of Me.

58. *maccittaḥ sarvadurgāṇi matprasādāt tariṣyasi* |
atha cet tvamahaṅkārān na śroṣyasi vinaṅkṣyasi ||

With all your thoughts enmeshed with Me, by my grace you will cross over all difficulties. But if from egotistical conceit you don't listen, you will perish.

59. *yadahaṅkāramāśritya nā yotsya iti manyase* |
mithyaiṣa vyavasāyaste prakṛtis tvāṁ niyokṣyati ||

Indulging in egotistical concerns (self-conceit, misplaced honor) you think, "I will not fight." That intention is deluded. Your own nature will compel you to act.

60. *svabhāvajena kaunteya nibaddhaḥ svena karmaṇā* |
kartuṁ necchasi yanmohāt kariṣyasyavaśo 'pi tat ||

That which you do not want to do when confused, O Son of Kuntī, that you will do even against your desire, bound by your actions from your own material nature.

61. *īśvara sarvabhūtānāṁ hṛddeśe 'rjuna tiṣṭhati* |
bhrāmayan sarvabhūtāni yantrārūḍhāni māyayā ||

O Arjuna, Īśvara is standing in the heart of all beings, causing all these beings to turn round and round by the power of māyā as if riding on a vehicle (*yantra*).

62. *tameva śaraṇaṁ gaccha sarvabhāvena bhārata |*
tatprasādāt parāṁ śāntiṁ sthānaṁ prāpsyasi śāśvatam ||

Go to it for refuge with all your heart and being. From that grace you will obtain supreme peace and timeless abode.

63. *iti te jñānam ākhyātaṁ guhyād guhyataraṁ mayā |*
vimṛśyaitad aśeṣeṇa yathecchasi tathā kuru ||

And so this wisdom, the ultimate secret of secrets, has been revealed by Me to you. Contemplate it deeply so there is no residue and act as you choose.

64. *sarvaguhyatamaṁ bhūyaḥ śṛṇu me paramaṁ vacaḥ |*
iṣṭo 'si me dṛḍhamiti tato vakṣyāmi te hitam ||

Listen again to my ultimate word, the final secret of all. You are the dearly beloved of Me; therefore I will tell you for your own good.

65. *manmanā bhava madbhakto madyājī māṁ namaskuru |*
māmevaiṣyasi satyaṁ te pratijāne priyo 'si me ||

Fill your mind with Me, loving Me, sacrificing to Me, make salutations to Me. In this very way you will really, *truly* come to Me. I declare this, for you are precious to Me.

66. *sarvadharmān parityajya mām ekaṁ śaraṇaṁ vraja |*
ahaṁ tvā sarvapāpebhyo mokṣayiṣyāmi mā śucaḥ ||

Give up all dharmas and take refuge in Me alone. I will set you free from all evils. Do not worry.

67. *idaṁ te nātapaskāya nābhaktāya kadācana |*
nā cāśuśrūṣave vācyaṁ na cā māṁ yo 'bhyasūyati ||

This should not be spoken by you to someone who has no tapas, who has no bhakti, who does not want to listen, nor to one who speaks indignantly of Me.

68. *ya idaṁparamaṁ guhyaṁ madbhakteṣvabhidhāsyati* |
bhaktiṁ mayi parāṁ kṛtvā mām evaiṣyatyasaṁśayaḥ ||

Whoever explains this supreme mystery to my devotees performs the highest devotion to Me and without a doubt comes to Me.

69. *na ca tasmān manuṣyeṣu kaścinme priyakṛttamaḥ* |
bhavitā na ca me tasmād anyaḥ priyataṛo bhuvi ||

Nothing gives more joy to Me than this one among humankind. And no one else on earth will be dearer to Me.

70. *adhyeṣyate ca ya imaṁ dharmyaṁ saṁvādamāvayoḥ* |
jñānayajñena tenāham iṣṭaḥ syām iti me matiḥ ||

One who studies, inquires, and contemplates our dialogue together will be loving Me with the sacrifice of knowledge. This is my thought.

71. *śraddhāvān anasūyaśca śṛṇuyād api yo naraḥ* |
so 'pi muktaḥ śubhāṁllokān prāpnuyāt puṇyakarmaṇām ||

One who listens with great trust and free of malice is also liberated and attains the joyous worlds of those of purest actions.

72. *kaccid etacchrutaṁ pārtha tvayaikāgreṇa cetasā* |
kaccid ajñānasaṁmohaḥ praṇaṣṭaste dhanañjaya ||

Listen to this, O Son of Pṛthā. Have you heard this with one-pointed concentration of mind? Has your delusion caused by ignorance been dispelled, O Conqueror of Wealth?

arjuna uvāca
73. *naṣṭo mohaḥ smṛtirlabdhā tvatprasādānmayācyuta* |
sthito 'smi gatasandehaḥ kariṣye vacanaṁ tava ||

Arjuna said:
Delusion is gone. Recognition and memory (smṛti) have been gained by me by your grace, O Ācyuta. I stand firm with all doubt gone. I will act by your word.

sañjaya uvāca
74. *ityahaṁ vāsudevasya pārthasya ca mahātmanaḥ |*
saṁvādam imam aśrauṣam adbhutaṁ romaharṣaṇam ||

Sañjaya said:
In this way I have listened to this wondrous dialogue of Kṛṣṇa the Son of Vāsudeva and the Son of Pṛthā, the great being, making my hair stand on end.

75. *vyāsaprasādāc chrutvān etad guhyamahaṁ param |*
yogaṁ yogeśvarāt kṛṣṇāt sākṣāt kaṭhayataḥ svayam ||

By the grace of the poet Vyāsa I have heard this ultimate secret yoga from Kṛṣṇa, the lord of yoga, narrating it himself right before our eyes.

76. *rājan saṁsmṛtya saṁsmṛtya saṁvādam imam adbhutam |*
keśavārjunayoḥ puṇyaṁ hṛṣyāmi ca muhurmuhuḥ ||

O King, as I contemplate again and again this amazing and sacred dialogue of Keśava and Arjuna I am thrilled every moment, again and again.

77. *tacca saṁsmṛtya saṁsmṛtya rūpam atyadbhutaṁ hareḥ |*
vismayo me mahān rājan hṛṣyāmi ca punaḥ punaḥ ||

And mindfully recollecting, again and yet again, the extremely amazing form (rūpa) of Hari, my astonishment is huge, and I am thrilled again and yet again, O King.

78. *yatra yogeśvaraḥ kṛṣṇo yatra pārtho dhanurdharaḥ |*
tatra śrīrvijayo bhūtir dhruvā nītirmatirmama ||

It is my thought that wherever there is the lord of yoga, Kṛṣṇa, and the Son of Pṛthā, the archer, there is beauty, victory, well-being, and certainly morality.

ACKNOWLEDGMENTS

WRITING A BOOK is always a challenge, and the notion of writing one about the Bhagavad Gītā was daunting when the thought first arose. On so many levels we knew we were not qualified, yet the idea floated our way time and again. We got swept into the process of study and questioning that the text itself demands and decided to give it a shot. This book is what came about: a glimpse into the vastness of this timeless classic. We hope our words contribute to the ongoing dialogue, communication, and insight that the Gītā has and will continue to inspire.

We are deeply grateful to those who have encouraged, helped, and supported us in various ways throughout the writing of this book. First, of course is the amazing support from Shambhala Publications. To our dear friend and fellow practitioner, Sara Bercholz, thank you yet again! You breathe life and enthusiasm not only into so many concepts for books, but into those who work with you to get thoughts on paper. A huge thanks to Beth Frankl, our editor, who has been patient, supportive, and clear in helping us at every turn along the way. Thanks to the discerning eyes of associate editor Audra Figgins, copy editor Jill Rogers, and proofreader Emily White. We'd also like to give a special thanks to Shambhala's design team, who listened and patiently responded to our sometimes quirky perspective on aesthetics, as well as the marketing and publicity team.

There have also been many fellow students who have contributed by sharing recordings of lectures, which served as an early skeleton for the book, and who gave us feedback along the way, in particular, Michele Loew, Sascha and Romana Delberg, Olle Bengtström, and Julia Naiper. Thank you to Callie Rushton for jump-starting the writing by diving in to transcribe. Finally, we'd like to thank our dear friend and mentor, Robert Thurman, who always presented objections to literal interpretations of the many different schools exposed in the Gīta and for listening deeply to our perspective of what Kṛṣṇa represents.

APPENDIX: EMBODIMENT EXERCISES

COMING FULL CIRCLE to the end of this book and perhaps taking the invitation to look for an appropriate path toward awakening, we may ask ourselves again, "What does it mean to be human?" With insights gleaned from Kṛṣṇa's teachings on interconnectedness and inspiration from Arjuna's insatiable appetite for questioning, we are one step closer to finding some answers, yet here we are still, embroiled in the particulars of our unique life, our perceptions, feelings, thoughts, sensations, and embodied form. Where do we go from here? When faced with uncertainty or when conflicts and crises arise, how do we harness these teachings in order to act in alignment with the truth of who we know ourselves to be? How do we act with conscience, compassion, and joy in this complicated world?

We are told in the Gītā that the way through this kind of confusion and out of suffering is to stabilize and steady the mind. So that is where we start: with a step-by-step process of training ourselves to repeatedly come back to center and drop into the physical sensation of what it feels like to be embodied and to see through the brilliant illusions spun into storylines of separate self that our minds are prone to create. When we finally trust and find refuge in the process of life to the point that we know viscerally, consciously, and unconsciously on an intuitive level that we can never be separate from the whole of existence, *then* we can be assured that, supported within the infinite ocean of love, we are doing the best we can to meet any crisis head on. Rooted in that state of clarity our actions are automatically fueled by a spirit of inclusiveness, kindness, and generosity.

In this appendix we offer practices that help to train us from the inside out. With practice the exercises can help us to pay attention to our immediate embodied experience, to let go of our preconceptions and attachments, and to trust not only our conclusions about but also the process of life. The exercises build upon one another so it is best to work through at least the first four in sequence as a means of developing tools that can help still and steady body, mind, and emotion. By practicing them consistently, a couple of times or more a week for even just a month or so, you'll notice that you'll have developed a stable foundation from which to quickly drop into the present moment and take action, even in times of crisis! The remaining exercises are designed to give insight into the embodied sensations of kindness, compassion, and connecting to the truth of who you are on a deep level.

Embodiment through Sound (Pair with Chapter 1)

In the story of the Gītā it is when Kṛṣṇa and Arjuna sound their conch shells as they ride onto the battlefield that Arjuna hesitates—being struck by a gut sense that something is not right, that senseless killing and thoughtless destruction lie ahead. It is here that the story and teachings held in the Gītā begin. Here too, within the vibratory sensation of sound and the inherently grounding aspect of a long, smooth exhale (known in yoga as a prāṇāyāma exhale), any of us are likely to be brought back into the present moment so that we may discern the most skillful, most compassionate course of action.

If you don't happen to have a conch shell lying around, you can practice *bhramarī* a classic prāṇāyāma (yogīc breathing) exercise that, like blowing into a conch, helps to focus the mind through the vibration of sound. The word *bhramarī* means "honeybee" or "bumblebee" and in the exercise you hum, extending the exhalation and making a vibrating sound that is somewhat like a bee in flight. It only takes a few minutes and can be done any time the mind is unsettled or foggy to help bring you back into the experience of the present moment.

1. Find a comfortable seated or standing position in which the spine can lift easily out of the pelvis without tension in the hips, neck, shoulders, or head.
2. Take a moment to notice sensations in the body. Bring your awareness to the base of your body, the sitting bones and thighs or the feet connecting to the surface you're sitting or standing on. Feel the support beneath you.
3. Soften your tongue and your jaw slightly and release tension in your face, lips, and the inside of your mouth—your palate. Your eyes may be closed or open, whatever feels easy and comfortable.
4. Take a full breath in. As you breathe out, keeping your lips slightly closed, begin making a one-note humming sound, any pitch. Keep that tone for the entire length of the exhalation. Then breathe in through the nostrils, without making the humming sound, keeping your tongue soft and jaw relaxed. At the very top of the inhalation, again begin making a humming sound, the same or a different pitch as previously, as you exhale.
5. Continue this pattern of breathing for a few minutes, making an audible sound with each exhale and then soften into a smooth, silent inhale.
6. Conclude the practice by taking a moment to notice your mind state and any residual sensations in your body.

Moving on the Wave of the Breath (Pair with Chapter 4)

Within the teachings of the Gītā, we are repeatedly reminded that everything we experience is in a constant pattern of change—the "guṇas acting on the guṇas." To experience an embodied sense of this we can move in a pattern of synchronized form, combining movement, gaze, and breath. By repeating the form a few times, we actually begin to embody the inherent nature of the guṇas, the process of change. In time, conceptual mind automatically softens, and the natural intelligence of the body can come to the forefront of our experience. Once you have practiced this pattern of movement and felt the unifying impact it has on the body, mind, and breath, it can become a "quick fix" if you find yourself in a state of imbalance.

1. Stand with your feet about ten to twelve inches apart, knees slightly bent. Scan your body to notice if there is any tightness or tension in your neck, shoulders, throat, or tongue. Bring awareness slowly down through your torso, arms, belly, legs, and feet, just noticing if there is tension.
2. Now bring your attention to your breath and on both the inhalation and exhalation, make a soft aspirate sound, like whispering the word *ah* with your lips closed.
3. Now open your eyes and let your gaze settle on something in front of you, maybe a pattern in the floorboards, carpet, or tile. Count five rounds of breath (inhale and exhale), if possible shifting your mind away from identifying the object by name and simply looking.
4. Now, as you are inhaling, begin to lift your arms up and out in front of you, turning your hands so the palms face one another as the arms lift toward the ceiling. Maybe the arms come up high, maybe not. Perhaps the hands come together, or not. No problem either way. Simply move the arms in sync with the inhalation and try not to create tension in your neck as the arms lift. Allow the movement of the hands and arms upward to take one full inhale.
5. Exhaling slowly, lower your arms down to your sides. Repeat the pattern several times, reaching up as you inhale and drawing the arms back down by your sides as you exhale. Stretch out both ends of the breath and coordinate the movement of your arms to coincide with the pattern of breath.
6. Next, add the gaze into this pattern. As you inhale and reach up, tilt your head to gaze at your hands. As you exhale and your arms come down by your sides, let your head return to neutral and gaze softly in front of you. Repeat this pattern three times, inhaling, reaching up, turning the arms, and gazing at your thumbs. As you inhale and reach up, notice the sensation of your feet planted

firmly on the ground. Then, as you exhale and bring your arms back down by your sides, notice the sensation of lightness in the core of your chest and heart.

7. Stand still for just a moment and bring your awareness into the feelings, thoughts, and sensations that are present. Notice your overall mind state and places you were holding tension at the beginning of the exercise.

To extend the exercise, you can add four more movements coordinated with the breath.

1. Inhale as you reach up, turning your arms as above.
2. Exhaling, bend your knees and, keeping your spine straight as you look ahead, fold at your hips to place your lower arms on your thighs. Gaze forward. As the exhalation comes to an end, curl your head down and look at your feet.
3. On the very next inhalation, lift your head and straighten the spine again, then exhale and look at your feet once more.
4. On the next inhalation, lift your head, begin straightening your spine and legs, and using your arms to push into your thighs, come back up to standing. Partway to standing, about midway through the inhalation, reach up overhead with your arms turned as before, and gaze at your hands.
5. At the very top of the inhalation, soften your gaze as you allow your arms to float back down by your sides. Repeat this pattern slowly several times on the wave of the breath.

Reflect on the feelings, thoughts, and sensations you experienced during the exercise. You may notice that after some rounds of breath, the synchronized pattern of movement, breath, and gaze seems almost to happen spontaneously. Your physical, mental, or emotional states may have changed without you *doing* anything to make that happen. This is a way of truly experiencing that although you are engineering the motions, much of what happens—mood shifts, change in flexibility, stilling of mind—is simply happening on its own, the guṇas on the guṇas.

Making Space for Mind: Simple Sitting Meditation (Pair with Chapter 3)

The "wise ones" are described in the Gītā as those who, through the practices of yoga, learn to still and stabilize the mind. It sounds quite simple yet, as Arjuna says, the mind is as hard to control as the wind, creating theory after theory, story beyond story, in an endless stream moving at breakneck speed. Thoughts seem to come out of nowhere and to eventually disappear into oblivion, dragging our mind states and emotions along with them.

Contemplative practices reveal that though there is immense value in the ability to think with agility, the unstable nature of mind can hinder clarity when we are faced with crises or other challenging circumstances. Under duress the ability to focus clearly without letting our thoughts and emotions skew our judgment is crucial if we are to act skillfully.

One form of meditation that helps with stability of mind is to choose a field of awareness, like our breath, and to bring the awareness back to this field when we notice it has wandered off. This sounds simple, but even for very experienced meditators it can be quite challenging. However, even setting the intention to bridle the mind in this gentle way can have a remarkably positive impact on levels of distraction, stress, anxiety, and confusion we may experience.

It is best to give this practice some time to build. Start with a short practice—perhaps five minutes—then build slowly to ten minutes or more on a daily basis. Begin practicing this form of meditation in a structured way, defining a specific time of day to meditate and sticking with it to establish a pattern and train the mind. More important than when or where you practice is that you set the intention to practice on a regular basis.

1. Begin by setting aside about five minutes (or more) when you will be undisturbed. Make sure the temperature in the room is comfortable, the lighting is not harsh, and that your clothing is comfortable and nonbinding.
2. Have a timer nearby. The passage of time can seem distorted while practicing meditation, so it is helpful to remove one more source

of distraction. Set the timer for the amount of time you've chosen to give to this exercise.

3. Find a comfortable seated position. You could sit on the floor or in a chair, depending on what works best for your body. Most important is that you arrange your body so that your pelvis is vertical, with your sitting bones dropping down into the seat. It can be helpful to elevate your pelvis by sitting on the edge of a folded blanket.
4. If you are sitting in a chair, let your feet rest evenly on the floor, perhaps placing a cushion behind your back for support or arranging a firm pillow beneath your feet, so they rest comfortably with thighs parallel to the floor. If you are sitting on the floor, make sure your knees and legs are folded into a comfortable position, placing support beneath the knees if needed.
5. Close your eyes and notice the sense of support beneath you. Then bring your attention to your upper body and make small adjustments to your posture so you feel as though your spine is rising naturally up out of your pelvis. Relax your shoulders and allow your body to rest comfortably. When you get the pelvis tilted correctly and are able to relax, you should feel that you are sitting straight without much effort at all!
6. Relax your neck, jaw, and tongue. Keep your lips soft, barely touching, and allow your tongue to rest naturally in your mouth. Keep your head in a neutral position, chin neither tucked nor dropped and your neck neutral.
7. Drop your arms to hang naturally by your sides, softening your shoulders. Bend your elbows and place your hands, palms down, on your thighs wherever they happen to land. Your upper arms should remain neutral, not reaching forward or back.
8. Now, open your eyes and gaze gently down, eyes softly resting a few feet out in front of you.
9. Bring your awareness to your breath: the inhalation, a natural gap, the exhalation, and another natural gap. For ten rounds of the breath, simply notice this pattern, making no particular effort to modify the breath. Perhaps your breath is even, perhaps not. Maybe it is smooth and long, or it might be rough or short. Don't try to change the breath; simply watch what is naturally occurring.

10. When you notice that your mind has wandered away from focusing on the breath, invite the mind back to focus on the breath.
11. The point of the practice is *not* to force your mind to stop producing thoughts but instead to learn to redirect your mind to a chosen field—in this case your breath—when and if you notice that it has wandered off. So it is wonderful when you notice your mind has wandered because you are noticing what's happening. Don't be hard on yourself or think, "I'm a terrible meditator" when your mind wanders. If only once in ten minutes you notice your mind has moved focus from the breath to something else, that's fantastic! Even if you only notice the mind has wandered when you hear the timer sound, and you think, "Oh right! I was supposed to be noticing my breath." That's great. You're training your mind to notice what's happening in the present moment.

Sitting and watching your breath for ten minutes or so a day is an excellent practice for training the mind to be stable and steady. Keep it really simple and be nice to yourself. Slowly over time, it will become easier and easier.

Once you have become comfortable with observing the pattern of breath, you may wish to do other sitting and breathing practices. Set up the body evenly as described above, whatever sitting practice you choose. For example, you could notice any simple sensation of breath—what it feels like entering and exiting your nostrils or the sensation of your chest rising and falling on the wave of the breath. With the intention to return to that chosen field of awareness when you notice that your mind has wandered, set a timer and begin.

Sitting practices such as these, in combination with a conscious practice of moving in sync with the breath, are a wonderful foundation to work with, expanding upon them or keeping them very simple, for years.

Body-Mind Balance (Pair with Chapter 6)

Balancing is anything but formulaic. It requires focus, quick reflexes in response to feedback and, possibly most importantly, the trust to let go of all theories you may have of how to balance. This simple embodiment exercise is a demonstration of the precarious interplay between clear vision, attachment to ideas, and not knowing.

1. Come to standing with your feet about hip width apart. Take a couple of rounds of breath to drop awareness into your body, settle your mind, and feel your feet connected to the surface beneath you.
2. Steady your gaze, slightly downcast, on an object or point that is about six feet out in front of you.
3. Exhaling, shift your weight to your left foot, and bend your right knee to lift your right foot off the ground, making sure not to lock your left knee. Put your right foot back down on the ground.
4. Keeping the gaze steady and your left leg strong and slightly bent, again lift your right foot off the ground. If it is possible while maintaining balance, turn your right foot so the sole of the foot is facing the inseam of your left leg. Place your right foot on your left shin or thigh. Do not place your foot on the knee joint.
5. For about a minute, keep balancing on one leg in this way. If you begin to lose your balance and need to put your right foot back down, that's perfectly fine. Just do so, take a couple of extra breaths, and try again.
6. Take a few rounds of breath, then switch sides, balancing on your right leg with the right knee slightly bent and bringing the sole of your left foot up to rest on your right leg. Repeat at least two times, balancing on each leg and observing the subtleties and interplay between mind and body, theory, the desire to balance, and how your mind softening its conclusions about what you must do can be helpful, until you forget what you're doing!

Reflecting on the experience you may notice that if your mind was scattered and your gaze unsteady, or if you were emphasizing the inhalation rather than the exhalation, balancing might have been difficult. Cultivating the embodied sense of groundedness and stability can be helpful, though not always. It's interesting to note that if you think you have the precise formula for balancing and use it, rather than responding instinctively to circumstances, it is almost impossible to balance. This exercise demonstrates the importance of staying alert without becoming rigid or attached to your ideas.

Life Is a Dewdrop (Pair with Chapter 2)

In the Buddhist text the Diamond Sūtra, the nature of the world is revealed to be that of interconnectedness and constant change—impermanence. These two underlying truths, or global themes, play a critical role in the telling of the story of the Gītā as well, and though they are intuitively simple and for most easy to agree with theoretically, when we apply them to our own storyline or our own everyday interactions in the world, they can become sources for confusion and fear.

If we comprehend interconnectedness to be a foundational aspect of life then our interactions in the world (which by definition are an extension of ourselves) require that we be transparent, vivid, and truthful not only in our dreams and ideals but also in our actions and communication.

When we see impermanence in the context of interconnectedness we become more comfortable observing the beauty and interconnected nature of all things as they change, and the notion of impermanence starts to become more palatable too.

Before you begin the practice, arrange to have a cup of hot liquid—tea, coffee, hot chocolate, or whatever suits you. There is more leeway in timing if you are planning to have something that is steamed or whisked, but even just pouring hot water for tea into a teacup with any type of milk will work.

1. Set up a seat at a table or counter.
2. Once the drink is prepared, check to be sure there are at least a few bubbles floating on the surface of the drink. If not, whisk the drink gently for just a moment until some bubbles appear.
3. Place the drink in front of you and bring your full focus to observing the bubbles: how many there are, how big they are, and if they are of varying size. Pay attention to their surface color and sheen and notice if they all seem to be the same or if some are shinier than others or more curved or flatter than others.

4. Spend a few moments simply watching the transformation and movement of the bubbles.
5. When a bubble or several bubbles pop, what do you see? How do the other bubbles seem to respond or not respond to this change? What, if anything, changes on the surface when a bubble pops?
6. After a few moments take a sip and enjoy the beverage as you reflect on what you observed.

It is likely that although the bubbles were impermanent and completely independent, you witnessed change within the context of interconnectedness. This happens all the time, all around you, from the sun rising to your own emotions and moods changing—all in a steady pattern, absolutely embedded in their background context.

Cultivating Happiness (Pair with Chapter 7)

It is said that a basic right of all beings is to be happy; in fact His Holiness the Dalai Lama goes so far as to say that our *purpose* in life is to be happy. Yet many of us live in a shadow of discontent. The world is filled with so much suffering! Just as Arjuna discovered on the battlefield, beyond the obvious external sources of suffering, we seem to be quite skilled at creating mind states that perpetuate our own unique take on misery.

When we give up our theories about what will give us happiness, searching for it in the things we think we need or want, we finally find it in the last place we're likely to look: within our own heart. It turns out that it's been there all along and that happiness, the seed of compassion, is what intimately connects us heart to heart with every other being on earth. This insight is rooted too in the teaching of nonattachment: letting go of the fruits of actions and even setting down and sacrificing into the fire of awareness, wisdom itself.

The following practices build upon and enrich one another. You may find them most helpful if you first follow the simple instructions below in the context of a meditation practice. They are ways of shining the light of awareness onto mind states that help us to cultivate happiness. Once you've become familiar with how this shifting of mind state works, you can "practice" happiness in virtually any daily situation.

There are positive mind states, such as kindness, forgiveness, generosity, trust, and love, that generate a heartfelt sense of happiness. There are also negative mind states, such as anger, jealousy, impatience, hatred, or inertia, that generate unhappiness. We each have specific visceral sensations associated with positive and negative mind states, but we may not notice them. By bringing conscious awareness to the embodied experience of the process of mind, body, and emotion rolling through our awareness, we can begin to cultivate lasting happiness.

1. Find a comfortable seated position, arranging your body so you feel at ease, as if you were setting up for meditation. Bring your awareness to the pattern of your breath entering and exiting your body.
2. Now check in with your physical experience, quickly scanning your body from head to toe. If you come across any areas of the body where you experience tension or strain, pause and focus on your breath. Perhaps the tension or strain will dissipate, and perhaps not. It's fine either way. Simply observe the sensations in your body.
3. Now direct your attention to the center of your chest, what we will refer to as "the heart." Take note of what you feel emotionally and what physical sensations you notice as you bring focus to this part of your body.
4. Bring to mind a time when you did something small but nice for someone. Perhaps you saw a stranger who looked really tired on the subway and you offered them your seat. Or maybe you fed a stray cat.
5. Imagine that moment or situation in detail and see if you can recall what you felt physically and emotionally. Perhaps you remember details, perhaps not; it's fine either way. Simply remembering the act of genuine kindness is a good starting place for familiarizing yourself with what it feels like to give something to others without expecting anything in return.
6. After a moment or two, bring your awareness back to the sensation of your breath entering and exiting your body. Then take a moment to reflect on the practice.

This practice is one that is helpful to repeat once or twice and then to take out of the meditation setting and into everday life. For one week set the intention to do one nice thing for someone—with no strings attached. Sometimes it's easier to do this for a stranger than someone you are close to. When you do something kind, pause and notice the physical sensations in the core of your heart. Do you feel happy, unhappy, or not much of anything at all? Whatever you feel simply notice it and move on.

Shifting Mind States (Pair with Chapter 5)

A related exercise emphasizes cultivating positive qualities associated with happiness when you are unhappy, stressed, or emotionally imbalanced. In this exercise you can observe the tendency to become attached to the wonderful feeling of happiness (like when you do something nice for others and then find yourself clinging onto that feeling rather than doing more nice things for more people) or being fearful of the dreadful feeling of despair. This exercise helps you not only to let go of mind states and attachments but also to see both positive and negative mind states equally. Over time, bringing equanimity to the perception of your own mind states can facilitate the ability to see others clearly and calmly.

1. When you notice a negative mind state such as anger arising, take a moment to consciously bring your awareness to the quality of your breath. Don't try to change it, just notice it.
2. Now, bring your awareness to your heart. What physical sensations do you notice? Do you feel spaciousness, tightness, heaviness, heat, coolness, dullness, or something else?
3. Then ask yourself, "On a scale of one to ten (one being not at all, ten being very much), how happy do I feel?"

This exercise is a way of beginning to notice the connection to the embodied sensation of happiness and your mind states. It is possible to shift mind states—and therefore your embodied experience, perceptions, and actions—from uncomfortable and unhappy to comfortable and happy.

1. For the next step, rescan your body. Don't be surprised if some of the discomfort you first experienced when beginning the exercise has changed. It's quite likely and normal since often just by bringing our attention to discomfort, the body releases patterns of holding on to tension.
2. As you come across uncomfortable places in your body, pause for a breath or two to direct awareness there and then move on.
3. Then bring to mind the image of looking into the eyes of a very innocent being, like a tiny baby or a kitten. Imagine you can look directly into those eyes and that they look back at you with awe and innocence. Neither of you is expecting anything in return, but you are both totally captured by the moment. Imagine this in as much detail as possible. Bring your awareness into your heart and notice what sensations are present.
4. Though what you feel may be subtle, this feeling is the seed of happiness, which in turn is the root of compassion.
5. Remind yourself that it is through the willingness to remain open and welcoming, to tap into the physical sensation of vastness that is deep within your heart, the same place that intimately connects you to others, that you find intrinsic happiness.
6. Again, ask yourself how happy you feel. It is likely that you feel happier than you did when you were absorbed by irritation.

To reflect on this practice, ask yourself whether you prefer the physical experience of happiness or unhappiness. Choosing to be happy, even in difficult circumstances, is a practice. If you honestly want to be happy, to work toward lasting happiness and the ability to help alleviate suffering in this world, then set the intention to cultivate the embodied experience of a happy, open heart whenever possible.

Watering Seeds of Happiness (Pair with Chapter 9)

1. Begin by recalling the feeling of deep, unconditional happiness—like that of looking into the eyes of another innocent being. Do this as often as you wish during the day, pausing for a moment to

recall the sensation of connection to other, *noticing* the embodied sensations of happiness, love.

2. Then at times when you notice negative mind states such as anger and jealousy arising, consciously decide what you want for yourself and the world. Do you want to water seeds of negative mind states by clinging to the unpleasant sensations within your heart that lead to negative storylines and unhappiness? Or do you want to shift the sensation in your heart to one that is pleasant and that leads to a connection to other, to kindness and compassion? Whichever you choose, do so knowingly.

Ultimately, every day each one of us makes the decision countless times (consciously or not) as to whether or not to be happy. How *we* feel impacts others, and the happiness or unhappiness of those, in turn, affects still more. The only part of that equation that is within our control is how *we* feel. The simple decision to cultivate happiness increases happiness, not only for you but for others as well.

Tuning In to the Suffering of Others (Pair with Chapter 8)

If we see a baby crying, there is a heartfelt urge to help relieve their suffering. If we encounter someone who is happy or we are in the presence of someone who is full of a seemingly boundless exultation for life, it is almost impossible *not* to feel joyful ourselves, and we welcome them into our heart. However, when we meet someone who is angry, violent, mean, and harmful to others it can be very difficult to connect, let alone invite them anywhere near our heart. Yet, as we've learned in the Gītā, the path out of our suffering is to keep all beings in our heart.

This simple practice can help us to see the suffering of others without becoming overwhelmed. In that way, not only can we keep them in our heart, but we will become more clear about what, if any, action we can take that will serve the person or situation as a whole. Keeping others in our heart when we face a crisis is essential.

For a few days as you navigate through the world, consciously notice when you see someone who seems to be suffering. This is not an exercise to explore ways of helping to relieve suffering but rather an exercise to give you insight into building clarity in times of intensity or crisis when you may need to take action in the future. Of course, if you happen to observe a situation that requires help, and there is something you can do, do not hesitate.

1. When you notice someone suffering, look closely at the whole situation. Then shift your focus to feel your feet connected to the earth as you breathe out.
2. Bring your awareness to your heart and answer the following questions: "What physical sensations do I notice? Do I feel happy, sad, or neutral? Do I want to help? Do I know what to do to alleviate the suffering?" If you feel compelled to act, ask yourself, "Am I acting to get something in return?" (If you do act, do so without expectations of outcome.)
3. Keep the practice and reflection short and simple. Just notice what's arising for you in that moment of witnessing suffering, whether you want to help, and if so, what you expect to gain from helping.
4. Next take an instant to remind yourself that love and happiness are intrinsic parts of human nature. Recall the visceral sensation of connecting to other from the previous exercise. Cultivating a deep connection to others is directly related to happiness.

The obvious next step is to help when appropriate.

5. If you decide to help, it is very important to let go of any expectations. Truly helping another is support and service. If you want something in return for offering love and happiness—a thank you even—then you will perpetuate the chain of suffering. For example, if you see a bug in the sink, struggling and failing to climb out, maybe you find a piece of paper and help lift it out to safety. In this case, it's pretty easy to not take it personally if the bug doesn't turn back and wave with gratitude. When it comes to people, however, it's often difficult to let go of our need for recognition or the outcome; the fruits of our actions. Just notice this.

6. Regardless of whether or not gratitude is offered to you when you do something kind, pay attention to how good it feels to simply offer help with no strings attached.
7. Practice this frequently—offering help and expecting nothing in return.

Step-by-Step: Dharma, Intention, and Motivation (Pair with Chapter 10)

It's often said that through yoga and meditation we are not learning new ways of being, but rather we are peeling away layers of habitual behavior that keep us confused, stuck, and out of touch with who we truly are on a deep level. Contemplative practices are not ways of learning, but of *un*learning. But it's easy to become dominated by behaviors that obscure our true nature—that of goodness. As layers of physically holding on to our sense of separateness and negative mind states begin to fall away, our true essence begins automatically to emerge. Then one day we suddenly wake up, as did Arjuna on the battlefield, and we ask, "Who am I *really*, and why am I here?"

No matter how separate and alone we may feel from time to time—and we all do—the truth is that we are part of something much bigger than ourselves. The taproot of suffering is that we continually forget how amazing and wonderful it is to be intimately connected to everything else—other people, animals, the oceans and lightning, even a dewdrop on a leaf in the park. Once we get a taste for this, things are never the same. In the background of our awareness there is always the gnawing sense that things are just not right when we fall into habitual patterns of separating ourselves out from the background of circumstance and others. When facing difficulty or a crisis, if we don't remember the truth of interconnectedness, we cannot act with the full intelligence that our mind, body, and spirit possess.

The following exercise is a series of contemplations designed to give you insight into who you are as part of the bigger picture of life. It is helpful to complete the exercise, to set it aside, and then to revisit the questions from time to time with new eyes so that you can update and deepen your understanding.

1. Find a comfortable seated position and drop into the embodied experience of your breath entering and exiting your nose. Focus on the sensation of breath, allowing your mind and nervous system to settle.
2. Now ask yourself the following questions, beginning with the first and working through them all slowly. You may wish to write down your answers or simply think them through in your mind; either is fine, but don't rush. For each question, note whatever first pops into your mind. Then take a breath and allow the answer to sink in. Then ask the same exact question again and pause after answering. Repeat this process for each question five times.
3. This full exercise can be completed over the course of one day, off and on, or over several days, coming back to unanswered questions after sitting with those you've considered. The important thing is to sit with your answer, then look again to see if something different, unexpected, or more detailed emerges for you.

The questions are as follows:

- Who am I? Look beneath the surface and then look again.
- What am I good at? Look beyond your job or position in life and consider what people say they relate to in you. Consider not only what you do but also your inherent character traits such as a sense of humor, integrity, loyalty, and so on.
- What gives my life meaning? Beyond the superficial acquisitions you have in life, what truly inspires you or makes you feel fulfilled?
- What is my underlying intention for living my life? To be helpful or truthful or alleviate suffering, for example.
- What is the purpose of my life? Start small, then look again.
- What motivates me?

Once you've established grounds for understanding what strikes you as your essence—who you are and what your purpose is in life—then you have a stable place from which to navigate when crises arise. You can, and should, always refine your answers, but this is a good start. You'll find that when you are faced with a crisis, if you drop your awareness into your body to become steady and stable, feeling your feet firmly connected to the earth, you can quickly assess the situation you face. Bring to mind your purpose in life. This is a guiding principle that can help you choose what action to take. Once you act, always look for feedback and adjust your actions accordingly. Throughout the course of taking action it is vital to check your motivations, your attachment to what you believe the fruits of your actions are, and to set them aside. Being honest and open, keeping happiness alive in your own heart, and always looking again will help you to navigate virtually any complex situation.

INDEX

abhyāsa (continuous practice), 51, 65–66, 184
action, 17, 39, 64
  context of, 14–15
  as creative power, 79–80, 192–93
  and dharma, interrelatedness of, 7–9, 13
  freedom from bonds of, 164, 201, 258
  fruits of, letting go of, 44, 45, 57, 60, 169, 170, 176, 223, 250–52
  fruits of, three types, 252
  guidelines for, 8–9
  guṇas and, 232, 233
  imagination determining, 27
  and inaction, interplay of, 44–45, 98, 160, 162, 169–70, 255
  renunciation and, 174–76
  as sacrifice, 35, 160–61, 172, 220
  tyāga rooted in, 127–29
  and yoga of knowledge, comparison of, 159–64
  See also attachment: fruits of action
Agni, 33–34, 206, 217
ahiṁsā. *See* nonviolence/nonharming
Ananta (nāga), 89, 207
anger, 109, 240, 276
  absence of, 156, 168
  arising of, 28, 157, 279
  of demonic beings, 243
  freedom from, 178
  giving up, 258
  rajas and, 39, 165
anukampā ("trembling along with"), 88–89
apāna, 49, 60, 76, 87–88, 171, 178
Arjuna, xii
  attachments of, 28–29
  confidence of, 90
  crisis of conscience of, 16–17, 148
  discernment of, 124–25
  doubt of, xii, 17, 49, 65, 70, 79–81, 96–98, 111, 185
  evolution of, 19, 20, 133, 261
  hesitation of, 4–7, 8, 9, 12, 142–46
  inquisitiveness of, 108
  insight of, 48
  and Kṛṣṇa, inseparability of, 68, 88–89, 93
  love for Kṛṣṇa, 98–99
  mind, softening of, 84
  need to know, 38–39, 48, 49, 125

ABOUT THE AUTHORS

RICHARD FREEMAN began his practice of yoga in college in 1968 and in that same period he attended the Zen Temple of Matsouka Roshi in Chicago. As a student of philosophy, the political and cultural circumstances of the times took him to India to practice and explore schools of yoga and bhakti. As a monk he traveled throughout India and Southeast Asia, and in 1974 he began teaching yoga in Iran. He has been an avid student of both the Iyengar and the Ashtanga methods, their relationship to similar practices, and their application to each individual. To this day he remains a student of comparative philosophy and is interested in the interfacing of different cultures and practices both historically and, most importantly, in our current world. He and Mary Taylor currently teach ways of practicing yoga and meditation in the context of relationship to other people.

MARY TAYLOR began studying yoga in 1972 primarily as a means of finding balance and reducing stress while working as a professional chef and training in a Gestalt Center. She soon became absorbed by the profound impact āsana, when coupled with yoga's other limbs, had on all aspects of life. Diving more deeply in search of intersections and differing (often complementary) underpinnings between yoga and other disciplines such as Buddhism, psychology, health care, politics, science, and art, she continues to study and practice daily, incorporating the residue that is produced on the mat into her work and life. Taylor cofounded, with Richard Freeman, the Yoga Workshop in Boulder, Colorado. They now split their time between Boulder and Thailand when not traveling to teach throughout the world.